Buyouts

Founded in 1807, John Wiley & Sons is the oldest independent publishing company in the United States. With offices in North America, Europe, Australia, and Asia, Wiley is globally committed to developing and marketing print and electronic products and services for our customers' professional and personal knowledge and understanding.

The Wiley Finance series contains books written specifically for finance and investment professionals as well as sophisticated individual investors and their financial advisors. Book topics range from portfolio management to e-commerce, risk management, financial engineering, valuation and financial instrument analysis, as well as much more.

For a list of available titles, visit our Web site at www.WileyFinance.com.

Buyouts

*Success for Owners, Management,
PEGs, Families, ESOPs and
Mergers and Acquisitions*

SCOTT D. MILLER

John Wiley & Sons, Inc.

Published by John Wiley & Sons, Inc., Hoboken, New Jersey.
Published simultaneously in Canada.

For general information on our other products and services or for technical support, please contact our Customer Care Department within the United States at (800) 762-2974, outside the United States at (317) 572-3993, or fax (317) 572-4002.

Wiley also publishes its books in a variety of electronic formats. Some content that appears in print may not be available in electronic books. For more information about Wiley products, visit our web site at www.wiley.com.

Library of Congress Cataloging-in-Publication Data:

Miller, Scott D., 1949–
  Buyouts : success for owners, management, PEGs, Families, ESOPs, and mergers and acquisitions / Scott D. Miller.
      p.   cm. – (Wiley finance series)
  Includes bibliographical references and index.
      ISBN 978-1-118-22909-5 (cloth); ISBN 978-1-118-28695-1 (ebk);
      ISBN 978-1-118-28400-1 (ebk); ISBN 978-1-118-28274-8 (ebk)
  1. Consolidation and merger of corporations–United States.   2. Business enterprises–United States–Purchasing.   3. Business enterprises–United States–Finance.
I. Title.
  HG4028.M4.B896 2012
  658.1'6–dc23

                                                                    2012012434

Printed in the United States of America

10 9 8 7 6 5 4 3 2 1

To my wife, Jayne,
and my children, Melinda and Mark

Contents

Acknowledgments

I wish to extend thanks to all of the individuals and companies that appear in this book as case studies. Every company is privately held, and all have generously shared information in order to provide readers with the benefit of invaluable experience in successful buyouts. Too numerous to mention here, the key contacts and principals have allowed me to identify them in the case studies as appropriate.

I would like to recognize the team at Enterprise Services, Inc., for suffering through the many mood swings, short notice on editing deadlines, and providing technical support to this otherwise analog author. To my partners Sandy Paavola and Greg Carlson, thank you for your understanding and patience in helping me with direction and purpose during the many long hours and weekends it took to get this book written.

I acknowledge the leap of faith taken by so many associates, friends, and organizations that provided speaking opportunities for me and allowed me to develop instructional materials. Their support has enabled me to gain the experience and confidence to keep moving forward. Thank you to Parnell Black, cofounder and CEO of the National Association of Certified Valuation Analysts, for being the first to let me serve the membership. I would like to especially mention Corey Rosen and Loren Rogers with the National Center for Employee Ownership; J. Michael Keeling, president of the ESOP Association; and Peter Christman and Dennis Gano with the Exit Planning Institute. I thank the board of directors of the Middle Management Investment Banking Association, including Dennis Roberts, Andrew Smith, Parnell Black, Richard Jackim, and Andrew Sherman. Their help has been instrumental in my understanding of the investment banking community. Dennis Roberts also graciously reviewed several of the chapters and perfected the art of tactfully encouraging enhancements to strengthen the content. I also thank the many individuals and departments at the American Institute of Certified Public Accountants for assistance in editing seminars and publications by offering suggestions to make them more complete.

Thank you to Lloyd Dickenson and John Michael (Mickey) Maier for the good conversation and inspiration at our council of advisors' meetings over appropriately chilled sudsy Wisconsin beverages and salty munchies.

I extend another thank you to Dennis Tomorsky, who as a friend and committee chair for the Wisconsin Institute of CPAs graciously allowed me to bend his ear about starting the consulting business that has led to this book.

Special recognition must go to the team at John Wiley and Sons that have been so instrumental with bringing this book to life. John DeRemigis, Executive Editor, was kind enough to listen to my "elevator speech" pitching the concept of this book and enthusiastically embracing the idea. Jennifer MacDonald, Senior Development Editor, and Natasha Andrews-Noel, Senior Production Editor made sure that due dates where honored and the manuscript was thoroughly reviewed. Brandon Dust, Senior Editorial Assistant sent me the color rendering of the proposed dust cover that drove home the point the book was really going to happen.

Finally, I offer a heartfelt thank you to Leon Danco, my longtime mentor, cheerleader, and friend. When I was alone in my basement as a new entrepreneur, Leon provided reassurance and early vision for the career that I so thoroughly enjoy today. He graciously allowed me to stand on his shoulders to gain perspectives that otherwise would have escaped me. One of Leon's favorite quotations, which he puts into practice and relentlessly pursues, is:

Dream no little dreams. They have no magic to move men's souls.
                                                            —Jeremy Bentham

Buyouts

The New Reality for Business Owners in 2012

First things first, but not necessarily in that order.
—Anonymous

Historically during the past 10 to 15 years business owners had little to fear about the failure to sell their businesses to third parties. There was the perception that there were many buyers waiting for the opportunity to acquire a business, bank resources were generally available to finance such transactions, and capital gain taxes were at historic lows. This thinking is not reflective of today's business environment. There are several important forces at work in our current economy, and the confluence of their impact has broad and far ranging significance for business owners that challenge the too comfortable thinking of the past. Circumstances for business owners have unalterably changed, and this book will help you make decisions in the upcoming uncertain future.

First, we passed a significant milestone with the financial meltdown of Wall Street in the fall of 2008. Within just a few weeks the entire face of the financial industry was systemically changed as one whole segment of investment banking capabilities was irrevocably altered. Linked to the implosion of the housing market and the subsequent torrent of bad debt, the banking industry shifted to preserving capital and avoiding most lending activities with any significant risk attached to it. Suddenly, commercial credit for middle market firms literally disappeared or was significantly reduced.

Second, there is a wave of "boomers" coming of retirement age. The oldest of the baby boom generation (1946–1964) are turning 65 in 2011. While many refuse to face reality regarding aging and reaching retirement,

1

the fact is that an estimated 80 million of them will be retiring in unprecedented numbers during the next 10–15 years. Much of the wealth of the boomer generation is committed to equity in closely held businesses, and releasing those resources for retirement purposes will have a telling impact on our economy. It is estimated that there will likely be far more sellers of businesses than buyers as the torrent of boomers seeks to ease into retirement.

Third, there is an almost certain material increase in taxes coming by January 1, 2013. The tax increase legislation has already been passed and signed into law. The increases are the direct result of "sunset" provisions in the tax cuts passed in the early 2000s often referred to as the Bush Tax Cuts. Tax rates such as the capital gain and ordinary income taxes will reset to the comparable rates in 2001. For example, at the Federal level, capital gain taxes will increase from 15% to 20%. Additionally, the new Patient Protection and Affordable Care Act passed in 2009 will impose surtaxes on certain capital gain and ordinary income taxes. State and local taxes on the sale of a business combined with Federal obligations will have a substantial impact on the net proceeds realized by a business owner.

In summary, there will be far fewer buyers with cash waiting to acquire companies. Business owners are well advised to be proactive and begin today to consider options that do not involve third-party buyers. There is a whole range of candidate buyers for the business including managers, key employees, family members, Employee Stock Ownership Plans (ESOPs), and private equity firms in concert with management. Selling to one or a combination of these buyers often results in a desirable outcome, but such a positive conclusion takes careful planning and above all, time. This book will demystify and provide a detailed look into the complex world of inside buyouts.

THE MIDDLE MARKET

This book is addressed to the stakeholders in middle market companies. The stakeholders include a wide range of interests including business owners, their families, key employees, professional advisors, communities, suppliers, and customers. The list is almost endless.

For my purposes the middle market is loosely defined as closely held companies with an overall value between $1 million and $250 million. There are thousands of companies with modest valuations under $1 million. Those businesses typically have few employees, little management beyond the owner and operate from a single location. These are the companies we find on "Main Street." Those companies are briefly addressed in Chapter 18.

The succession options for them are often limited due to size and a restricted market presence. Companies with a value over $250 million are typically divisions of public companies or public companies themselves. They have market dynamics beyond the scope of this book.

Middle market companies, as defined here, represent closely held businesses that most often have been founded by one or a few individuals with a vision of doing things better. With vision, hard work, and a positive attitude it is just possible such attributes will lead to the evolution of a successful company. According to the Middle Market Investment Banking Association it is estimated there are over 20 million privately held companies with sales under $1 million, and most of those businesses have no employees. There are approximately 1.2 million companies that meet the arbitrary definition of middle market companies as defined herein. Many of those companies are owned by aging baby boomers. As a generation, every day that passes thousands of boomers turn 65. The end of the working career is approaching rapidly for many.

This book will be of value to business owners and the employees in those companies. The book will also be of assistance to professional advisors to privately held businesses. Too often outside advisors assume the company has to be sold to outsiders if there is no logical family member to assume the mantle of leadership. As you read the book, it will be shown that business owners have many attractive options, but they must recognize that the options involving the transition involving insiders will take time to complete.

NOT ANOTHER MERGERS AND ACQUISITIONS BOOK

This book is focused on *buyouts*. Most significantly, the emphasis is on inside generated buyouts, typically not the sale of the company to a third party. First I examine common attributes with all business transactions such as the state of the economy, financing resources, valuation insights, the consideration of professional advisors, and how to minimize taxes.

There is a tidal wave of retirements coming as the boomers begin to exit the workplace. It is likely to be a buyer's market for many years. The face of acquisition financing has changed, as banks become more risk averse in the post 2008 Wall Street debacle. Strategic business thinkers will recognize the forces at play and will work to optimize options. Those few exceedingly successful companies with strong growth and demonstrated profitability will always attract buyer attention. There are fewer of those companies. There are a vast number of attractive, profitable, closely-held companies that will likely be under the radar screen of outside buyers.

This book addresses one option often not recognized by business owners; the inside buyout. The reason business owners often do not consider such an option is that there is the perception that "insiders" do not have the financial wherewithal to acquire the company. It is true that such buyers cannot typically write a check for the business. After 2008 fewer outside buyers can do the same thing. I suggest that many business owners take a deep breath and think about exiting the business over time. With a longer time horizon, inside initiated options are now far more likely. The benefit to inside buyouts is that the seller is dealing typically with employees and people that have been known for many years.

CHAPTER ORGANIZATION

There are a series of chapters that consider inside initiated buyouts from many perspectives. Beginning with Chapter 9, I look at management (or key employee) buyouts. The management buyout is considered from the perspective of overall advantages and common cautions or issues that need to be addressed. Valuation considerations are part of the analysis followed by observations on the viewpoint of the seller and buyer. The analysis considers professional advisors and a risk analysis that could threaten the transaction. Finally, technical matters impacting the structure of the proposed transaction are considered. All the succeeding chapters follow a similar outline.

Buyouts involving the assistance of private equity firms, or private equity groups (PEG) are considered in Chapters 10 and 11. The distinction is made between PEGS where management has been instrumental in the selection of the PEG (Chapter 10), and where the seller has been instrumental in the selection of the PEG (Chapter 11). ESOPs are addressed in Chapter 12 where the ESOP is one of perhaps many investors; and the case where the ESOP is the 100% shareholder. A special 100% ESOP in Chapter 13 is included because of the extraordinary tax benefits and operating environment of such a capital structure.

Professional service firms, including engineering firms, public accounting firms and management consultants, are addressed in Chapter 14. Many of those professional service firms embrace broad based employee participation. The use of "parallel companies" is considered in Chapter 15, a strategy employed when the underlying company is subject to high revenue volatility or cyclical results typically found in construction companies.

Succession within family businesses is the topic for Chapter 16. There is currently an enhanced opportunity to transfer family company ownership to the next generation of family members because of newly enacted gift tax legislation. Employee cooperatives are a little known option due to restrictive state laws, but when properly applied as discussed in Chapter 17 they may be an exciting option to explore. The last chapter on buyouts addresses the smallest privately held companies, Chapter 18.

The comparison between inside buyouts and selling to a third party is considered in Chapter 19. This is a summary chapter on options for the business owner and his advisors to consider.

CHAPTER 1

Buyout Examples

*Opportunity is missed by most people because it is dressed in
overalls and looks like work.*

—Thomas Edison

Throughout this book I reference many case studies of real companies
that have gone through the buyout process. Additionally, there are many
illustrations of buyout principles without naming specific companies for confidentiality reasons. Years of speaking and consulting have me concluding
that the reference to appropriate case studies is a time honored and preferred
means to communicate key concepts. Case studies with real life applications
are so much more viable than dry technical narrative.

This first chapter is intended to introduce you to a select number of
thought leaders, visionary thinkers, and hands-on business entrepreneurs
that illustrate how to roll up your sleeves and work toward accomplish-
ing extraordinary results. In order of presentation we will explore SRC
Holdings Corporation in Missouri; SSG Financial Services a public accounting and consulting firm in Ohio; and Quality Assembly and Logistics, LLC
in Wisconsin. The last case study is Jumbo Heater and Manufacturing Company, Inc. in Cleveland with some personal lessons learned.

CASE STUDY—SRC HOLDINGS, CORPORATION

Perhaps one of the most celebrated management buyouts of a business is the
case of the International Harvester's ReNew Center Repair Division which
was started in 1974. The Division became known as Springfield ReManufacturing. Mr. Jack Stack joined the company in 1979 and played an integral

part in the buyout from Harvester. As part of International Harvester's Construction Group in Woodfield, Illinois, the unit focused on remanufacturing engines and components used as replacement parts in Harvester equipment. In 1981 International Harvester itself was realizing financial difficulties and that stress was making its way throughout the entire organization. A recession was gripping the country and Springfield ReManufacturing was already experiencing a wage freeze.

Jack Stack, General Manager for Springfield ReManufacturing, was thinking of ways to save jobs at the plant. The Springfield ReManufacturing Division was still profitable even as the fortunes of the parent Harvester were deteriorating. The thought of buying the operation from Harvester was broached, but Harvester was having so many of its own problems at the corporate level the proposed buyout was delayed. After a succession of new Harvester managers in a short period of time, the management proposal was lost in the increasing mountain of Harvester problems. Compounding the stress, Harvester placed the Construction Group on the sale block and one large international company was bidding on the bundle of operations. At the darkest hour, Jack was convinced that the plant would be sold to a third party.

The proposed sale kept getting delayed. Jack was aware that negotiations were very complex. Suddenly in the middle of negotiations, Jack received a call from a lead Harvester negotiator stating that talks were at an impasse, and some of the issues involved Springfield ReManufacturing. In reference to an earlier purchase inquiry from the management, the Harvester negotiator said they could have the plant for an additional million over the preliminary offer of $6 million. Jack was "tapped out" for financial resources at $6 million. Virtually all that amount was debt, and finding another $1 million seemed impossible. With his creativity hat on, Jack proposed the extra million be in the form of an unsecured one year note from Harvester to Springfield ReManufacturing. On paper it is an extra million with "terms." Nothing like some delayed payments to overcome lack of cash today. Harvester was Springfield ReManufacturing's largest customer and they could see that repayment on the note was likely. The deal was accepted.

Management succeeded against impossible odds to acquire the business unit and in 1982 SRC Holdings Corporation (SRC) was formed. The structure of the transaction still is haunting today. Management, numbering 13 individuals, in 1983 was able to raise $100,000 in equity between them toward the eventual purchase price of approximately $9 million. When we look at the math SRC was leveraged approximately 89:1 debt to equity. In an era when financial institutions like to see debt to equity ratios of 2:1

or 3:1 it is easy to understand the miracle of SRC. Under the category of "more good news," SRC was in a delicate position of not being able to make any operational missteps due to the heavy debt load. The first year SRC posted an operating loss of approximately $60,000. Employment was maintained among the staff, operations were strengthened and most of the "equity investment" was now on the balance sheet as a debit balance (loss). The SRC stock was valued at just 10 cents a share that first year. A consortium of 13 management investors along with a recently created Employee Stock Ownership Plan and Trust (ESOP) were the new SRC owners.

From those dark moments one may ask what has SRC done in the intervening 30 years since 1982? What began as an engine and components remanufacturing facility has grown into a diversified company with over 12 operating units, annual sales exceeding $350 million, and with over 1,200 employees. SRC has been recognized as one of the top 100 places to work and is acknowledged as a leader in management systems.

Starting at Ground Zero

Jack was fortunate to have a management team that was trusting in its leader, and committed to making SRC a financial success. The team instituted open book management long before it became a popular buzzword on the speaking circuit. Financial information was routinely and openly shared with all the employees. The feeling was that the employee stakeholders were not going to feel like owners unless they were in fact treated like owners. Daily and weekly meetings were held to analyze the financial performance at the plant. Together as a team, obstacles were addressed and solutions found. Methodically, the operational issues on the plant floor and in the administrative offices were vetted and resolved. When you are leveraged 89:1 from a pragmatic standpoint there is only one way to go. At that point decreasing the leverage to 60:1 is a victory. The story is substantially better than that and by 1986 only three years after the buyout, revenue was increasing by 30% annually and sales exceeded $42 million. SRC was flirting with genuine financial respectability.

The Great Game of Business

The success of SRC was becoming legendary. Through the 1980s the company was growing and diversifying. As an employee-owned company they succeeded in building a culture of ownership. All the employees had a direct financial interest in the success of SRC. In 1992 Jack along with Bo Burlingham co-authored the book *The Great Game of Business*

(Currency/Doubleday), which detailed the shop-proven management strategies and philosophy so instrumental in the financial success of SRC. *The Great Game of Business* was so successful that SRC started an affiliate The Great Game of Business, Inc. to teach the lessons SRC learned on the production floor. One central theme that is emphasized, is why they teach employees how to make money. By insisting on financial literacy, SRC has succeeded in promulgating a spirit of cooperation and ownership. The employees know how important their contributions are to the financial health of SRC and their own financial well being.

Following the first book, Jack and Bo co-authored *A Stake in the Outcome: Building a Culture of Ownership for the Long-Term Success of your Business (Crown Business)* in 2003. This second book details the trials and tribulations SRC experienced since the first book in 1992. The Company was having growing pains and second thoughts about its future as an employee owned business. An employee-owned company is great on paper until the stock of investors has to be redeemed. The stock redemption obligation seemed as a crushing burden to the original investors. They wanted to remain employee owned, but they also wanted to convert their now substantial equity stake in SRC into cash for retirement.

The solution that SRC embraces is to sell more of the stock of departing individual investors to the ESOP. With time the percentage of stock owned by the ESOP has increased. There are substantial tax benefits to both the individual shareholders and the ESOP to encourage more employee ownership. ESOPs are discussed at length shortly.

Looking into the Future

During 2008 SRC was on the cusp of a crucial decision. SRC had grown into a complex company with many business units and management wanted to have a structure that enabled the employee teams within the various units to have some significant control over their future. If it made sense, SRC would sell a business unit to its employees, in much the same spirit as Harvester sold SRC to its employees. SRC elected to have the ESOP acquire the last of the outstanding shares of individual investors and is today a 100% ESOP Company.

Having the ESOP as the sole shareholder enables the Company to access the vast financial benefits of being an S corporation. SRC is able to redeem the stock of departing employees and recycle it to the remaining stakeholders. The Company has succeeded in building and maintaining an ownership culture. Hundreds of companies representing thousands of employees have journeyed to Springfield, Missouri to learn the Great Game of Business.

Only those that are interested in building long-term value and a culture of ownership will likely find the investment in time and money worthwhile. Jack Stack and his team have demonstrated a serious flaw in short-term thinking and chasing financial results of the moment.

CASE STUDY—SSG FINANCIAL SERVICES

The public accounting firm of Saltz, Shamis, and Goldfarb (now SSG Financial Services) was founded in 1987. The principals of the firm were concerned that in that era the traditional and conservative career path for many certified public accountants (CPAs) was to be promoted into the partnership as an equity holder or leave the firm. This "up or out" protocol was challenging to the SSG partners, and they wanted to think about options to this potentially hostile employee environment. Many accounting professionals don't want to become "partners" because of the professional commitments, demands, and liabilities that come with the territory. In the world of changing family values and with a high percentage of women CPAs, the up or out philosophy was hurting the profession in the opinion of Gary Shamis, President of SSG.

SSG believed that providing a career path for CPA professionals with a competitive compensation program without becoming a traditional equity partner was a worthwhile goal. Embracing this non-traditional approach to the team was attractive to the partners because it provided SSG with a distinctive brand literally not seen in the profession.

In 1996 SSG introduced what is technically a non-qualified stock purchase program (Plan). The concept is to allow the professionals to purchase "stock" in SSG. Partners Gary Shamis and Mark Goldfarb worked on the Plan along with a compensation consultant to refine the details. The non-qualified stock purchase program is in essence a phantom equity plan. Participants have to acquire the "equity" in SSG with their own after-tax dollars. From the beginning days:

- Eligible participants had to be CPAs (based on existing Ohio law barring non-CPA ownership).
- Participants had to meet a minimum employment period.
- Full time and part-time employees are eligible.
- 90 percent of the investment is unsecured debt with a fixed interest rate.
- The balance of the investment is in non-voting stock.
- There is a minimum investment required.

The Plan provides for participants leaving the employment of SSG, voluntary withdrawals for personal circumstances, and there is a non-competition agreement.

Impact of the Plan

When the Plan was introduced SSG had approximately 80 employees centric to the Akron-Cleveland area. Today the firm has grown to over 400 professionals in multiple offices throughout Ohio and Kentucky. Gary Shamis contributes the dynamic growth and financial success of SSG in large measure to the approach of treating their associates as partners.

The risks of introducing the Plan at first were numerous. Remembering the Plan was introduced in 1996, this "outside-the-box" thinking was not part of the CPA profession's career protocols. Most partners are loath to share any information regarding the financial performance of their firm, let alone with just staff members. It was believed that staff members would not responsibly handle the confidential financial information being shared. Since the Plan was voluntary, non-participation could be embarrassing to individuals and damaging to the moral of the firm. A catastrophic legal judgment against the firm would put the investments at risk.

The SSG partners considered these issues at length but decided that the benefits would outweigh the disadvantages. There are many positive aspects that tipped the decision in favor of installing the Plan. The professional staff members understand SSG has two distinct career paths. One career path is the traditional one that culminates in an equity ownership in the firm. The second path offers a career to those professionals that want to be affiliated with SSG and still have a lifestyle compatible to their needs. According to Gary Shamis the SSG professionals are distinctive from those of competitors because they are also owners, imbued with an ownership outlook. The commitment to the firm-client relationship is reinforced because of the employee investment that has been made. Due to the Plan, everyone may share in the success of the firm. Ohio law has subsequently been changed permitting non-CPAs to be shareholders in the firm. The invitation to become an owner is now extended to all eligible employees.

Intangible Benefits

The SSG partners had a "gut" feeling that installing the Plan would have a disproportionately favorable impact on the firm. Treating all associates as partners including part time professionals; has been exceedingly beneficial. Many outstanding professionals have stayed with SSG for that very reason. Gary Shamis notes that the structure of SSG is advantageous in recruiting

because SSG offers an immediate opportunity for new associates to participate in the success of the firm. The value of the stock in the Plan is a function
of the dividend that is paid, and also the growth in cash receipts. SSG has
been growing at a double-digit rate since the Plan was introduced. This has
led to an attractive increase in the value as everyone is focused on providing
the best client service and developing new business opportunities.

Several important lessons have been learned according to Gary Shamis.
You cannot assume that the financial benefits will be self-evident. The advantages of the Plan have to be carefully and repeatedly communicated to
the employees. The existence of the Plan is intended to be a winning circumstance to SSG and the employees. This commitment to communication
is a lynchpin with other firms that have embraced employee participation
with similarly positive results. The Plan needs to be communicated as an
attractive investment vehicle for the future of the employees. Address what
the firm will do with the influx of investment cash; in the case of SSG
the capital is committed to growing and expanding the firm. The Plan is a
"buy-in" program for those employees that want a part of the ownership
of SSG.

Looking into the Future

SSG maintains equity participation for select individuals, which follows
a more traditional public accounting firm template. Professionals will be
invited to participate at this level. When the principals retire or leave SSG,
their equity is redeemed according to a shareholder agreement. Professionals
that aspire to this level of responsibility are most often those that have also
elected to make an investment in SSG through the Plan. The connection with
ownership, commitment, and professionalism combines to make SSG one
of the leading employers in the region.

The recent recession has momentarily slowed the historically strong
growth rate. Gary Shamis believes that the attributes of SSG are so strong
that they will continue their trajectory of continued growth. Currently one
of the largest public accounting firms in the region, SSG continues to think
"outside the box" and is affiliated with the Leading Edge Alliance of like
minded public accounting firms.

The creative thinking by the leadership at SSG and their approach to
the professionalism of their entire team sets the groundwork for expected
continued success. SSG has expanded into many other service areas not
necessarily associated with being a CPA. The open culture and having the
Plan is an invitation to a wide range of career minded individuals that
SSG offers an attractive future of significance. With over 400 motivated
associates the likelihood of continued success is assured. When asked if he

and his partners had any regrets regarding the Plan, Gary Shamis had one: "Not starting the Plan sooner." Gary Shamis, meet Jack Stack.

CASE STUDY—QUALITY ASSEMBLY AND LOGISTICS, LLC

In a garage in 1979, founder Mr. Dave Brandt started Engineering Research and Design Associates (ERDA) with five employees making specialized lightweight seating for the airline industry. This is a classic entrepreneurial initiative started with little more than some good ideas and enthusiasm. With time ERDA grew and branched into specialized manufacturing and assembly with particular expertise in the medical industry in addition to the airline seating focus. In 2000 the Company was acquired by DeCrane Aerospace, Inc. (DeCrane) largely for its airline seat manufacturing expertise.

DeCrane manufactures interior products and completion kits for aircrafts as well as systems integration for aircrafts. DeCrane works within a broad spectrum of the various facets of the aviation industry including commercial airlines, military applications, individual aircraft owners, and original equipment manufacturers (OEMs). In 2009 Mr. Guy Meyerhofer, Vice President of the DeCrane Seating Division, approached DeCrane about the possibility of acquiring the ERDA Division. Mr. Meyerhofer was interested in the opportunity to acquire the Division and determined a price he was willing to pay. The Division was profitable, but it ceased to be a strategic fit for DeCrane.

There are several attractive attributes of the Company including ISO 9001 Certification, which is indispensable when negotiating with large quality-conscious accounts. The Company also employs Kanban point-of-use inventory. Kanban is a visual signaling system to trigger action on the production floor. The system reduces waste, provides quick responses to changes, and provides the tools for ongoing review of production processes. They are Food and Drug Administration Registered, Electrical Testing Laboratories Certified, and Underwriters Laboratory Certified. They occupy a modern facility with 56,000 ft of floor space in Marinette, Wisconsin. The location provides for virtually unlimited expansion opportunities.

Mr. Meyerhofer was tasked with putting in place an offer acceptable to DeCrane. He partnered with Generation Growth Capital, Inc. (Generation) in Milwaukee, Wisconsin who provided some of the financing for the buyout. The Company was renamed Quality Assembly & Logistics (QAL), LLC. in 2009, in concert with the buyout. Mr. John Reinke, Managing Director with Generation, indicated they took a flexible approach to financing the

QAL management with the buyout. The assets were acquired from DeCrane using a combination of equity provided by management for a controlling block of common stock; an investment in preferred stock by Generation that carried a dividend and warranted for a percentage of the QAL stock; proceeds from a local bank and assistance from Marinette County and Marinette City.

Generation's flexibility was particularly helpful in putting all the financial pieces in place. Their investment in Preferred Stock was the equity needed to permit the debt leveraging provided by the bank loan package. QAL has an option to redeem the Generation Preferred Stock and common stock warrants once certain financial goals have been met. According to Mr. Reinke, "Generation provided financial assistance to the QAL management so that with time they will own the Company. The business plan will take several years to complete, but QAL is growing and remains under local management control." QAL is an integral part of the Marinette business community thanks to the team approach and long-term vision provided by the financial partners.

Success Factors

For those following the timeline, QAL was acquired at the height of the recession in 2009. The Company was negatively impacted by the recession as most other businesses. During this time there were very few management buyouts, particularly in the risk-averse heartland. If the transaction was going to be completed with the retention of many skilled employees, the buyout needed to be accompanied with a significant amount of equity financing provided in a manner allowing the management to retain control during the buyout period.

Generation understands the core capabilities of QAL and knew the management was capable of strong cost and quality controls. The prospects for growth would provide QAL with an exit from the acquisition leverage with time. If QAL was capable of increasing sales and profitability, and needed additional capital to grow, Generation is in a position to understand the requirements and structure a growth continuance that is a winning situation for management, Generation, and the community.

Management has financial goals that enable it to redeem the equity interest of Generation upon an agreed process. This creative approach allows management to best direct the operations of the Company while Generation is a non-controlling financial partner. Generation's interest may be redeemed without the Company having to be sold through an auction process that puts control of the Company into the hands of a potential buyer that may over-leverage the business and destroy it. The flexibility provided by Generation is a lynchpin to the success of this management buyout. While a budgeted period of time has been planned to redeem the equity interest of Generation, that timeline is not absolute. If QAL requires additional time and resources to complete the transition, the partnership with Generation will provide for that. The management buyout of QAL in the middle of a recession is unusual. The overall structure of the transaction relates to a middle market company and it was accomplished with reasonable leverage. When so many buyouts of the 2000s are in trouble due to overly optimistic or unrealistic projections, having a pragmatic perspective will serve Generation well going forward.

The longer-term time horizon is already paying dividends. The flexibility accorded the management proved to be a tremendous benefit when QAL found an opportunity to acquire a complementary line of business in 2011. Just a short time following the leveraged buyout, QAL went back to its primary financial backers and secured additional resources to purchase what is now called QAL Medical. QAL Medical produces Continuous Passive Motion (CPM) devices that assist patients in the recovery following joint surgery such as knees, hips, ankles and toes. QAL did its financial homework demonstrating the strong complimentary fit with the acquisition and the current product line. QAL Medical completed the ISO 13485 certification further enhancing their commitment to quality. With the addition, approximately 20 new jobs were added at the Marinette plant. The acquisition is assisting QAL with some needed product diversification. While the QAL Medical acquisition was accomplished with additional debt, the added profitability of the CPM products puts QAL on track to manage all its financial obligations.

CASE STUDY—JUMBO HEATER & MANUFACTURING COMPANY, INC.

Founded in Cleveland, Ohio just after World War II, the company specialized in the design, manufacturing, and distribution of cast iron soil pipe plumbing specialty fittings. The founder returned from military service and was one of the few members of his generation to have a college degree. With modest financial assistance, Jumbo Heating and Manufacturing Company, Inc. (Jumbo) was started occupying an old building in the heart of the industrial landscape in Cleveland. Enjoying the economic bounce following the end of the war, the business steadily grew and an old but dedicated facility was purchased in 1957. Jumbo featured a line of proprietary soil pipe fittings each designed and patterned after standard industry specifications. The process of bringing new products to market included rendering a design and delivering the hand-drawn design to a pattern maker to produce a master wood rendering of the product. The wood master is then used to produce aluminum production tooling that was shipped to cast iron foundries to make the rough green sand castings. The castings were shipped to the main facility where they were tapped and threaded as required and inventoried for eventual shipment to customers.

With time the cast iron soil pipe industry began to feel the pressure of competition from other types of materials, particularly PVC plastic. The cast iron foundries were coming under increasing scrutiny from the Environmental Protection Agency (EPA) as sources of air and ground pollution. At best Jumbo was going sideways financially during the 1960s, and the future was challenging. While the company was financially surviving, the family was able to provide outstanding educational opportunities for the children. The founder was a heavy smoker and living in industrial Cleveland compounded an already dire health environment. Upon graduation from an MBA program, the son had no interest in returning to Cleveland and assuming the leadership of Jumbo. He knew little about the business, and there was always friction with his father. As the founder's health began to fail, the son decided to return and learn the family business. Owning a business was a long-term goal of the son and there was this family company waiting for an heir apparent. The Company consisted of an antiquated manufacturing facility and a separate foundry in another state.

Tensions and Failure

The return of the son provided a brief respite from an otherwise bleak financial future. The product line was rapidly becoming obsolete, the EPA was proactive against most foundries for pollution related issues, there were few resources to invest in new products to remain competitive, and the health of the founder continued to deteriorate. The declining financial circumstances of Jumbo were a source of frustration for the son. The founder was hesitant to risk personal assets that had been carefully saved and set aside for retirement. Without such a commitment, the future of the company was particularly bleak. The son soon realized the lost cause and began to consider career options. After a promising start, the reality of a lack of attention to re-investment and the corresponding product obsolescence came back to haunt the family. Another opportunity presented itself and the son eventually resigned from Jumbo, moved to another state, and started a new career in business. Broken-hearted and in failing health, the founder succumbed to cancer within another year. Before his demise Jumbo was sold to an investor for a bargain price with the assistance of an astute business intermediary that was knowledgeable about foundries.

LESSONS LEARNED

Not all of the case studies in this book have happy endings. If you have not guessed, the founder's name was George Miller, father of Scott Miller, the author of this book. From this personal tragedy, there are some strong take-away lessons. It is always helpful to try and see both sides of a story. Jumbo's demise is a result largely of failed communication.

Dad pulled back from his industry and did not attend a trade association meeting for countless years. Isolated and withdrawn, he lived in the past and could not imagine how to deal with changing circumstances. His key "advisor" was an old family attorney even more removed from the world of current trends and out of touch with the needs of a succession strategy. The attorney had known the family from the days of my grandfather and his plumbing and mechanical contracting company (circa 1920s).

Dad had developed a "circle the wagons" mentality. This is a perspective of just holding onto the financial resources that have been pulled out of the family business, never to reinvest them if at all possible. The risk appetite was gone, and Dad just wanted to coast and enjoy his remaining days at peace drawing a modest return from the business he spent his career building. It was not fair that the market was passing him and posing a threat to his hard-earned wealth. This is the creative destruction aspect of our market-based capitalistic economy. It was not fair to my dad that the market was migrating away from cast iron plumbing fittings; however, it was great news for injection molding companies manufacturing PVC plastic pipe.

My heartfelt advice to all business owners is replete throughout the pages of this book. It is essential that business owners address the topic of succession planning with earnest and focus. Fulfilling your personal dreams and goals is possible with diligence and an acute awareness that things do not stand still for very long in our dynamic economy. Surround yourself with the best advisors you can find and afford. I think they overwhelmingly pay for themselves if you elect to listen to the voice of experience.

Privately held middle market companies occupy a strategic position in our economy building wealth for owners, employment for associates, and a future of hope for our economy. I hope you enjoy this book. It is available because my decision was made years ago to flex my intellect, embrace my own dreams and work diligently and with passion for a cause that I fully embrace.

SUMMARY

This chapter should have you thinking about buyouts both from the standpoint of what is possible and also from the view of what can go terribly wrong. The emphasis is on the positive with special care to indicate some best practices that will lead to successful buyouts.

CHAPTER 2

The Economy

None of us really understands what's going on with all these numbers.

> —David Stockwell, U.S. Budget Director

Things are going to get a lot worse before they get worse.

> —Lily Tomlin

The state of the economy will have an impact on the ability to get a transaction completed. As this book goes to print, the economy is mired in one of the worst recessions in memory. The beginning of the great recession had its first warnings in 2007 when certain problems with the housing industry were becoming evident. The economic cancer began to spread into the financial markets largely as a result of problems with how housing was financed. In hindsight many exotic financial instruments were invented and designed to provide investment opportunities for large institutions. Many of these financial vehicles were not understood by those making investments in them. Just imagine trying to understand the following investment vehicle: Credit Default Swaps on Double AA Tranches of Mezzanine Subprime Collateralized Debt Obligations (huh?).

Eventually, the inherent problems on Wall Street largely relating to the housing market were discovered along with a disproportionate amount of leverage. The financial catastrophe will have an enduring impact on the markets for many years.

BRIEF OVERVIEW OF THE CURRENT RECESSION

Generally, the economy really faltered with the failure of large financial institutions largely centered in New York and closely related to Wall Street investment banks. The high-profile financial bailout of Bear Sterns in the spring of 2008 was the first sign of impending gloom. By September and October of 2008, the financial markets were rocked with the reconfiguration of the investment banking community on Wall Street, and a pronounced ripple effect throughout the financial sector. By way of a quick summary the following nearly unbelievable string of events occurred.

- On September 7th, 2008, Fannie Mae and Freddie Mac are nationalized.
- September 14th, Bank of America announces its purchase of Merrill Lynch.
- September 15th, Lehman Brothers is bankrupt. This really sends signals of shock and angst through the financial markets.
- September 16th, the Reserve Primary money market fund "breaks the buck." A dollar is actually less than a dollar that day.
- September 16th, the same day the Fed provides AIG with an infusion of $85 billion in return for an equity stake of almost 80%.
- September 22nd, traditional investment banking as it was known for decades is irrevocably changed as both Goldman Sachs and Morgan Stanley become bank holding companies. This election approved by the Federal Government allows both of them to have access to bank liquidity permitted by the banking system. As bank holding companies they will be regulated much differently.
- September 25th, FDIC seizes the assets of Washington Mutual, the largest bank failure to date in history.

Within only a few short weeks Lehman Brothers filed for bankruptcy, Merrill Lynch was forced into the arms of Bank of America, Goldman Sachs—no longer viable as an investment bank—becomes a regular deposit seeking bank to avail themselves of support by the Federal government, and so it went. From my standpoint I could not believe what was being reported. It is fair to unequivocally state I did not see it coming. Perhaps those much closer to the financial centers knew of problems, but the full impact of so many material developments and spectacular announcements on an almost daily basis shook our market-based capitalistic economy to its core.

It is no exaggeration to state that the status of the free market capitalistic economy of the country was at grave risk unless something dramatic and draconian was done by the Federal government. After the fact, there are now a number of sensational books highlighting the inner workings of the power corridors in New York and Washington, D.C. My favorite reading on this topic is listed in the companion Web site to this book (www.wiley.com/go/ millerbuyouts) regarding references. If those insights are to be fully believed, our economy was really at the brink of a near total breakdown. Credit was at the point of being frozen as fear gripped the major financial institutions. If credit was frozen under the most draconian scenarios the reverberations through the economy would be nearly instantaneous with disastrous results. In ways unimaginable to the average market participant, events could have quickly gotten out of control cascading into a global financial meltdown.

Financial Armageddon was averted during those crisis weeks because the Federal Government decided to open the liquidity floodgates and provide funding to ease the threat of panic. While the financial sector was spared in the immediate future, the economic shock waves continued through the end of 2008. The new administration led by the Democratic Party in the Executive Branch (President Obama) and the Legislative Branch in both the Congress and the Senate inherited an economy on a steep slide into recession. The unemployment rate steadily climbed to over 9%, the highest in decades. It seemed that every month in 2009 witnessed the announcement of hundreds of thousands of workers finding themselves unemployed. The reality of a terrible recession was now spreading as the layoffs were impacting all sectors of the economy and virtually all major metropolitan areas.

Crises Following Wall Street

As 2009 progressed, the crises spread from the financial industry to other pillars of our economy. The automotive industry was on its own precipice of collapse. With the financial bailouts of financial institutions and the insurance leader AIG, the decision had to be reached if the automotive industry would also be assisted. Eventually the decision was made to allow a programmed bankruptcy of both Chrysler and General Motors. Both Chrysler and General Motors were destined to emerge from bankruptcy protection with a dramatically altered cost and capital structure that was intended to permit them to be competitive in the newly reorganized economy. Chrysler and General Motors survived but at great cost to secured creditors and other vendors. On main street the feeling often suggested that the major players in the economy (examples: large banks, major insurance companies, large automotive manufacturers) receive preferential treatment with taxpayer support, but the rest are left to pay the price. What additionally hurts is that the many true sources of the financial mismanagement that led to the crises on Wall Street became publicized, leaving the impression that those that largely caused the damage are the ones being helped with taxpayer dollars.

It is almost laughable that according to the "official" scorekeeping regarding recessions (trends in the number of quarters of activity), the recession apparently ended sometime in 2009. That may be the more academic approach to the analysis, but on Main Street where unemployment hovers above 9% after three years and counting, the recession still burns.

Prospects for the Immediate Future 2012 and 2013

This title suggests an all-knowing forecast, which is of course not possible from this author. An educated guess is forthcoming. What is apparent is that as 2011 comes to a close, we are entering the national theater known as election season culminating with a presidential election in November 2012. During 2011 the political posturing of both the Democrats and Republicans was a near-nightly spectacle on the daily news channels. As the year progressed you sensed the palpable hardening of the political positions. The current administration was receiving terrible press about the deteriorating economy and the lack of an economic rebound. The challengers knew the administration was in trouble as countless surveys documented a steady erosion of confidence and frustration at the lack of economic progress.

The strategy of the opposition is becoming clear as the 2012 election gets closer. That strategy is to provide as little cooperation as possible while unemployment remains high in the hope that the public anger will vote the current leadership out of office in November 2012. The political brinkmanship is serious and results in new financial crises on an ongoing basis. The Federal government came within hours of a partial shutdown in July, 2011 as partisan fighting over the budget came to a head. The crises were averted in time, but shortly following the deadline the Federal Government credit rating was downgraded by Standard and Poor's. The credit downgrade was perhaps more symbolic than substantive, but it was a warning shot to the ruling political class that the global community is watching with displeasure. More on the impact of the global community shortly.

One may ask: What is the practical impact of this terrible economy? The correct answer as in so many endeavors is "It depends." What is a disaster for some is a bright opportunity for others. One quick example will drive this point home. If you are a business owner seeking to retire or transition your company, it may be almost impossible to put together a suitable transaction that will satisfy your requirements. If you are a family business and the company is struggling, this may be a perfect time to involve family members with an equity stake by gifting or "selling" a block of deeply discounted stock. The goal in this case is the transfer of significant family wealth to favored members of your clan. Generally, the existing economy is a severe depressant on getting transactions completed absent the more unusual situation of those actually looking for a depressed value.

There are entire broad segments of the economy that are suffering disproportionately such as construction and manufacturing. There are other segments of the economy that are more resistant to the wide swings such as healthcare and retail food sales. The key point is to realize that trying to perfectly time the exact moment to effect a transaction is an exercise in great speculation. The current downturn may well extend across four to five years. Even when the economy is ready to turn after such a prolonged period and business owners have delayed taking action in some cases for years, ask yourself how many other countless thousands of business owners are thinking the same thing?

NEAR TERM REGULATORY ENVIRONMENT— TAX INCREASES

One specific matter of great interest to my audience is the tax environment at both the Federal and the state levels. Since approximately 2001, the business community has largely enjoyed the benefits of Federal tax cuts from the Bush Administration era. First, the passage of the Economic Growth Tax Recovery and Reconciliation Act of 2001 (EGTRRA) was passed lowering a number of tax rates including the maximum Federal personal income tax rate from approximately 39.5% to 35%. Legislation in 2003 further lowered other highly visible tax rates including the Federal capital gain rate from 20% down to 15%. Additionally, C corporations received a tax break on dividends along with other limited tax benefits. The economy experienced growth following the legislation. What few people realized is that the tax reductions were only temporary, they were not made permanent. There was a "sunset provision" that stated the tax reductions were set to expire on January 1, 2010 and be reset to the Federal rates in effect just prior to the enactment of the legislation. There was a temporary extension of the tax reductions until January 1, 2013 as part of the political compromise late in 2000 under the Tax Relief, Unemployment Insurance Reauthorization and Job Creation Act of 2010.

Tax rates will automatically reset to the levels of the early 2000s. There is no debate, it is a done deal. The only way the tax rates do not reset is if there is a dramatic Administration change in the national elections in November 2012. The rates may be extended for a period, but it is highly unlikely that permanent rate reductions will be made. Due to our political processes, it takes 60 votes in the Senate, along with a majority in the Congress and a willing President to pass the permanent law. Add to this the input of a wide range of vested interests and the likelihood of permanent tax rate reductions is really remote bordering on the impossible.

For business owners in a transition mode, exposure to those tax increases is largely elective. Decisions may be made ahead of the tax increases to facilitate the sale of a business (avoiding the tax increase with financial and tax engineering). Business owners may wait for a date after January 1, 2013 and hope that the economy improves enough to garner a higher price that more than offsets the increase in the taxes. Good luck trying to time that event.

Additional Regulations Coming

It bears mentioning that the Federal Government is also adopting legislation to address the excesses of the financial industry. Legislation known as the Dodd-Frank Wall Street Reform and Consumer Protection Act (Dodd-Frank Act) is working its way through Congress. While some momentum has stalled, the comprehensive legislation is targeted to reform Wall Street. A few of the key provisions will address such things as: reduce market volatility, study the causes of flash crashes, establish greater transparency regarding complex investment vehicles, and raise capital requirements for banks. Following the 2008 financial crises, the newly elected Administration rightfully sensed the public outrage of seeing those that are perceived to have exacerbated the crises being bailed out with taxpayer dollars. The Dodd-Frank Act seeks to impose a regulatory net over the industry to insure that such a potential tipping point is never again realized.

Saying "never again" in a political or economic environment is dangerous, but the intent is apparent. One clear goal of the Dodd-Frank Act is to impose discipline on the financial industry so that the egregious behavior is curtailed. The financial industry cannot be trusted to manage itself, as the crises proved. Unvarnished self-interest on many parts nearly destroyed our economy.

THE LONGER VIEW

There is a good case to be made that this time things are different. The "Great Recession" gripping the economy will force a number of systemic changes. Things may never fully return to what was known and comfortable before 2008.

The protracted recession is teaching business owners to think strategically, and the most astute owners will adopt a longer-term time horizon. This book is dedicated to those strategic thinkers today that recognize that at least for the foreseeable future for several years, fulfilling optimal transition goals will take time, imagination, and an acceptance that circumstances have changed. The emphasis here is on optimal goal achievement. Business owners may always refuse to accept the changing circumstances and wait for bad if not very bad events to happen, such as a turn in health or worse.

Some economists are estimating that the return of unemployment rates in the 4–5% range may take years, with unemployment being a relative sign of a healthy economy. Business owners are well advised to take corrective actions to size their businesses to the economic activity that enables them to remain profitable. The risk environment is very substantial, and with the tremendous uncertainty magnified by the political behavior in Washington, D.C., most business owners rightfully are taking a wait-and-see attitude. Financial and business journals suggest that many companies are saving their ready liquidity for what may appear as a protracted period of economic malaise.

Global Perspective

A few thoughts on the global economy are appropriate. During most of my career through an arbitrarily assigned date of approximately 2000, my entire orientation was to the American market. While international business was somewhat considered, my focus was on things here in the United States. During the past 10 to 20 years the international business community has evolved to the point where the influence on the global community by the United States is shrinking, and perhaps shrinking at an accelerating pace. We (the United States) have major global competitors for a finite pool of natural resources.

One of the new acronyms we all need to know is the "BRIC" economies of Brazil, Russia, India, and China. The population of the BRIC nations dwarfs that of the United States and those economies are growing at rates far in excess of our economy. There is a race to the top, and we are seeing greater competition from corners of the global community not seen to any material degree before. The European Union (EU) has developed a single currency and a host of agreements designed to build economic transparency within their borders for greater cooperation and growth. The forces of globalization have been unleashed, and the inexorable push for improved living conditions literally guarantees a future much different from anything we experienced prior to my arbitrary date of 2000.

SUMMARY

My point in mentioning the above matters is to pass along the obvious insight that our economy is changing, and changing in many unimaginable ways. We will face growing global competition, and the traditional and customary way of approaching business and commerce will be dramatically different moving forward.

CHAPTER 3

Finance

There have been three great inventions since the beginning of time: fire, the wheel, and central banking.
—Will Rogers

We have to continually be jumping off cliffs and developing our wings on the way down.
—Kurt Vonnegut

Did the financial crises of 2008 have a significant effect on the ability to obtain commercial financing? Of course, the answer to the question "Is financing available?" is almost always "It depends." This chapter will provide an overview of the major segments of the world of finance in the domestic economy today for middle market companies. Scale is a matter of consideration for this book. The middle market is addressed, which includes companies and owners that depend on more traditional sources of funding. In this light, those traditional sources include such options as commercial banks, community banks, private equity funds, the Small Business Administration (SBA) programs, mezzanine funds, and ultimately seller financing. The chapter does not address truly substantial financial requirements running into billions of dollars that are served by such options as Sovereign Funds, the Federal Reserve, the European Union (EU), and other substantial sources.

The prior chapter on the economy set the stage for changes in the way funding is both available and managed. Generally, the financial industry suffered a severe financial bloodbath through the early years of the recession (2008–2010). Many financial institutions suffered substantial losses, often related to real estate credits. The equity positions of many banks were severely harmed, with capital being consumed by loan portfolio losses. Preservation of capital against future erosion was a common industry rallying point. Preserving adequate capital was one of the best strategies to stay off the FDIC watch or close list.

Access to financing is integral to success in transition planning. We will examine a few of the more common resources with observations on the state of those resources and the likelihood they will provide the funding required for middle market transactions.

COMMUNITY BANKS

Community banks are a good place to begin the analysis. For many closely held companies this is the place where trust is developed and a long-term relationship evolves. The community bank is in the region and for our purposes loan decisions are based close to where the funding is placed. Entrepreneurs and business owners typically place great reliance on the ability to make a single phone call and talk about financial requirements with a decision maker at the community bank. Such relationships typically evolve over years and the parties get to know one another. In many instances both the community bank and the business owner are financially conservative and eschew over reliance on too much debt. The banking theory suggests that the community bank will stand with a business owner even when economic times are challenging because the two have experience with one another. As long as the fundamentals are still solid (such as a viable business), the community bank will likely be more flexible in arranging terms that are workable for a troubled account.

One possible issue with community banks may be their size. As commercial accounts grow they may outstrip the ability of the community bank to fund the operations. When both an operating company and the real estate owned by the controlling shareholder are financed by the same community bank, the dollar amount in absolute terms may approach many millions of dollars and become an unwelcome risk in relation to the legal lending limit. While the community bank may have a correspondent bank relationship (a relationship with another bank to share the loan risk), this places the debtor in the awkward position of not knowing where the next dollar or the marginal dollar of funding is coming from. Typically, the originating community bank will try to maintain the primary relationship, but a business owner must now balance the interests of two banks instead of one. The solution to the issue of size is for a business owner to select a community bank at the beginning with a sufficient legal lending limit to accommodate reasonably foreseeable requirements into the future. Ask the community bank what their limits and comfort ranges are.

Another potential issue with community banks is that they may not have much of a commercial loan appetite. The skill set required for commercial loans is much different than that required for home and retail loans. An interview with the senior loan officers should address this concern.

The exceedingly positive attribute of many community banks is that there is a good chance they know you, and understand your business. This sense of security is reassuring to the risk-taking business owner. Contrast this to a larger regional or money center bank where it is likely that staff turnover often precludes any significant continuity of relationships. The bank wants a commitment from the business owner, it is fair (to that business owner) to ask the same understanding of the bank. Let's not forget that the bank must extend credit in its judgment to worthwhile borrowers, and it is a business decision. It is still of comfort for business owners to know to whom they are indebted.

The financial crisis has had an impact on the community banks. For those that made the unfortunate decision to invest heavily in real estate development in California, Florida, and Arizona (among a few other markets) that strategy has been a financial disaster. Many community banks are sufficiently conservative and did not lend disproportionately into the real estate development market. I am most familiar personally with community banks in the heartland and they have generally not been hit with the massive loan default positions on the coasts.

Impact of Pending Dodd-Frank Act

The concerns of the community banks are summed up by Mark Mohr, president of First Bank Financial Centre in Wisconsin. He expressed concern about the uncertain future of bank regulations. At the time of this release, the Federal Government was still negotiating portions of the Dodd-Frank Act. It appears that one hallmark of the pending legislation is to increase the capital requirements for banks so that if another financial crisis occurs the banks themselves will have a much greater capital cushion and not have to rely on the Federal Government for a bailout. As we have seen in the evening news, financial institution bailouts are very unpopular with the current mood of the electorate. The clear message to bankers is to protect the capital base of the bank today and substantially avoid credit requests with a high perceived default risk. High credit risks today are equated with commercial loans related to buyouts and other heavily leveraged environments. When asked about buyout loans the past few years, Mr. Mohr indicated there were very few at his bank. That sentiment has been echoed by many other senior community bank loan officers.

In such an environment and in the anticipation of higher capital requirements, community banks have a few strategies to consider. They may focus on preserving existing capital by avoiding risky loans. They may suspend some dividends while the capital base is being increased or cut operating costs to improve profitability. Finally, more stock may be issued with a corresponding dilution to existing shareholders. Discussion in the community banking network suggests more will option preserving capital and improving profitability rather than issuing more stock.

Secured Loans

The community banks focus on "secured" loans, where the borrower is able to provide proof of adequate collateral to protect the bank should a default on the loan payments arise. In this spirit, the focus is more typically on the assets supporting the loan request. Acceptable collateral are often classified as "hard" assets such as accounts receivable, inventory, fixed assets, rolling stock, and real estate. The commercial borrower has to demonstrate an ability to service the loan requirements including interest and debt principal repayments. For the business owner, expect to sign an unlimited personal guarantee on the loan. The benefit to this rigorous analysis is often a very competitive interest rate on the funds. It is exceedingly rare today for a community bank to extend an unsecured loan supported by little more than likely cash flow from the borrower. If a cash flow loan is required that is not supported by the assets in the businesses or personal assets there are other resources to consider.

REGIONAL AND NATIONAL MONEY CENTER BANKS

This level of banking offers the substantial benefit of being large enough to address virtually any single source credit requirement for a closely held middle market company. It is almost impossible to outgrow the financial resources of such a bank, of course subject to their credit analysis and approval. The regional and national money center banks (money center banks) have exacting loan requirements, but they typically have substantial commercial relationships with the largest companies. Examples of these financial institutions include, Bank of America, JPMorgan Chase & Co., Citi, UBS, and Morgan Stanley. They are often in a better position to analyze and provide detailed cash flow analysis related to servicing the debt. When the credit request is sufficient large, business owners will almost always have to consider the resources of money center banks.

When certain major credit requests are quantified, the fear among business owners of money center banks often dissipates quickly. Such relationships are built on solid banking fundamentals and it is common for the customers to provide certified financial statements from a public accounting firm. The reporting requirements are more substantial as is the credit relationship, often amounting to millions of dollars.

Similar to the discussion regarding community banks, the evolving Federal regulatory environment is a concern for money center banks. Perhaps you are aware of the "too big to fail" concern in Washington that suggests that certain of the largest banks are so large that the economy cannot suffer the loss of one. The bankruptcy of Lehman Brothers investment banking in 2008 created a whole pandemic of foreseen and unforeseen financial issues. The unforeseen dangers really threw the economy into a crisis mode and the Federal government, we have learned after the fact, had almost no choice except to infuse countless billions of dollars to support an overextended financial system. There is a growing consensus that future regulations will place a higher capital requirement on the money center banks so that a crisis similar to the 2008 meltdown "never" happens again. History will be the judge of that statement, but in the near term the largest banks will have to think of ways to increase capital expressed as a percentage of their balance sheets.

The money center banks understand cash flow lending better than community banks, but pressure to avoid risky loans such as heavily leveraged buyouts is a fact of this economy. Presentations by the largest banks suggest they will carefully analyze credit applications, but lending multiples are reduced from the earlier more robust market from 2004 to 2007 for example. It is unlikely that the multiples for cash flow lending are going to improve until the regulatory issues are addressed.

Further complicating the issues of commercial lending in this country related to buyouts, the international banking industry has to concern itself with global issues. As this book goes to press the EU is struggling to save the Euro and the debt ratings of several of its major members including Italy, Spain, and Greece. Failure of the banking system in Europe will impact this country within days or weeks.

The money center banks are still in lending mode, but it is a fair conclusion to reach at least in the current economy that such lending will be conservative. These large lenders are still looking for secured loans, and most middle market companies can expect to have their credits well collateralized.

MEZZANINE FUNDS

Mezzanine lenders typically begin where most traditional banks end. The mezzanine funds will still carefully analyze credits, but they will typically accept relationships that are largely unsecured. They are typically introduced when the credit availability of the traditional banks ends. A mezzanine lender will anticipate being subordinated to the senior level bank, or the bank with the strongest collateral position. The mezzanine bank is still collateralized by the assets of the business, but its position is typically secondary to the senior or primary lender. In return for assuming this largely unsecured position, the pricing of this layer of financing will seem high to most business owners. The interest rate or the total consideration paid to the mezzanine lender is a reflection of the cost of funds to the mezzanine financer and the perceived risk of the credit.

The mezzanine lender is typically looking at the total return on the investment and may consider creative ways to realize the target return. In buyout situations involving significant leverage, the mezzanine debt may be interest only for a period of time while senior debt is paid down. Mezzanine debt may be structured to provide a higher return to the lender over time through a combination of such elements as warrants or payment in kind metrics. Whatever the method of computing, the consideration to the mezzanine lender is adopted, and the overall costs of this level of debt will be much greater than the cost of senior debt.

It is almost impossible to provide a range of returns and fees related to mezzanine debt, but as an example if senior debt interest rates are in the range of 4–6%, the mezzanine package may be providing a return in the range of 12–18%. This is approaching if not exceeding equity rates of return. Clearly, the use of mezzanine financing is limited to those few companies that can service the debt obligations to the satisfaction of the lender.

PRIVATE EQUITY

As the name suggests, this source of financing involves an equity investment in the company by a specialized resource. For our purposes the private equity resource is referred to as a private equity group (PEG). In fact the private equity resource may be a single source of funding and not a group. Typically, the PEG will have its own funds to invest along with funding provided by a number of other resources. Those other entities often include funding sources with a longer-term investment horizon such as pension funds, university endowments, insurance companies, and other similarly minded institutions. Typically PEGs will make presentations to a host of candidate funding sources with the promise of providing higher than publicly available market returns. The expertise of the PEG managers is represented as the "secret sauce" that enables the fund to earn those higher returns. The managerial expertise typically spans extensive exposure to targeted industries and operating a business with a significant amount of debt. Exacting orientation to management by the numbers is expected and there is often little room for errors of judgment.

Once the PEG has secured its own level of funding, it will make investments with companies using a combination of its own resources (much of it may be borrowed from long-term investors) and funding from a commercial bank. The commercial bank is still likely to be the secured lender, and the PEG will be subordinated to them. The amount of leverage or debt in such structures may be substantial. Ultimately the PEG is looking to convert its investment in the candidate company to a return that justifies the risk.

The PEG is an investor in the candidate company and serves a viable purpose of getting the target from one level of operations to another level that requires the use of considerable financial resources. Later in this book we will consider PEGs with both a short-term and a longer-term investment horizon.

The PEG is there to make money for its investors and the day an investment is consummated, the PEG has already strategized about its own exit vehicle. For our analysis, we assume the PEG is acquiring the controlling interest in the candidate company and is working with management to attain predetermined targeted results. While all facts and circumstances are different, most PEGs will want to have an exit within four to seven years. The exit strategy will often be developed to maximize the investment made by the PEG. Common exit strategies are to sell to management and an Employee Stock Ownership Plan and Trust (ESOP), sell to a larger strategic buyer, sell to a larger PEG, or exit via an initial public offering (IPO). Selling to management and an ESOP is not likely to result in the highest return, but it has happened on occasion. An IPO is less likely today given the turbulence in the public markets for new issues. Finding a strategic buyer is often the most common solution. Finding strategic buyers with cash in today's market is often a daunting challenge.

For many PEGs the only thing they can do is hold onto the investments they have made and hope for an improving economy and more confidence on the part of candidate buyers. The "frothy" and "irrational exuberance" of the earlier 2000s may never fully return. PEGs will have to carefully select investment targets with great care giving more credence on exit strategies.

SMALL BUSINESS ADMINISTRATION AND GOVERNMENT SOURCES

This section is included because the SBA is a favorite finance tool for many community banks in particular and smaller commercial banks in general. The SBA program provides funding for closely held companies under exacting loan requirements. Once the document and qualifications are addressed, they are popular with traditional banks because the Federal government will guarantee a substantial portion of the loan principal. For the bank originating the loan, the loan loss default exposure is greatly reduced. This is a tremendous advantage to those banks interested in preserving capital.

The SBA program offers the additional advantage of having a substantial lending limit. At this time that limit may be as high as $6 million. This is an amount that will address the requirements of a significant percentage of all closely held companies. When the company is in an industry that is perceived to be higher risk, an SBA loan may be one of the few options available to many business owners.

Other Federal loan programs may be available, but they are often so specialized it is beyond the scope of this overview chapter. Banks that offer SBA capabilities typically specialize in such placements and have substantial demonstrated experience with such loans. A successful history of placements with few defaults is a competitive advantage for those banks offering SBA services.

SELLER NOTES

This is a catchall category and is included as the balancing amount to get many transactions completed in today's economy. As discussed, the general market of buyouts is deemed to be very risky by most financial sources, and they will expect to be compensated for the level of risk being assumed. Unless there is a well financed PEG, most buyouts are going to have some component of seller finance, and many transactions will be heavily dependent on seller notes. In my experience the seller note will be subordinate to the senior lender of the buyer. Unlike a mezzanine resource that will expect a higher rate of return, the seller will typically not have that degree of negotiating leverage with a buyer. The interest rate on a seller note is most typically somewhere between a senior bank position and a mezzanine rate, but likely closer to the senior bank rate.

In certain types of buyouts the seller note will be a substantial part of the financial package. The seller is advised to obtain as much security and collateral as possible, but there are often limits on that attribute. A seller note typically does not have the legal documentation of a commercial note. The seller note will stipulate such obvious things as interest rate, debt amortization, default remedies, and other material aspects. Accelerated payments, preemptive covenants, and personal guarantees are typically not as well documented. The seller will have to decide if he wants the transaction to conclude or not based on some level of participation.

In smaller middle market companies, the seller may be more than willing to provide the assistance because he knows the management team and has worked with them for years. Additionally, the effective control of the company may reside with the seller by stipulations as to who selects the board of directors while the seller debt is outstanding. Many sellers may be hesitant to provide significant financial support if control of the business must also be surrendered.

One significant development for business owners to consider is the ability of the company to repay the seller note. Debt principal payments are generally only repaid with after tax dollars. Interest expense is deductible, but principal payments are generally not deductible with one notable exception. There is the special situation where an ESOP-based note may be repaid with tax-deductible interest and principal. This strong tax advantage is discussed in later chapters on ESOPs. For the business owner, this is a substantial development since the principal is tax deductible. For example, if the company is an S corporation in an approximate combined Federal and state income tax rate of 40%, the tax deductible principal payment is often repaid in approximately half the time. For debt-adverse business owners this is an attraction over the sale to another party where the debt is repaid with after-tax dollars.

SUMMARY

Middle market companies have a spectrum of financial options as discussed. There may be a few more exotic offshoots, but the expense and limited applications make them of little use for most companies. Today's economic environment has made the commercial banking community cautious about extending risky loans for fear of damaging capital investment. If transactions are to be closed, the business owner will likely have to have a more open mind about the terms of the deal. Getting mostly cash at closing is less likely today, so there will almost certainly be some component of seller financing.

CHAPTER 4

Valuations

Price and Terms

The formula "two and two makes five" is not without its attractions.
—Fedor Dostoevsky

It's clearly a budget. It's got a lot of numbers in it.
—George W. Bush, Former President

This chapter is intended to provide insights into the valuation process and considerations that drive the determination of valuing a privately held company. The insights are a blend of such things like traditional valuations for tax-oriented assignments such as gifting, investment banking insights relating to the actual acquisition of a business, and rules of thumb most commonly applied to smaller companies. This book is written with the economic backdrop of the worst recession in memory, and the application of valuing a privately held company today takes into consideration the overall economy.

There are a myriad of methods and methodologies to determine the "consideration" being paid for the company. I have specifically avoided using the term "price" because that suggests there is a single amount to be paid in cash, or cash equivalents. Today transactions that are being completed are accompanied by a wide range of additional factors that are integral to the "deal." For our purposes these factors are generally referred to as the "terms" of the transaction. Clearly, few transactions will be completed with the buyer paying all cash at the closing. Transactions are typically subject to a range of contingent covenants and conditions, the terms. A few of the more common terms are escrow accounts, seller financing, contingent payments or earn-outs, management and consulting agreements, and personal guarantees. This leads me to conclude that with today's economic environment in particular, the value of the business will be a function of the price and the terms. The more generous the terms extended by the seller, the more likely the total consideration will be higher.

We will first examine a number of fundamental concepts regarding valuations before becoming more specific on valuation methods and commonly encountered terms.

> This chapter is intended to provide insights and vocabulary regarding the business valuation discipline. There are too many valuable books that consider a thorough analysis of how to conduct and complete valuations without repeating that understanding here.

PURPOSE OF THE VALUATION

The first appropriate question to ask regarding valuation is, "What is the purpose of the valuation assignment?" Immediately establishing a valid purpose for the valuation will typically imply many other facets of information required to complete the analysis. Often, the purpose of the valuation will lead to a determination of the "standard of value," which often suggests appropriate valuation approaches and methods.

There are many purposes for a valuation assignment. The following non-comprehensive list illustrates many of the common reasons for a valuation.

- Selling a business to a third party
- Transferring ownership to family members via gifting
- Litigation between shareholders
- Divorce action between husband and wife
- Establishing value for estate tax determination
- Installing an Employee Stock Ownership Plan and Trust (ESOP)
- Acquiring a business

In addition to the valuation purpose, it often is significant who initiates the assignment. Consider the case of a highly contentious divorce: The overall parameter of the valuation assignment is almost certainly affected by the party bringing the initial complaint. This situation stands in sharp contrast to a transaction that is predicated on parties that are friendly and wish to conclude a successful result.

DETERMINING THE TRANSACTION CONSIDERATION

There are countless opportunities and procedures to determine a "transaction" price. For our purposes, we will assume that the transaction price is a function of future economic benefits that the owner of the asset will derive through its ownership. We have also assumed that the business is a going concern with a perpetual life.

The world of transactions is most often driven by rational parties, and we will assume that those parties are influenced by traditionally proven valuation techniques. There are a number of more common types of economic analysis embraced in determining the transaction price, and they will be briefly examined in this chapter.

Price and Terms Briefly Examined

While traditional methods of financial analysis may lead to a transaction price, the "price" is a relative term. It frequently makes a significant difference if the price is paid in cash at closing, or if the price is a function of many other transaction attributes negotiated by the parties.

One old saying regarding transactions is, "You tell me your price, and I will tell you the terms." In the world of business transactions, it is a rare event when the total transaction price is paid in cash at closing.

Typically, the transaction deal will be a process of detailed and often intense negotiations to arrive at a mutually accepted agreement. To illustrate the difference between price and terms, the following non-exclusive listing demonstrates typical issues that impact the final outcome of the transactions.

- *Hold-Back of Proceeds*—The buyer requires that a portion of the transaction price be typically held in escrow following the transaction date. This form of transaction "insurance" provides the buyer with some recourse against the seller if the facts surrounding the transaction are not as they are represented and more favorable to the exiting seller.
- *Seller Financing*—The seller is required to provide partial financing for the deal. The buyer will pay only for a portion of the requested transaction price with other sources of financing. Seller financing is a time-honored practice to have the seller bear a significant part of the responsibility for the future success of the deal.
- *Performance Payments: Earn-Out Provision*—The buyer requires that the transaction price is in part dependent on representations of future prospects advanced by the seller. This is a form of insurance for the buyer should future prospects prove to be unrealizable; then, the seller is at risk for a portion of the transaction price.

- *Non-Competition Agreement*—This agreement is commonly invoked to bar the seller from going into competition with the buyer. While the spirit of the non-competition agreement is valuable to the buyer, the tax treatment of the accord is most decidedly negative. The agreement is treated as an intangible asset for tax purposes subject to a 15-year amortization.
- *Employment Agreement and/or Consulting Agreement*—Such agreements are typically very favorable to the buyer. The amount of the agreement is deductible in the current year as it is paid, and it is ordinary income to the seller. This is also a strategic move on the part of the buyer to extract extended terms from the seller.
- *Contingent and Unknown Liabilities*—At the time of closing, often many categories of assets and liabilities may only be estimated based on preliminary numbers prior to closing. Transaction documents often specify how the use of estimates will be considered in the final determination of the transaction price. Commonly, such items as the collection of aged accounts receivable or the realization of inventory amounts are examples of estimated assets at closing, subject to adjustment. On the side of liabilities, a frequent item that requires an estimate is product warranty exposure.

There are many types of terms that are possible, limited only by the imagination of the principals to the transaction. There may be many iterations and enhancements to this listing. The key point is that there is typically some underlying price on the asset being acquired, and the longer-term total package of compensation to the seller additionally will be a function of the transaction terms.

STANDARD OF VALUE FOR TRANSACTIONS

The term "value" is going to indicate different things to different individuals. This section is intended to indicate the more common understandings of valuation standards. In many instances, there will be a legally imposed standard of value, such as the value determined for gifting and estate tax returns or for ESOPs. States and other local jurisdictions may impose a discrete standard of value for such actions as divorce litigation and shareholder disputes. In other instances, the standard of value appears to be a number negotiated by the parties to the transactions. The following definitions and illustrations indicate the more common understandings of the standards of value.

Fair Market Value

This standard of value is the most widely recognized for business valuations. It is the standard of value for virtually all tax-related issues relating to business valuations in such matters as gift taxes, estate and inheritance taxes, income taxes, and ESOPs. It is also frequently cited as the standard of value in many other applications, such as litigation. The definition of FMV in Treasury Reg. § 20.2031-1(b) is stated as

- *Fair Market Value*—The price at which the property would change hands between a willing buyer and a willing seller when the former is not under any compulsion to buy and the latter is under no compulsion to sell, both parties having reasonable knowledge of relevant facts.

The above definition has been refined over time to encompass a number of other significant items. The definition of FMV is between a "hypothetical" buyer and a "hypothetical" seller. This distinction is significant, because it excludes a consideration of a "specific" buyer. A specific buyer may be a strategic buyer bringing to the transaction table many synergies and economies discrete to that buyer.

The hypothetical buyer is understood to be a financial buyer. A financial buyer typically brings only the purchase price to the transaction table and not things that a specific or strategic buyer does, such as industry-specific acumen and value-added synergies. Under FMV the transaction terms are understood to be "cash only." The terms will not be impacted by such matters as special financing arrangements, contingencies, and other provisions. FMV is based on information known and knowable or reasonably foreseeable as of the valuation effective date but not subsequent events that could have an impact on valuation.

This standard of value is further refined in IRS Revenue Ruling 59-60, which details the various factors to be considered in establishing FMV. Rev. Rul. 59-60 is detailed in its discussion of factors to be considered in arriving at FMV. In general terms, FMV is established by a careful consideration of several broad requirements including such elements as:

- The nature of the business and history of the enterprise
- The economic outlook in general and the condition and outlook of the specific industry
- The financial condition of the company
- The earnings capacity of the company
- The dividend-paying capacity of the company

- The existence of goodwill or other intangible value
- Prior sales of stock
- The market prices of comparable companies

This is of course an abbreviated summary of the requirements. The determination of FMV is intended to be a thorough examination of the company from a valuation viewpoint.

FMV is broadly referenced, but in the world of actual business transactions it is rarely the standard of value that is used. FMV is the standard of value commonly adopted for tax-related transactions such as gifting, estate tax determination, and selling to an ESOP.

Adequate Consideration (Employee Stock Ownership Plan and Trust Specific)

In addition to the IRS, the Department of Labor (DOL) also has oversight responsibility for ESOPs, including the valuation of stock being sold to a plan. The DOL has a similar but not identical definition of value as it relates to ESOPs. The DOL has issued proposed regulations in May 1986, 29 CFR Part 2510 *Regulation Relating to the Definition of Adequate Consideration, Notice of Proposed Rulemaking* (Regulation), that defines their understanding of the standard of value for ESOPs. The definition is similar to FMV as stated, but it is expanded to embrace attributes of an ESOP that are unique to those transactions. While the Regulation is technically only "proposed," the DOL and the Federal Courts have relied on this definition since 1988. Every valuation professional doing ESOP work assumes the Regulation to be in effect.

The Regulation raises the issue of the ESOP paying for control when there is control in appearance and control in fact. Control in appearance suggests a majority of the stock is sold to the ESOP. Control in fact addresses the governance of the subject company following the sale of stock to the ESOP. The Regulation indicates it may be proper for the ESOP to pay a premium for control only if the ESOP will actually be acquiring the ability to direct the company, the extent to which a third party paying a similar price would have control. The Regulation also indicates that the ability of the company to honor the repurchase obligation, which is a requirement to make a market for the stock of departing employees, has to be considered. One other major point of emphasis is that Adequate Consideration requires the stock to be valued at FMV determined in good faith. The determination of what constitutes good faith is a long discussion, but for our purposes it is emphasized that this standard means that the Trustee must conduct a prudent investigation of the facts with the sound application of valuation principals in arriving at a determining of the value. For ease of presentation, the DOL standard of valuation is "adequate consideration" which is an extension of FMV with a consideration of ESOP attributes.

> Our purpose with this discussion about adequate consideration is to indicate that the DOL and IRS have similar but slightly different definitions of value relating to ESOPs. Throughout the balance of this book we will refer to the standard of valuation for ESOPs as FMV.

Investment Value

According to the *International Glossary of Business Valuation Terms*, a handy reference for a working definition of "investment value" is

- *Investment Value*—The value to a particular investor based on individual investment requirements and expectations.

There are some pronounced differences with the definition of investment value and FMV just discussed. There are a few major distinctions. Investment value relates to a specific investor, whereas FMV relates to the "hypothetical" buyer. Investment value considers specific individual investment requirements and expectations; FMV considers a hypothetical transaction where the terms are cash. Investment value may consider the synergies that exist between the investor and the subject investment, and such value may be significantly impacted by this factor. No such consideration is applicable in FMV.

When we are considering business transactions, individual investor considerations are typically a driving and determining factor in the structure of the deal. Consequently, investment value is often the standard of value for transactions.

Fair Value

This standard of value is most often used in the context of financial reporting purposes. When applying generally accepted accounting principles (GAAP), the Financial Accounting Standards Board (FASB) defines fair value.

- *Fair Value*—The fair value of an asset (or liability) is the amount at which that asset (or liability) could be bought (or incurred) or sold (settled) in a current transaction between willing parties, that is, other than in a forced or liquidation sale.

Fair value differs from FMV in that it may consider a wide definition of the market for the asset or liability, including all potential buyers. The candidate buyer for example may be a strategic buyer willing to pay a premium price for the asset.

"Emotional Value"—What a Buyer and Seller Perceive

This is a catchall concept with very little empirical support. The value is what opposing negotiating parties agree to. In business transactions, and in this author's experience with smaller closely held businesses, there often is a "gut" feel for the value of the business. The parties to the transaction will negotiate the overall value, often accompanied by a healthy dose of terms. Such transactions are almost impossible to quantify from any rational economic approach. Such instances occur typically with smaller closely held businesses, with a total value under one million dollars. They just happen.

TYPES OF BUYERS AND SELLERS

In the perfect real world one expects that business transaction buyers and sellers are fully informed of all relevant facts before entering into a deal. Unfortunately, there is no perfect world of business transactions. In most instances where business transactions occur, there is typically some amount of disproportionate negotiating leverage enjoyed by one side over the other. This discrepancy in negotiating strength is often the source for a creative application of transaction terms and conditions. As discussed in the definitions of value, a number of buyers and sellers have emerged.

- *Hypothetical Buyer and Seller*—These legal creations have been developed as an extension of the definition of FMV and promulgated by Federal and state authorities. The attempt to define the hypothetical buyer and seller is to remove the taint of such things as strategic knowledge, insider advantage, synergies, and other benefits that will impact the transaction.
- *Financial Buyer*—Often thought of as being the same as the hypothetical buyer, the financial buyer typically comes to the transaction table with a perceived ability to complete the purchase only expecting financial returns not impacted by any synergies or other advantages that may exist as a result of the transaction. The financial performance expectations of the financial buyer are most typically embodied by rates of return that

investors may expect from investments in publicly held corporations. Such investments in public companies are typically open to any investor with the resources to make the equity purchase.

- *Strategic Buyer*—In most transactions involving a closely held business, the buyer of the business would typically be considered a strategic buyer. The *International Glossary of Business Valuation Terms* refers to this investor as a "special interest purchaser," with the understanding that the acquirer of the business believes they can enjoy post-acquisition economies of scale, synergies, or strategic advantages by combining the acquired business interest with their own.
- *Management and Employees*—Technically such candidate buyers are insiders and they will have specific insights into the business. They typically have limited access to financial resources and will be restricted on the amount that may be tendered for an acquisition.
- *Family Members*—Obviously "insiders," family members typically are not dealing on an arm's-length basis. Often the goal is to pass wealth between family members on the most tax-preferential basis possible. That suggests a business valuation environment that is conservative.

ATTRIBUTES OF OWNERSHIP—CONTROL AND MINORITY POSITIONS

A well-documented and understood principal in the financial community generally finds that the value of an asset is enhanced the more that control is associated with the asset. The value of an asset is often a qualitative concept until we begin to specifically identify the attributes of the asset relating to the likelihood of future economic benefits. Future economic benefits are typically greatly enhanced when the owner exercises more control over the property.

For our purposes, we are assuming that the property or the asset is an investment in an operating company. The extent to which ownership of the investment is accompanied by the ability to control the operations and decisions of the company, determines by how much the investment is almost certainly going to be enhanced.

Control Position (Enterprise Value)

Within the business ownership context, if 100% of the stock in a company is owned by a single shareholder, clearly this is the strongest position to be in, as that shareholder has dominant control over the operations. Valuing such a position of ownership is commonly referred to as the control position of the business, an understanding of value that includes the ability to make and enforce the wide range decisions.

The control position value is often referred to as the enterprise value. There is no common definition of enterprise value, but it is often understood to mean the market value of invested capital, which includes both equity and long-term debt. Sometimes you will see the value of a company expressed as the market value of invested capital (MVIC), which includes market capitalization, preferred stock, and debt. Regardless of the specific understanding, enterprise value typically encompasses the value of the business that considers the attribute of control. For our purposes, the enterprise value is generally understood to mean the control position of the business.

While the example of a single shareholder owning all the stock of a company is clear and easy to understand, there are degrees of control that may be enjoyed depending on the facts and circumstances of each situation. Depending on the amount of stock owned or depending on shareholder agreements or applicable statutes, the degree of control may vary and be subject to interpretation.

The following non-exclusive list indicates common elements of control position attributes within the context of owning a business:

- Establish company policy
- Appoint the board of directors
- Establish employee compensation
- Declare dividends, acquire or divest assets
- Issue or redeem stock
- Change bylaws and articles of incorporation
- Recapitalize the company

Absent the situation where total and complete control of the business is established, determining the value for an interest in the company for less than complete control is subject to interpretation of all relevant factors. As the attributes of complete control are diminished, the value of the subject investment is correspondingly impacted since the investor has less control over the business entity and less control over the decision-making process.

Certain empirical data that is available for business valuations produces an implied minority position, for example data from Morningstar, Inc. (d.b.a. Ibbotson and Associates). It is beyond the scope of these materials to develop the detail to estimate an adjustment for a minority position. The point to emphasize is that empirical data exists to estimate such an adjustment.

Generally when the discussion is centered on buyouts we are considering the acquisition of the entire organization and a control position analysis. In circumstances that span a longer time horizon with multiple transactions, we often see minority position valuation analysis. This is the case with the transfer of ownership in family companies, and often with the sale of a smaller block of stock to an ESOP.

LACK OF MARKETABILITY

Converting an investment in a company into cash is easily done if your investment is in a company actively traded on a public market. Liquidity for our purposes is understood to mean converting an investment in a business to cash with minimum transaction and administrative expenses. Often the analogy is converting an investment in a marquee company like Microsoft or Ford to cash. Such large and respected companies have their stock listed and traded on the premier global markets. In this instance, liquidity is not a problem.

Liquidity becomes a significant issue when the investment is in a closely held company where there is no active market established for its stock. Converting an investment in a closely held company to cash may be an activity subject to significant uncertainty and substantial risk. Investors generally place a high premium on liquidity and favor investments that offer the advantage of rapid conversion to cash. The relatively more complex situation of converting an investment in a closely held business to cash is often referred to as a "lack of marketability."

If we are using as a valuation benchmark for closely held businesses data derived from publicly held companies, then some adjustment for a lack of liquidity is appropriate. Much of the data embraced by the valuation community to determine value is largely derived from sources dependent on the analysis of public company returns. Correspondingly, such data represents an environment where the investment in a public company is converted to cash with a minimum of time and effort.

There are other sources of valuation data that are not directly related to the analysis of publicly held companies. For example, transaction databases representing the sales of closely held businesses indicate value with no reference to public markets. In such instances, the data reflects actual transactions of closely held companies between parties that have negotiated the deal. No adjustment for lack of liquidity is appropriate in such circumstances.

ADDITIONAL ADJUSTMENTS TO VALUATION

In certain select circumstances, additional adjustments, whether a discount or premium may be applied to the asset being valued. When the circumstances are more "qualitative," understood for our purposes to reflect a real issue but almost impossible to directly quantify, it is often crucial to indicate the reasoning for considering the adjustment.

The following are examples of considerations that may justify in part some additional adjustment. An intense concentration of credit either in customer sales or vendor supply is often seen. A key person adjustment, especially where the skills are very difficult to replace, is another common application. An example is a renowned product researcher and inventor that has been a wellspring of patents and new products. The size of the block of stock may also be a consideration. An example is what the IRS calls a "swing vote" attribute, or the situation where a relatively nondescript minority block of stock has inordinate value because it could enable another shareholder to gain control of the company when it is added to his or her block of stock.

Often such issues are very real considerations in the valuation of the business. Since standalone reliable data for such adjustments is often not available, most business valuation professionals will add or subtract an amount for a consideration of the issue in question in the lack of marketability discount.

THREE VALUATION APPROACHES: INCOME, MARKET, ASSET

The discussion relating to valuation approaches will take on a sharper focus since we have considered two very important candidates for adjustment. We need to consider first the ownership attributes of the asset being valued and a potential lack of marketability adjustment. As the three approaches to valuation are considered, we will illustrate how ownership attributes and lack of marketability impact the determination of value.

Income Approach

The essence of business valuation is an expectation of future economic benefits as a result of an investment decision. The income-based approach to valuation in its simplest format is the present value of expected future economic returns during the period the asset is owned. Under such an analysis, the net present value of the economic benefit stream entails taking the future economic benefits of the investment and discounting them by your required rate of return.

There are two primary methods of analysis within the income approach: the discounted future returns method and the capitalization of earnings method.

Discounted Future Returns Method (Discounted Cash Flow) The discounted future returns method is also known as discounted cash flow, which we will refer to it as "DCF." DCF enjoys sound business valuation theory, but it is also exceedingly difficult to apply correctly.

DCF entails a specific projection of future economic benefits for a set number of years. The projection period is typically 5 to 10 years. At the end of the set projection period, a "residual value" must be computed. The residual value represents the economic benefits' stream into perpetuity, which is appropriate theory in investment-oriented valuations. Once the projection is developed, the economic benefits are discounted to the present by an applicable rate of return in order to arrive at the net present value.

So far the stream of "economic benefits" has only been generally defined. What is critical is that however the economic benefits are defined, they must be discounted by a rate of return that is appropriate for that definition of economic return. It is beyond the scope of this overview of valuations to discuss in more detail the discount rate.

There are a number of ways to define the stream of economic benefits to the investor. Common references include:

- Pre-tax income
- Earnings before interest and taxes (EBIT)
- Net income (NI)
- Earnings before interest, taxes, depreciation, and amortization (EBITDA)
- Free cash flow

The economic benefits that are used in the valuation often depend on the purpose of the assignment. The more common definitions used are EBIT and EBITDA.

Normalized Financial Results Most typically we begin an analysis with financial statements prepared to GAAP. If we are fortunate, we have financial statements that are professionally reviewed or audited by a public accounting firm, and the financial statements are accompanied with full financial footnotes. This is a good first step.

For the purposes of valuation we are interested in the "economic financial results" of the organization. The economic financial statements are "normalized" with adjusting entries to recast the results into what the company could have done under reasonable predicable operating results. A description of the most common types of normalizing adjustments will make this point clear.

- *Non-Recurring Events.* As the heading indicates, these items represent non-recurring or extraordinary costs (or income) not typically associated with ongoing operations. Examples include such items as the costs associated with closing a division or subsidiary; most litigation particularly that which is related to personnel; and uninsured inventory or asset loss. The sale of assets resulting in a one-time gain is an example of non-recurring income.
- *Discretionary Items.* Virtually all candidates under this category are expenses to the company that are not deemed to be necessary to customary operations. Candidates for this classification include company helicopters (only those not required of course); many executive bonuses (however some senior level bonuses are typically expected); and employee benefits well in excess of industry averages.
- *Tax Related Adjustments.* This is a narrow classification and most often the only candidate is an adjustment to convert last in first out (LIFO) inventory to first in first out (FIFO) inventory.

Often historical financial information is first normalized using the three categories so that applicable financial ratios and profit margins are recomputed regarding economic results. The adjusted results are then used to build a forward looking forecast. One of the most common adjustments is senior management compensation based on an estimate of what it would cost to employee competent individuals and not what has been the total historical compensation including disproportionate bonuses.

Discounted Cash Flow Advantages and Cautions   DCF is theoretically sound, as it places an emphasis on specific future economic benefits. It is often the single most important technique for analysis regarding mergers and acquisitions. This makes sense because mergers and acquisitions typically reflect a longer-term look into the future, combining the best attributes of the parties involved in the transaction.

The method may account for specific material events, both favorable and unfavorable, that are anticipated in the future. The method may specifically consider such things as a new product, an acquisition expected to close in the future, the loss of a major account, or adding a new product line.

The method assumes that whoever is putting the projection together has a successful history of accurate forecasting. Without some history of prior success forecasting multiple years into the future, the validity of a "first-time" effort has to be seriously considered.

One question to ask is if the DCF a result of a minority position or a control position analysis. If the projections include adjustments and assumptions only a controlling shareholder is capable of making, then the resulting cash flow analysis is on a control basis. For example, one common adjustment is normalizing the executive compensation to some amount approximating market rates. This type of adjustment indicates a control position analysis.

There are often so many variables in the DCF that the results are easily manipulated to almost any desired end result. One of the strong attributes of DCF is that it can consider a myriad of variables in determining value. This is also the very reason why DCF is successfully challenged. Having so many variables makes it easy to manipulate the end result to virtually any desired number.

Capitalization of Earnings Method   This method is complementary to DCF, but there are some significant differences. Whereas DCF is predicated on a specific projection of results into the future for a period of time, the capitalization of earnings method does not employ a specific future multi-year projection. With the capitalization of earnings method, a single representative number indicating economic return is used to develop value. This single number is "capitalized" by an appropriately developed rate of return that takes into consideration future long-term sustainable growth, which includes inflation.

There is often confusion between the "cost of capital" referenced in the DCF section and the "capitalization rate" mentioned previously. The two are easily reconciled. The capitalization rate begins with the cost of capital, but there is typically one additional adjustment. We must adjust the cost of capital by subtracting long-term sustainable growth. This is required so that the capitalization rate has a consideration of future growth in its computation. Long-term sustainable growth is subtracted, and that is growth into perpetuity. Long-term sustainable growth rates often include a consideration of inflation and some nominal amount of real growth. Correspondingly, the growth rates frequently seen are in the range of 1% to 4%. Any sustainable growth in excess of 4% may be very hard to justify. Remember, the company may have near term growth that is attractive, but the financial model is projecting results into perpetuity.

Capitalization of Earnings Advantages and Cautions   One of the strengths of the capitalization of earnings method is its simplicity. A single number representing economic value is divided by an appropriate capitalization rate. An estimate of value can be facilitated rapidly by determining these two important determinants of value. Of course, the numerator and the denominator each have a number of considerations as imputed variables, but this is still a useful technique for determining value.

This method enjoys the perception that it is easily understood and reasonably expeditious to compute. An estimate of value is typically developed in short order, which is a decided plus in preliminary feasibility analysis. Where there is no history of successful and believable projections, this method is likely to be as valid as one predicated on a spurious and perhaps self-serving projection. This method is more valid where subject operations are well established and reasonably stable. Correspondingly, a single economic benefit to be capitalized is more readily determined, as historic results are a good proximate indicator of future prospects.

Similar to the DCF analysis, one question to ask is, is the capitalization of earnings a minority position or a control position analysis? If the projections include adjustments and assumptions only a controlling shareholder is capable of making, then the resulting cash flow analysis is on a control basis. For example, one common adjustment is normalizing the executive compensation to some amount approximating market rates. This type of adjustment indicates a control position analysis.

One significant caution is that this method is often overly simplistic for many companies that are dynamic. Such firms may be in evolving business sectors that are changing rapidly. Often the bias is to imagine a growth industry situation, such as the recent "dot.com" excitement (and subsequent bust). The opposite may be true, where an industry is in sharp decline and it may be appropriate to provide a specific projection considering unfavorable developments.

Market Approach

Conceptually, the market approach to valuation is linked to the ability to identify prior "comparable" transactions that are useful in the financial analysis of determining value. Finding comparable transactions for analysis is rapidly evolving in the era of Internet data. Valuation professionals have enjoyed access to rapidly evolving technology and transaction databases since the early 1990s. Greater and more sophisticated data collection and identification has enhanced this valuation approach.

Generally, when we think of the market approach for business valuations, there are two primary bodies of data to consider, and a less accurate analysis involving "rules of thumb."

First, we can examine the ever-expanding and accessible arena of publicly traded companies, or the "guideline company method." Publicly held companies must disclose a torrent of useful information about operations, and financial markets track performance with exacting detail. The combination of such factors along with near-instant information access via the Internet provides a rich background for analysis.

Second, merged or acquired companies offer an increasingly attractive baseline for analysis. During the past decade a limited number of readily accessible databases accumulated useful information on transactions involving the merger or acquisition of both closely held and public companies. Referencing complete sales of businesses is referred to as the "guideline transaction method."

Finally, we will consider the analysis related to "rules of thumb." This analysis is less precise than the other methods, but it may offer a cost effective way to approximate the transaction value of the smallest companies. Such companies typically have only a few employees and lack a professional management team.

Public Company Guideline Method   The best news about this method is the existence of a tremendous amount of transaction data relating to publicly held companies. There are thousands of publicly held companies, and they represent a majority of the market capital in this country. Many of the public companies traded on major markets are household names such as IBM, Coke, and Microsoft. Public companies are also listed on less frequently traded markets such as over the counter, regional markets, or on "pink sheets." All such companies are subject to stringent reporting requirements that accompany the public listing. All publicly held companies are also followed by analysts on their respective markets. Clearly, higher profile companies will receive a disproportionate amount of media scrutiny.

The overwhelming source of valuation validity for this method is the daily trading of stock in public markets. Every day investors buy and sell stock in arm's-length transactions. Such sales often represent smaller "minority position" blocks of stock. Based on the analysis of the daily trading, a rich resource of financial information is obtained for each individual company, as well as information for broader indices. The broader indices may involve such items as financial returns for market segments, industry groups, or the entire market as a whole. Public company trading information serves as the foundation for a wide range of financial data that is useful in business valuations. A number of more common valuation indicators are listed.

- Multiples of earnings or cash flow to equity such as the price to earnings ratio (P/E) multiplier. Commonly the trailing 12 months' earnings of the public company are the basis for the P/E multiple, often listed as equity/net income or the P/E ratio.
- Equity to sales.
- Equity to book value.

- MVIC to sales, where MVIC includes both equity and the book value of debt. Commonly, this is expressed as MVIC/sales.
- MVIC to EBIT. Commonly expressed as MVIC/EBIT.
- MVIC to book value. Commonly this is expressed as MVIC/Book Value.

You must carefully match the valuation "multiplier" with the correct baseline variable. For example, it is important to understand the underlying earnings. There is a potentially significant difference between such income measurements as NI, pre-tax income, EBITDA, and EBIT. In the financial analysis, you must make sure that the valuation multiple is correctly applied to the proper variable.

Public Company Guideline Method Advantages and Cautions   Subject to finding comparable guideline companies, the indicators of value represent actual sales of stock on public markets. This empirical data is very defensible and enjoys a high degree of validity. The data is typically very current, further adding credibility to the analysis.

It is very difficult to identify truly comparable guideline companies, particularly when the subject company is closely held. Public companies typically have a much broader product and service capability than closely held companies, which is often a compelling advantage when managing risk. Most readily traded public companies have hundreds of millions of dollars in sales. Demands of the public markets often dictate that only larger companies can be truly actively traded. Since it often is inappropriate to compare large billion dollar public companies with closely held businesses, the challenge is to find smaller public companies that may be considered comparable. Finding enough comparable companies is very difficult.

The requirements of being publicly traded are such that public companies are fundamentally different from closely held businesses. Investors in public companies often have notoriously short holding periods. That is not typically the case with ownership in a closely held company, which is typically much longer in the time horizon. Finally, doing research trying to find comparable companies is time consuming, costly, and with no guarantee of success. The method is most often applicable with larger closely held companies and with a significant valuation budget.

Guideline Transaction Method   This method is focused on the sale of an entire company to another buyer. The theoretical strength of this method is that once we identify comparable company transactions, this method produces valuable data for valuation purposes. Until recently, say the later 1990s, this method typically received scant attention because there was little reliable and consistent information regarding the sale of closely held businesses. While information regarding larger public companies has been available, there was not much on closely held companies.

This data shortfall was recognized, and a number of transaction databases were refined during the 1990s with an emphasis on developing useful valuation indices. Regarding the sale of closely held businesses, a number of useful transaction databases have evolved including the following: Capital IQ; FactSet Mergerstat Review; Pratt's Stats; and Business Reference Guide (only for the smallest companies).

Practical Applications of the Guideline Transaction Method Cutting through the theory of valuation, the rhetorical question by a business owner may be what is the value of my company? Of course, no one actually wants to pay for a formal analysis, and business owners want a "ballpark" number as a reality check. One approach to take that is exceedingly easy to employ if not perfectly statistically validated is to apply the "Rule of Five" as defined by Dennis Roberts in his insightful book, *Mergers & Acquisitions, An Insider's Guide to the Purchase and Sale of Middle Market Business Interests* (John Wiley and Sons, 2009), John Wiley and Sons. Dennis brings to the valuation discipline decades of front-line experience with hundreds of real world transactions in addition to teaching and writing about the topic.

The practical insight is to suggest that middle market companies with a value of between $5 million and $150 million obtain a sell price approximately 5 times normalized cash flow. Cash flow may be defined in many ways such as EBIT, EBITDA, or pretax income.

Exhibit 4.1 indicates a bell curve with the most common pricing multiple of 5. This equates approximately to a pretax return of 20% (1/5). The

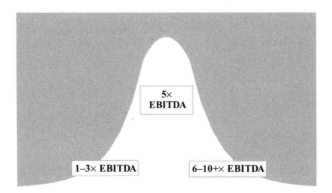

FIGURE 4.1 Pricing Multiples
Source: From Dennis J. Roberts' *Mergers & Acquisitions: An Insider's Guide to the Purchase and Sale of Middle Market Business Interests* (John Wiley & Sons, 2009). Reproduced with permission of John Wiley & Sons, Inc.

multiple will be adjusted for such factors as the risk of business, the economy, and prospects for future growth. Multiples of 3 and 4 are more common with seasonal and volatile businesses (such as construction), and multiples above 5 are for companies with low risk or a strong likelihood of above-normal growth.

Guideline Transaction Method Advantages and Cautions   Sales reported in the transaction databases typically reflect control position acquisitions or mergers. This represents the enterprise value of the company. The buyers of the companies in many cases are within the same industry. Such buyers are often referred to as "strategic buyers." Strategic buyers bring synergies to the table that form part of the deal structure. This consideration is important because it may differ significantly from a hypothetical buyer, which is the standard of value when determining FMV.

The transaction databases typically indicate the total consideration paid for the businesses. But in such transactions, the "terms" of the deal often have a significant impact on the consideration being paid. Terms in such circumstances often represent such things as seller financing for a percentage of the total deal; "holdbacks" on sale proceeds subject to satisfaction of certain contingent events; non-competition agreements for shareholders and managers of the acquired company; earn-out provisions over time pegged to financial performance of the company in the post-acquisition time period, and so on. The transactions represent actual deals that have been completed. This is valuable empirical data representing valid sales of businesses.

The transactions are typically analyzed in relation to common industry measurements. The business brokers often refer to the transaction value as a relationship to EBITDA. Other indicators of value may be stated as a percentage of revenue or book value.

Transactions are often completed by "strategic buyers," or entities that are in the same industry as the subject company. Data has to be very carefully analyzed if an assignment includes establishing FMV for tax purposes.

The "terms" of the transactions have to be understood. Terms may often add a material amount to the ultimate transaction consideration exchanged between the parties. Terms in FMV assignments are understood to be 100% cash, which is potentially significantly different than data in the transaction databases.

Rules of Thumb   This section is included to highlight worthwhile valuation information for the smallest companies, generally those with a few employees and under $1 million in revenue. The traditional valuation methods already described are on a scale that is often not suitable for a small company. In those circumstances having a rule of thumb as a guidepost is a reasonable way to approach the pricing of such an entity. Often the personal and the commercial costs are so intertwined that it is difficult to separate them.

One of the best books on this subject is the *Business Reference Guide: The Essential Guide to Pricing Businesses and Franchises* by Tom West, published annually by Business Broker Press. The book contains literally hundreds of small business classifications in addition to insights on the valuation of franchises and licensing arrangements. The source of the information is the reporting by business brokers into the database maintained by Mr. West. The transactions span many years so the rules of thumb are not especially timely representing today's economic climate. The valuation insights have the benefit, however, of considering many transactions per each industry classification so the effect of volume is helpful. No single transaction is likely to have a disproportionate impact on the information. This is a useful reference and a good place to begin the valuation analysis of smaller companies.

Other sources for approximating values based on limited information are trade associations. Some of the trade associations comprised of similarly sized members that are most often small companies, will have data on member transactions. Contacting a specific trade association regarding such information is the only way you will know. If the trade association does maintain some transaction data, it will likely be hesitant to share that information with a non-member. Access to proprietary information such as transaction data is one benefit to being a dues paying member.

Asset Approach

The asset approach to valuation certainly enjoys solid theoretical support. The assets of a business entity have some inherent value, or replacement cost. Additionally, assets are routinely reported on financial statements, the balance sheet, on a historical cost basis.

For the purposes of this course, the income and market approaches to value are typically far more appropriate. In business transactions, buyers are typically motivated to complete a deal by anticipated future economic benefits. Such economic benefits are often determined largely by "employing" assets in useful endeavors, not necessarily "owning" the assets. Without a reasonable expected return on an investment, the underlying asset may be sharply discounted in value. An asset approach is an implied control position analysis.

Clearly, in the world of business transactions determining the "purchase price" is often a function of determining future economic benefits. That determination is most commonly tied to an income approach to valuation.

Yet, when the deal is being finalized, most commonly the assets of the target company are being purchased or acquired.

The amount a buyer will spend for a business is most commonly a function of future economic benefits. Structuring the actual deal is a function of applied tax code and limiting liability in most cases. Asset purchases typically afford tremendous benefits to the buyer, and most typically the buyer is in the dominant negotiating position.

Once the transaction purchase price is determined and the buyer is resolved to acquire the company assets, then tax efficiency agendas generally prevail. The consideration or purchase price in an asset acquisition is allocated to the various asset categories for tax purposes. Under this process, generally referred to as compliance with IRS Code Section 1060, the full purchase price is allocated to various asset categories. The IRS favors allocating the total purchase price in this manner.

Asset Approach Advantages and Cautions Parties to transactions are most often familiar with assets and are comfortable thinking through the deal in terms of the assets. Many of the assets are reasonably known quantities such as accounts receivable, inventories (when inventory is bought and simply resold as in distribution), rolling stock, equipment, and real estate. If the value or the price of a deal is in excess of such reasonably verified asset values, the "balancing" (a.k.a. "plug") amount is an intangible asset most typically called "goodwill." Goodwill is commonly the catchall category of assets that do not have a highly refined definition and a place on the analysis schedule.

Analysis schedules using the asset approach are typically presented in a traditional financial statement format reflecting the company's balance sheet. The asset approach is helpful in understanding how to structure the deal for tax planning purposes. Most acquisitions of closely held companies are asset-based transactions, and tax planning is typically a driving consideration in the ultimate structure of the deal.

The allocation of the sale proceeds to the various assets illustrates which assets the successor owner deems most valuable in the long term. For example, if previously unrecorded goodwill is a significant asset, then the intangible attributes of the acquired company are of paramount importance to maintain.

The asset approach schedules indicate the allocation of sales proceeds, but the approach often tells us nothing about how the value is determined when a significant amount is allocated to an intangible asset like goodwill.

The approach may become very costly and an administrative nightmare in larger transactions. All significant assets may require appraisals for the transaction to be completed, which could be a tremendous burden if the assets include real estate located in multiple states as in a chain of businesses.

SUMMARY

This chapter is intended to provide an overview of valuations for the business transaction arena. We have examined different standards of value, which may apply to various transactions depending on the facts and circumstances of each case. We have also examined the three major approaches to valuation: the income approach, the market approach, and the asset approach. Finally, before the value may be assigned to any particular set of circumstances, we have to determine such things as ownership attributes and the degree of marketability.

CHAPTER 5

Industries and Businesses

*He who builds a better mouse trap runs into material shortages,
patent-infringement suits, work stoppages, collusive bidding,
discount discrimination, and taxes.*

—J. E. Martz

The preceding chapter on the economy introduces a number of often obvious factors regarding the financial health of the nation. We will be explor-
ing a wide range of buyout options, but those options are often a function
of the type of business. Some businesses exude an aura of excitement and
marketing sizzle and attract a disproportionate amount of attention. In this
instance, think about the near unimaginable success of a technology start-
up company that explodes on the economic scene with the founders falling
heir to a fortune in relatively short order. A few such incredible successes
will have the attention of investors seeking the potential of disproportionate financial gains. Our system rewards the financial risk takers and "high
rollers." Of course, our system also punishes those who fail, and often the
penalties are devastating. I'm sure you can think of business owners and
entrepreneurs that have both made and lost fortunes.

Other businesses are far more ordinary and provide daily or worka-
day services and goods. In this category think about convenience stores
and drycleaners. Not exactly the fodder for dreaming, but many business
owners have found just such an investment as the ticket to financial independence. This chapter will frame in general terms a limited number of
industries with the goal of emphasizing the relative risk environment and
the more common transition options that we have seen. Ultimately, we are
attempting to link the industry with the strategy more likely to result in a
successful buyout.

There is nothing like a consistently profitable business to attract the interest of potential buyers. In the mergers and acquisition industry, financial profitability is attractive, but the major companies also seek something that is often far more important, growth. From a sales and marketing standpoint, the profit "growth" is the intangible sizzle that often drives the premium valuation that business owners covet. Many closely held companies will feature some growth, if only for inflation, but longer-term sustainable growth or short-term material explosive growth is typically the attribute to a small subset of industries. Certain industries have an aura of glamour, often justified by past performance or the experience of a number of superstar financial performers. One such industry is "technology," which is so general that it may encompass a wide spectrum of qualifying players. Once a company has earned a specific industry label, that industry label will likely have a significant impact on the options before the business owner. Following are a few summary thoughts on a limited number of industry labels.

TECHNOLOGY AND SOFTWARE

Let's begin with the unquestioned champion of mystique and glamour. The technology industry today is somewhat infamous for the technology or "dot.com" bust in 2000–2001. The technology bust of course was preceded by an almost unimaginable run-up in the public stock markets beginning in the early 1990s and lasting until the bust. The Nasdaq stock market is the home for many technology companies and was the leading source for impressive equity gains in the 1990s. In spite of the dot.com meltdown, the technology sector did rebound and today it still offers significant upside potential for investors.

There is a residual effect to the aura generated from this industry. While there was a financial downturn in this industry segment, it has rebounded and the investment community holds major public companies in this sector with respect because of the earnings and growth that has been demonstrated. One view commonly voiced: Who will be the next Microsoft, eBay, or Google?

Technology companies with demonstrated earnings will attract desirable attention because such firms typically promise growth, and that growth may be highly regarded by a strategic buyer. Many private equity firms focus only on candidates with a high likelihood of future growth since that is part of the business model that involves substantial debt. The candidate company literally "grows" its way to financial ratio respectability through increasing profitability and revenue. Short-term results may prove to be very attractive, but there is also a high risk of obsolescence over time.

COMMUNICATIONS

This general industry category shares much of the same aura as technology. The communications revolution in this country has produced a number of financial superstars that have returned financial reward to its investors. Many of the major communications firms have already been combined to the point where the financial newspapers are sounding the alarm that further consolidation may be difficult to achieve at the national level. There are still a number of middle market equipment and service providers to the industry to attract attention.

ENERGY

This industry sector seems to be assuming the aura of high growth. The global market for energy, particularly carbon-based sources such as oil, coal, and natural gas, is growing. There are now far more growing economies that will be seeking secure energy sources. The competition for energy from such countries as Brazil, Russia, India, and China (BRIC) will continue to keep energy prices high into the future. While the energy industry is dominated by a number of household names and large utility companies, there are a host of service, testing, and support companies that will tag along in this sector.

COMMODITY GOODS—RETAIL FOOD AND AGRICULTURE

This general category did not attract serious attention from investors when technology and communications were strong. The industries growing only with inflation and population growth are stable and predictable. Companies are generally attractive to longer-term investors. The market is large, however, as expressed as a percentage of the national economy. There are many closely held companies that are retail grocers, convenience stores, niche food processors, and service firms. Following the financial market meltdown from 2008, these stable companies that are consistently profitable and have proven to be recession resistant are coming back into favor.

HEALTHCARE

Somewhat in the same vein as commodity goods above, healthcare is distinguished because of an aging population. The "baby boomers" (almost

80 million) are reaching retirement age and the demographic trend of an aging population is going to continue for the next few decades. The aging population will consume more healthcare resources on a per capita basis because older people experience more health-related complications. The industry is not really market driven, as there are only a few major providers in most large metropolitan areas. The healthcare providers typically do not compete on price, rather they compete on soft issues such as caring, sympathy, and service. The future of healthcare is positive and while it is often not demonstrating explosive growth, in certain practice areas investment is attractive. Because the industry is mature.

MANUFACTURING

This industry earned a negative tag when much of our industrial base seemed to be exported to lower cost global regions such as Asia and South America. While low-value commodity items (such as textiles) were exported, much higher value manufacturing stayed in the United States. The manufacturing sector automated and became ever more efficient. Often more production is achieved with fewer workers due to such things as innovation, applied technology, engineering and design, quality control, and transportation costs.

CONSTRUCTION

Notorious for its cycles, construction is currently at a low point driven largely by the financial crises in the housing market. While interest rates are at historic or near historic low levels, many if not most banks view construction as a high credit risk and a source of problems and not opportunities. In many parts of the country obtaining financing for new home construction is very difficult. Overall construction is still down from the levels of 2003 to 2006. Few construction firms are being sold in this depressed market, and it is likely that the few candidates that are available are experiencing difficulty attracting outside financing.

MAIN STREET BUSINESSES

This catchall category is intended to include the vast array of smaller retail stores, specialty companies, and service firms. This covers the wide range of businesses from franchises, licensing arrangements, hardware stores, many family companies, and distributors to mention a few. Generally these businesses are successful if they have survived past the first few years where there is terrible attrition. There are so many of them that few are distinguished as acquisition candidates by third parties and are therefore difficult to sell. Many business owners will have to decide if they will hold out for a period of time and hope for a stronger economy, or transact the business at fire sale pricing.

DISCRETIONARY PRODUCTS AND SERVICES INDUSTRIES

Companies in the entertainment business, restaurants, gift boutiques, many clothiers, and items that are not perceived as necessary are in general suffering during this recession. For many of these niche companies, there are fewer discretionary dollars available for spending and such firms have been squeezed to the point of barely surviving. These firms are unlikely objects of third party acquisitions and succession planning.

PROFESSIONAL SERVICES

Where these services are required or traditionally supplied as in public accounting, tax preparation, and financial planning, such firms are to a degree recession resistant and have largely escaped the severe economic recession. They are often still strong candidates for transactions because of the more certainty of predicable cash flows. Other services such as commercial consulting, process improvement, employee communications, and personnel placement are generally still feeling the crush of the recession. If their service capabilities are not required, many companies will not contract with them until the prospects for the economy improve substantially.

SUMMARY

The industry overview is at most a snapshot of what segments of the economy are likely to be attractive to outside investors. It is my experience that investment dollars often follow a herd mentality and there are more resources looking for fewer good places to invest. Once an industry has earned a blemish, such as home construction today, it will take a long period of time for investor confidence to return. There is often an industry "shakeout" as the weakest of the industry members fold, or are merged out if existence.

One key fact to emphasize is to keep the business profitable. Successful companies, with success defined as being profitable, will have far more options than those companies that are barely surviving. My experience is that thoughtful investors generally do not want someone else's problems.

CHAPTER 6

Professional Advisors

I have no use for bodyguards, but I have a very specific use for two highly trained Certified Public Accountants.

—Elvis Presley

Retaining knowledgeable transaction-centric and experienced advisors is essential in our experience. We will consider the various advisors and indicate the relative reliance on them from the buyer's side and the seller's side of the transaction. The strength of the advisor will depend on the service capabilities that are expected depending on the type of transaction considered. The various observations are offered not in any particular order, because the relative importance of each is a function of the requirement of either the buyer or the seller. The interest of the buyer and the seller are often very different and their reliance on advisors will change depending on the requirements. What follows is my listing of key professional advisors.

ATTORNEYS

Attorneys are often first considered regarding the buyer. The buyer is typically placing its resources on the transaction table and is mindful that its interests must be carefully guarded against unknown liabilities. Counsel for the buyer will typically be drafting the transaction documents to protect the financial and legal interests of his client. Major documents along with a cursory review of transaction due diligence is discussed in Chapter 7.

From the buyer's perspective, retaining an experienced attorney with a long history of successful closings is critical. The legal profession trains attorneys to be advocates for their clients and to be credible advisors to the full spectrum of possible outcomes, both good and bad. In my experience there are many ways for deals and transactions to unravel, but understanding the inherent benefits of the transaction is important to keep in mind. The rewards and risks of the transaction must be kept in perspective, not just an orientation to only what may go wrong.

It is important to make the distinction between transaction attorneys and corporate counsel. Transaction attorneys bring to the table a wealth of experience with negotiations, setting priorities, getting to "yes," drafting discrete and often complex documents, and the overall knowledge of how deals get consummated. Corporate counsel may not have this expertise but may have a command of such things as contracts, taxes, employment law, and corporate governance. The skills to succeed in transactions are much different than most areas of law, and with the stakes being very high this is a poor time to be training an attorney, no matter how trustworthy.

CERTIFIED PUBLIC ACCOUNTANT

The certified public accountant (CPA) is a more generic person that possesses practical accounting and tax expertise. It is not mandatory to be a CPA; it is our experience that for most middle market companies there is an accounting firm providing accounting, tax, and perhaps consulting services.

The buyer typically relies on the CPA for assistance on taxes, forecasts, and consolidated financial information. The world of transactions when multiple entities are concerned becomes complex very quickly. Tax issues may become complex particularly where there are corporations, limited liability companies, partnerships, and other legal entities involved in the same transaction. Consolidated financial statements often must be provided, with a consideration of intercompany eliminations, appropriate accruals, compliance with generally accepted accounting principles (GAAP), consideration of liabilities, and so on. Accurate reporting will be essential to avoid surprises as the transaction unfolds.

The seller often looks to the CPA for guidance on valuation, and thoughts on tax strategy. The CPA is typically a trusted advisor that has known the business owner for years. The CPA is familiar with the totality of the owner's financial situation since tax returns have been prepared in the past. Additionally, the CPA typically has had many clients pass through the transition process and is in a strong position to provide insights into the process that is surely a source of stress for the selling owner.

In larger companies, the owner has a CPA firm, and it is common for the company to use a range of services offered. Often there are a number of professionals that form a team at the CPA firm involved with the candidate. The range of services may include investment banking, wealth management, tax planning, organization assistance, and other capabilities.

There are a few caveats regarding CPAs. They are trusted advisors in most cases, but as a CPA myself, I always avoided situations on topics uncomfortable to me. This makes sense; things that are unknown are a risk to my professional expertise. It is virtually impossible to have the breadth of knowledge to be an authority on all relevant topics. Transition planning is a niche topic with tremendous stakes for the business owner. It is best for the owner to do some independent research on the topic at hand and to trust established authorities.

FINANCIAL ADVISORS

The financial advisor represents a discipline as much as an individual. It is possible that depending on the unique skill set of the individual, the financial advisor may be a CPA or less likely an attorney. There are many other professional designations, many of them specialty disciplines such as those involving insurance, retail investments, fee-for-service financial planners, wealth managers, and exit-planning professionals. We will assume that the financial advisor is a separate individual working in a financial advisory firm. The distinguishing hallmark here is that this discipline is represented by a known and trustworthy relation.

The buyer is particularly interested in the services of the financial advisor with a pending liquidity event (sale of the business) on the horizon. Figuring out investments in today's uncertain and risky economy is serious business. Structuring investments suitable to provide cash for retirement is an art form. Many retiring owners have dependents, and members of a family unit may together or singularly live for decades beyond a retirement date. One great issue today is making sure you do not inadvertently outlive your financial assets. Careful planning for retirement including provisions for long-term medical care, nursing homes, and having assets to retain independence as long as possible are examples of key considerations.

The best financial advisors have access to planning software that takes into account your lifestyle today and the lifestyle post retirement. The drop in expenses for a senior level executive or business owner in retirement may not be as substantial as imagined. It is best to model the costs so that there are no surprises for such things as healthcare, home maintenance, travel, and other expectations.

Case Study: The Maher Group

The Maher Group is an investment broker affiliated with a major wirehouse in the St. Louis metropolitan area. Jim Maher, JD, CPA, Founder, and President, is the quintessential entrepreneur. Born into a farm family in Iowa,

Maher worked his way through college holding part time jobs, playing D-1 football for the University of Missouri, was elected student body president, and along the way earned his CPA designation while graduating from law school. Shedding a safe salaried career with an international Big 4 CPA firm, he began working in the securities industry and eventually founded his own investment advisory firm. Maher brings to the client relationship a spectrum of skills second to none and rarely found in investment advisors. He understands the breadth and range of legal issues confronting owners of closely held businesses, and is knowledgeable about the tax environment. He is proactive in strategic thinking, offering options for his client's consideration. As a team player, he understands the roles played by other professional advisors. He complements the contributions of other advisors, and at the end of a discussion he and the Maher Group are able to implement the investment strategies. Team members in the Maher Group hold an impressive collection of professional designations including other CPAs, an attorney, chartered financial analysts (CFAs), and chartered retirement planning counselors (CRPC). It is no wonder why the Maher Group has walls filled with awards, recognitions, and volunteer acknowledgements, and they are recognized as a regional thought leader.

INVESTMENT BANKERS

Investment bankers are most often associated with selling the business to a third party, not quite the focus of this book. These professionals may be invaluable when the candidate company is of a sufficient size to preclude a straightforward management buyout. When a financial resource such as a private equity firm, discussed in Chapters 10 and 11, is an integral part of the succession process, it is a daunting task trying to find the right fit. There are perhaps thousands of private equity firms and even more additional resources to fund buyouts. Most business owners have no idea how to begin searching for a compatible partner, and compatibility is critical for a successful non-adversarial process.

Investment bankers spend a great deal of time studying industries and knowing the contacts within those industries. It is difficult being all things to all business owners and most of the credible professionals will have substantial specific industry expertise. These individuals will know where to begin looking for the best financial partners. Through their extensive networks, it is possible to focus on those few best candidates to provide a satisfactory solution to a business owner.

Investment bankers have experience in negotiations and understanding the many twists and turns that are common with transactions. They are an independent and professional resource that is in a position to remove the emotion from the transaction equation and focus on getting the proposed project completed. In my experience, the successful investment bankers are consummate communicators and technicians. They understand the angst and stress that business owners face when thinking about transitioning options.

They are also excellent resources in the analysis of valuation for transaction related purposes. They are experienced journeymen with insights into completed transactions and what drives value creation. They have a feel for market conditions and the likelihood of matching a need with available resources.

Case Study: The McLean Group

Founded by Dennis Roberts, CPA and Andy Smith, CPA, The McLean Group (TMG) is headquartered in Mclean Virginia, and has a national network of investment bankers. Mr. Roberts is a nationally known speaker and author, *Mergers & Acquisition: An Insider's Guide to the Purchase and Sale of Middle Market Business Interests* (John Wiley and Sons, 2009). He has dedicated a career to building the professionalism of the investment banking industry. Mr. Roberts has graciously contributed time and resources into a number of organizations dedicated to the investment banking community. Most recently he is one of the co-founders of the Middle Market Investment Banking Association (MMIBA). TMG investment bankers are organized into a number of industry specialty groups providing focused expertise in the mission of adding value to the client relationship. All of the investment bankers have obtained professional licenses through the Financial Industry Regulatory Authority (FINRA) as part their affiliation with TMG. This level of professionalism is rare within the discipline. Under the banner of full disclosure, I am affiliated with TMG as an investment banker, and they hold my FINRA licenses as the broker dealer. The hundreds of "tombstone" notices that line TMG corridors attest to the firm's success. The national affiliation of investment bankers under the TMG name will only grow with time.

BEHAVIORAL SCIENCE

The study of such topics as human compatibility and leadership qualities are often regarded as a lot of wishful thinking by many business owners. Too bad. The study of human behavior is a powerful tool for a businesses to have in assessing the strengths of the senior team. While the study of human behavior at all levels within an organization has merit, I think it is particularly essential for those few key employees that can make a significant impact. When the senior team is compatible and there has been no professional assessment of the key associates, I call this remarkable luck. I have witnessed numerous instances where the key employees have sharp differences, and such disagreement is often traced back to the fact that no assessment of likely behavior was ever completed. It may take years for the problems to surface, but when such conflicts arise it may tear an organization apart. Conflicting behavior may be predicted with a high degree of confidence, particularly when completed by highly trained professionals.

Business psychology services may entail leadership assessments, developmental assessments of current employees, career coaching, team building, succession planning, conflict resolution, organizational planning, human resource projects, leadership exercises, predictive testing, and aptitude testing among a wide range of capabilities. Firms that embrace this approach to human resource management often have high performance senior managements that have a solid understanding of organizational goals. Later in this book there are many examples of success stories where communications and building a culture of ownership have proven to be enormously beneficial to the financial success of the organization. As our economy increasingly shifts to a service based market, an emphasis on human relation skills becomes increasingly important.

Case Study: Humber Mundie & McClary

Humber Mundie & McClary (HM&M) is a professional firm of doctorate-level licensed psychologists who specialize in helping companies succeed through strategies that maximize talent and shape strong organizational culture. All of the principals bring to the client relationship an exceedingly high degree of scholarship, professional accomplishment, and experience. The partnership's services include leadership assessment, executive coaching, and international video assessments, as well as succession planning, team building, organizational planning, on-site selection testing, family business counsel, and vocational counseling. This book often references the importance of behavioral compatibility as an integral element to succession success. HM&M is a firm that helps businesses assess their most valuable asset, its senior leadership. It equips decision makers with information that can help them select individuals and form teams that fit best with the culture, values, and objectives of their companies. The possible costs to the organization of having the wrong individuals in leadership positions can be disastrous. HM&M Partner Emeritus Dr. Gordon Pederson has been one of the foundational assessment professionals in the Milwaukee area, home of

HM&M offices, for decades. He and his partners have worked with hundreds of national and multinational companies. According to Dr. Pederson, "An organization's future growth depends on having in place the leaders who have the talent and synergy to carry forward the vision. Psychological assessment and development is a proven tool for building such a structure." Dr. Al Mascitti, managing partner of HM&M, conducts each year an extensive number of international video conferences to assess leadership abilities in parts of the world. I am a firm believer in the merits of psychological testing for key employees, particularly when there is a marquee event in process, such as the succession of the company.

KEY EMPLOYEES

Most middle market businesses have key employees. Typically the larger the company, the greater likelihood there are several key employees. The precise contribution to the organization may vary, but key employees hold positions with titles such as: chief operating officer, chief financial officer, controller, sales and marketing manager, and officer designations. The entity will have key employees that have typically been with the business for many years and are thoroughly knowledgeable about operations both good and bad.

Key employees are first addressed from the seller's standpoint. My experience is that key employees retain that special status because they are critical thinkers and fully realize the challenges facing the company, including the retirement of the principals. Generally, taking a few key employees into confidence is a plus because it tends to allay their fears about the future of the company. While confidentiality is a hallmark of sensitive activity such as transaction planning, key employees may be a wellspring of reassurance for the selling shareholder if handled professionally. The key employees will almost certainly be interviewed by the prospective buyer at some point, and they are in a position to offer help with the transition planning or torpedo the efforts if they feel slighted or cheated.

My experience is tilted to bringing key employees into your confidence and letting them know your plans. If the owner suspects that this may cause considerable anxiety and prompt some to consider leaving, there are strategies to address this natural inclination. For truly key employees it is appropriate to consider perhaps a package of benefits. For example, a special retention bonus may be established to encourage key personnel to stay during the sale process. The retention bonus is paid upon the successful sale of the business. The retention bonus should be sufficiently substantial so that if the key employee elects to leave there will be a significant financial penalty. Other strategies include negotiating employment contracts with the buyer for the key employees, often one to two years or longer in the case of exceptional talent.

BOARD MEMBERS OR ADVISORY MEMBERS

These advisors are helpful for both buyers and sellers. Personally, I think having outside advisors with the best interests of the owner and the business are an integral part of fulfilling your goals. Outside advisors will be more objective and can see things that are often hidden to those too close to the daily routines.

Outside advisors are helpful to business owners to ask objective questions about pursuing the transaction. Once the momentum of a deal begins to take shape, the transaction often has a forward pull regardless of subsequent events or other roadblocks. The push to "close" often becomes unbearable. Outside advisors help provide balance and objectivity to the process. It is better when the outside advisors have personal experience with transactions and know the ebb and flow of emotions during the transition process. Their insights then become invaluable. Objectivity and experience are paramount qualities to have, particularly when the authoritative literature suggests that most transactions fail to meet objectives due to lack of planning and integrating the parties.

For the seller, outside advisors will provide insights into the process. I have found that without outside assistance or substantial independent research, most business owners are naive about the value of their company. Under my law of "selective facts," business owners "hear" and retain only what they want to know. Often the most favorable set of circumstances, the highest multiple, or the maxim price within a range is retained. Substantial effort was dedicated in the early chapters of this book suggesting that our economy has undergone material changes since 2008, and it may not return to how things were pre-2008 for many years if ever in certain industries. Business owners experience the changes and see what is happening on a daily basis, but are still in denial thinking that things will return to "normal" if enough time passes. An outside advisor will hopefully challenge the set manner of thinking and provide required support for the business owner.

FAMILY

Technically family members really do not comfortably fit within the ranks of other professional advisors. I believe that family advice for the business owner is often the most important resource above any of the other advisors.

A spouse, children, immediate family members or other close members provide the daily support for getting through the daily obligations of running a business. During the time of active involvement in the business, and assuming the activity of a family, the days seem to fly by and years seem to vanish. The pulse of the business is often challenging and rewarding. Most business owners are so thoroughly immersed in the business and with family that there is little significant time for many outside interests. Most business owners struggle with the thought of not having the company to dote over.

A spouse will be a wonderful sounding board to think about retirement. What will you do without the daily focus of the business? If not a spouse then another significant influence will serve much the same purpose. Hopefully the business owner has someone to share this critical decision.

One of the great advantages to an inside buyout is that the business owner likely has far more leverage in designing an exit that is consistent with personal goals. Selling to a third party typically negates an orderly exit. The buyer is in control following the passing of the business. A best practice in my experience is to have a plan of gradual exit, which may be adjusted if the business owner wants to accelerate the process. Most business owners considering an inside buyout care about the company and the employees and want to see the organization succeed. Having a good support group in the form of involved key employees will make the transition journey as good as it gets, knowing at some point there must be a break with the organization.

SUMMARY

Retaining experienced professional advisors is critical to the business owner having the best chance at realizing critical personal goals. The succession-planning environment is changing rapidly when the impact of such things as taxes, the economy, technology, product obsolescence, demographics, and political trade winds are considered. My admonition is to make sure those most trusted advisors have remained current on matters of succession planning in all of its multi-faceted dynamics.

CHAPTER 7

Documents and Due Diligence

People who fail to plan, have planned to fail.

—George Hewell

Trust everyone, but cut the cards.

—Finley Peter Dunne

Due diligence is often thought of as something only for the buyer to be concerned with. The buyer is perceived to be taking the greatest risk in acquiring a company, and therefore the thinking is that extra care should be exercised. I think the notion of due diligence should be more expansive with a considerable list of items for both sides of the transaction, the buyer and the seller. This book is focused on inside buyouts where there is the presumption that the parties to the transaction are familiar with the subject company and the risks that a truly third party would be concerned with are more limited by the insider knowledge.

This chapter is not intended to be a primer on how to draft and interpret legal documents most commonly associated with business transactions. While there is a discussion of the major documents likely to be encountered, the emphasis in this chapter is to implore business owners in particular to make sure your essential interests are represented by the most qualified and experienced professionals.

DUE DILIGENCE FOR THE SELLER

There are a number of issues that the seller should address in preparation for the exit-planning process. The following sections identify the major areas for advanced serious planning. The items are emphasized so that the seller has the opportunity to think about the impact of the issues in time to craft those areas into an overall plan that best accomplishes personal goals.

Have an Exit Plan—Know Your Options

In my experience the first due diligence step to be taken by a seller is to have an exit plan. This is intended to be more a conceptual mindset as opposed to a formal plan in a plastic jacket with topical tabs. A business owner should be thinking about the eventual exit from the business. Hopefully, the exit plan is updated with facts and circumstances that evolve over time.

The business owner should take control of the process of exit planning. This exercise should include studying the options that are available for exiting the business and also considering what will be done in retirement. What is intended is to provide a listing of issues I have found to be important without necessarily developing the insights on how to address them. Many issues are behavioral in nature and are best addressed by professionals better qualified to speak about the major concerns.

Among the most important considerations is deciding on the standard of living to be maintained. It is not enough to think that assets and resources must be maximized. If that was the simplistic goal, hold the business until you die and let your heirs figure out the mess. Failure to plan is planning to fail—a wonderful line. It is important to be pragmatic in your financial expectations. The goal is to approximate living expenses without the safety of the company providing the benefits. Remember that many costs will not change such as housing and food.

Address important personal goals. Many business owners genuinely feel it has been a privilege to be part of a growing and successful business. There is often a compassion for the local community, perhaps a feeling about the faith of the community and a strong feeling for the employees that have made success possible. There may be a consideration about the legacy of the founder. There are likely to be at least some qualitative issues, and the more successful the company the more likely there will be issues to consider. Finally, a spouse may have strong input into this chapter of thought.

Many business owners have some vague idea of succession options, but only a small percentage will have a circumspect comprehensive plan. Regrettably, most business owners wait until a crisis or some "mortality event" (the death of a family member, personal health crisis, or some other traumatic event) occurs to begin a planning process. Too often in this case time is short and many options that take years to accomplish are no longer a consideration.

Business owners that are in touch with the market will spend the time to research exit options. Generally, the options may be distilled into a few viable selections. Exit to family, exit to managers and employees, sell to a third party, do an IPO or liquidate the company. This book is centered on inside buyout options, which in many cases is the preferred route for many business owners if the transaction proceeds are sufficient to meet financial goals.

Review Legal Requirements

The list of things to do under this heading is often shorter. Some obvious candidates include making sure you or the company has clear title to the assets that are being passed to the new owner. Make sure obvious documents are current such as shareholder schedule, company leases, outstanding contracts, shareholder and board minutes, and state filings. If the seller owns the real estate occupied by the company, a lease be updated and environmental issues considered. Outstanding litigation, if any, should be reviewed. The buyer's attorney will almost certainly ask for representations and warrants by the seller related to the company. This is a standard practice to protect the buyer from unknown liabilities.

If you are in a marital property state, remember that spousal consent may be required for major decisions that impact the couple financially. Engage an attorney familiar with transaction to develop a comprehensive checklist of items to consider.

If real estate is involved, make sure it has been subject to environmental review. Buildings that have been associated with the business for many years or facilities with likely environmental issues have to be carefully considered.

Identify Advisory Team

Chapter 6 discussed advisors and the advice should be heeded. Depending on the circumstances, sellers often have a need to solicit the assistance of family members, financial advisors, industry colleagues, and other trusted advisors. The key item emphasized is to find those few individuals whose advice is valuable and in your best interests.

Optimize Value

The chapter on valuation discusses traditional approaches to valuing a private company. Many business owners profess an interest in maximizing the value of the business, but actions speak louder than words. The conduct of the business is a key indicator of the likelihood the operating results are in fact being optimized.

Many companies are managed to break even financially for tax purposes, with the result that the company is not being managed to make money. Net profitability can always be adjusted by payouts such as bonuses. Burying personal costs in the business does the owner a disservice because the real worth of the company is hard to determine. Additionally the morale of the employees is negatively impacted because of the perception the "owner" is running expenses through the business. While this is justified by the owner in good years as an appropriate prerequisite for taking the risk to start the business, the practice is suspect when the inevitable economic downturn arrives and everyone is being asked to sustain cuts in salary and resources.

> In my experience one of the most important things a business owner must do to enhance value is to clean the financial statements and purge them of excessive personal items before selling. Remove non-operating assets and end indefensible expenditures. Trying to normalize, "add-back," or just ignoring a long list of adjustments simply looks bad. It indicates that the company has not been professionally managed.

An open and collaborative company culture tends to produce the highest returns with time. Empirical studies verify this fact, and the more financially successful companies seek to have the employees buy into the notion of "owning" their jobs. There are substantial resources for you to consider in building a more collaborative culture.

Put the House in Organizational Order

This part is complementary with optimizing value. This section is intended to emphasize addressing the reporting and informational needs of the business. The employees need the most current tools available to discharge their jobs and optimize results. Make sure your information-reporting system and financial statements are understandable. Since this is a book on inside initiated buyouts it may not be necessary to go to the expense of having a CPA firm review or audit the financial statements. Often that level of detail and assurance already exists with larger companies that utilize bank financing. The higher level of financial reporting in such instances is often a loan covenant provision. If debt is to be a part of the buyout strategy, having an independent party such as the CPA firm review the financial statements is a recommended practice.

Address Key Employees

Successful inside-initiated buyouts will be mindful of the careful consideration afforded the key employees most often identified as the senior managers. The management team will be a crucial factor in the decision to transition the business internally. The business world today is typically dominated by having timely access to data for decision making, pricing issues, and strategic thinking. The key employees are integral to the organization because of demonstrated past performance in the discharge of responsibilities. These key individuals have portable skills and you do not want them to have an incentive to leave because of poor communications related to succession planning. I have found it is best to be honest with these key employees and they will respect your decision to embrace their trust. If the inside buyout is the choice, the sooner your key people are brought into the planning cycle the better.

A worthwhile strategy to consider when selling to an inside initiated buyout is to "jump-start" the process by allowing the key employees to participate in the success of the company through some form of ownership program. The ownership may be in the form of actual stock, but it may also include such things as phantom stock, stock appreciation rights, or stock options. Such programs provide an incentive for the key employees to remain with the company in a committed manner that aligns the seller's interests and those of the buyer.

DUE DILIGENCE FOR THE BUYER

When we think of a "sale" to a new owner, the topic of due diligence often reflects lengthy checklists of a myriad of details to be confirmed, corroborated, or discharged. The buyer is the party to the transaction that has the vast exposure of unknown liabilities if some material item is left uncovered. Even when the parties are familiar with one another, the buyer's due diligence is still a significant task that is to be addressed in a serious manner. The purpose here is not to introduce those lengthy checklists since they are readily available elsewhere. Rather, the intent is to consider major areas of investigation and a brief consideration of common transaction documents. As mentioned in Chapter 6 regarding advisors, relying on thoroughly vetted experienced professionals with transaction experience is one of the best protections for the buyer.

Key Employee Leadership

If an inside-initiated buyout is to occur, one requirement is to have leadership within the key employee group. Most typically a number of key individuals will be involved with the details of the transaction, but within that inner circle there needs to be a designated leader. At some point the future president of the company will have to emerge from among the inside team or from outside the company. It is typically much easier if there is leadership within the company.

The leadership may become an at-risk position during the exploratory stages when the current owners have not made a decision on succession plans. It may be presumptuous to be so forward as to suggest an inside buyout. Someone has to broach the topic eventually. Success in business often involves taking risky positions and hoping that circumstances work toward a happy ending. No one said it was going to be easy.

Selection of Advisors

Part of the leadership includes an analysis of the advisors on the transaction. In many cases where the ownership is predisposed to an inside buyout, they will be selecting the advisors who would protect their interests. In most cases the assistance of the seller is required for the transaction to work, and if that assistance is required the seller has a significant hand in the selection of the lead advisors. That said, it is a best practice in my experience for the buyer to have their own advisors even if their role is limited to reviewing the transaction as proposed by the seller. The buyer needs to be reassured that the proposed buyout makes sense and is fair to all parties.

In most cases a key advisor to have is an attorney that is considering the transaction from the buyer's perspective. Legal issues need to be thoroughly considered and an attorney will be an advocate for his client, in this case the buyer. If a third party is part of the buyout such as a private equity firm, they will have their own advisors and will likely be driving the terms of the transaction as well as the development of the legal documents.

Structuring the Transaction

In most of the cases of succession planning contemplated in this book, the seller will have a substantial hand in structuring the eventual transaction. The structure is typically intended to maximize sale proceeds after a consideration of transaction related taxes to the seller. Chapter 8 will consider the major taxes impacting transactions. The tax impact will typically determine if the transaction is a stock or asset sale and the terms.

Regardless of the goals of the seller, the transaction must make economic sense and it will have to involve cash flow. The reliance on outside financing, such as a bank, will compel a reasonable analysis because the bank will insist on some structure that has the greatest chance of success. It is unlikely the bank will support a transaction that has little chance of success.

In most cases the eventual structure of the transaction involving inside buyers will contain significant financial elements that are tax deductible to the company and the buyers. Candidates are items that are deductible such as deferred compensation, employment agreement, consulting arrangements, and Employee Stock Ownership Plans and Trust (ESOPs).

Some understanding of the pricing of the company needs to be established. Establishing a value might be a formal analysis by a reputable professional firm. The advantage to this is that the work product will likely be defensible to both the seller and the buyer. When leverage is a significant component of the transaction structure, an income approach will have the most merit. Using a discounted cash flow analysis will have the advantage of demonstrating how the acquisition obligations will be discharged over the next few years. When the valuation is so one-sided in favor of the seller; under those circumstances I have seen a significant number of failures because expectations could not be met. In most cases of failure, the future projections were simply too optimistic.

Financial Considerations

In concert with the other issues to be addressed, early consideration toward the topic of financing the transaction has to be addressed. In most cases, the help of the seller is instrumental. The one unanswered question is: How much assistance is required? The seller wants the buyer to feel some financial pain by buying the company, but there are limits to that pain threshold.

An appropriate first step is to determine how far a bank will go toward financing the transaction. As mentioned in Chapter 3 on financing, it is very challenging to engage traditional banks in financing buyouts because of the perceived high-risk status. The debt capacity of the candidate company needs to be assessed before the financial gaps can be filled in. Added to the bank financing, the buyer will be expected to provide some equity. In most cases the key employees will have limited financial resources so the equity is likely to be a modest amount.

Typically the company will be buying itself through future cash flows. At this point it is often apparent that the company will be able to afford a greater consideration of cash flows to the seller if those cash flows are tax deductible to the company. In this light such items as salary continuation, employment contract, consulting agreements, and deferred compensation are frequent options. The seller may have to accept extended payment terms in order to convert the investment in the company to cash for retirement.

Tax Planning

Closely related to financial issues, tax planning is an important attribute to consider. Once there is a "go" on the overall idea of the transaction, the focus is often on minimizing the taxes related to the plan. Financial consideration and tax planning are typically considered together because the absolute minimal amount of tax exposure (with a stock sale) may not be feasible from a cash flow standpoint. There is often a balancing of interests between taxes and cash flow.

Review Legal Issues

We have assumed that an inside buyer familiar with the intricacies of the business is one of the parties to the transaction. Even with inside knowledge, it is still essential to review legal issues with due diligence. Obvious items such as verifying ownership of assets, disclosure regarding litigation, and possible contingent liabilities are candidates for validation. If real estate is a factor, environmental studies must be completed to clear any possible exposure. An experienced transaction attorney will guide the buyer through the applicable legal issues.

COMMON DOCUMENTS AND KEY COVENANTS

The last section of this chapter is an abbreviated consideration of the most commonly encountered documents.

Term Sheet

This may literally be notes on the back of an envelope. The intent with the term sheet is to outline in aggregate the overall structure of a transaction, often with few details. This is the first-pass feasibility analysis to see if the two sides are in the same universe. Transition discussions have to begin at some point, and non-binding notes as part of an overview gets the process moving ahead. Candidates for consideration include ballpark price, first pass on financing the transaction, seller involvement (employment agreement, board membership, consulting), buyer resources, timing issues, and other material matters.

Confidentiality Agreement

This agreement is far more likely when a third party providing significant financing is involved, such as a private equity firm. A confidentiality agreement involving a seller and key management is less likely since they know one another. Having the agreement is still a good practice even if the intent is to make the point that no one should be careless with information while negotiations are in progress. When a third party is thinking of acquiring the business, a confidentiality agreement is virtually mandatory.

Letter of Intent

The letter of intent (LOI) is more common when unknown parties are negotiating since the signing of such a letter often starts the formal due diligence process. It is typically part of a "lock-up" or "exclusive" clause that stipulates the seller will not be actively shopping the business for a period of time. The LOI is not binding because it is still subject to a rigorous due diligence process on the part of the buyer that may uncover undesirable facts about the company. The LOI will typically be present when a third party such as a private equity firm is providing a substantial amount of financing. The content of the LOI is typically more detailed than the sketchy term sheet, but it will contain reasonably precise information about the major provisions of the proposed transaction. Candidates for inclusion are the overall purchase price, amounts and sources of financing, employment provisions, stock or asset purchase, contingent payments or earn-outs, and other material issues.

Stock or Asset Purchase Agreement

Up to this point it is possible that negotiations may have proceeded on little more than a handshake and good faith, particularly where the parties know one another. Once there is an agreement to agree and money is close to being exchanged, it is time to memorialize the understanding with a binding legal document typically referred to as the purchase agreement (Agreement). The Agreement will stipulate if assets or stock are being acquired. This Agreement will have a number of standard sections considered as follows.

- *Recitals.* This section states the parties to the Agreement and the fact that the parties wish to be bound by the terms of the Agreement as stated.

- *Agreements.* This section may be lengthy and includes a detailed description of the financial aspects of the transaction and other material provisions. Common elements found in the first few sections include the purchase price information, escrow amount (if any), seller financing, contingent purchase price or earn-out information, prorated items such as taxes and prepaid amounts, employment agreements for key employees, assumed liabilities (if any), indemnification stipulations (if any), and the handling of costs of the transaction. The list may be much longer reflecting the various interests of the parties.
- *Warranties and representations of the seller.* This section is often a listing of the known and unknown universe of things that can go wrong. This is the area where a fertile but appropriate imagination of counsel is crucial. Any number of terrible events or circumstances may happen after the transaction date, and this section attempts to assign responsibility for such events to the extent practicable.
- *Warranties and representations of the buyer.* Typically much less contentious than the section applicable to the seller, this section may include the statement that the Agreement is binding on the buyer.
- *Documents to be delivered at closing.* This is typically a listing of all the documents related to the transaction. The list may become lengthy depending on the complexity of the transaction. If you have ever seen a "deal book," you understand why transaction-related expenses are significant. The deal book is often in the form of a binder(s) with tabs that indicate the documents enclosed. There may be multiple deal books with literally scores of documents. The documents may include such things as:
  - Corporate resolutions approving the transaction
  - Articles of incorporation
  - Shareholder schedule
  - Escrow agreement
  - Bill of sale
  - Employment or consulting agreements
  - Leases
  - Loan agreements, copies of notes
  - Any other documents important to the transaction
- *General provisions.* This section typically states such things as:
  - Governing state law
  - Notice information
  - Waiver of provisions (must be in writing)
  - Survival of warranties and representations
  - Agreement binding on successors and assigns
  - Severability clause (if a provision of the Agreement is found to be invalid the balance of the Agreement continues in full force and effect)

Loan Agreement and Notes
(Bank and Seller Financing)

The financing documents are typically a major part of the transaction details. When transacting with a bank, the institution will have their own documents with a significant amount of standard language that protects the interests of the bank. Expect those documents to be exceedingly one-sided in favor of the bank; the bank will typically not waiver on the stipulations within their documents. There are a few "fill-in-the-blank" spaces stipulating such important items as interest rate, term of note, escalator clauses, and items considered default provisions. Be prepared for small print and language that is often difficult to follow. Before signing, make sure you understand the provisions. Have an attorney or loan officer explain all the provisions. If a personal or corporate guarantee is required, that will be a separate agreement.

When the financing is in the form of a seller note, the loan agreement is typically much less intimidating. The loan document should be drafted by the seller's law firm and will include such obvious things as the interest rate, term of the note, what constitutes late payment or a breech, penalties for late payment or a breech, remedies to a late payment or breech, and other material information.

There will only be one signed note, which represents the binding agreement to repay debt principal.

Employment, Non-Solicitation, Incentive,
and Retention Agreements

The key employees of the company may be subject to any of the above agreements. If management is making an equity investment or guaranteeing the obligations of the company, they should have the security of an employment agreement that states such matters as compensation, incentive payments, duties, benefits, and perhaps most importantly what happens if their employment is terminated for whatever reason. This fact may be considered in a shareholder agreement discussed shortly. Most of these agreements are written by the counsel for the company, and they are typically structured to primarily protect the interests of the company in case something goes wrong. If negotiating balance between the parties (employees and the company) is desirable, consider binding arbitration and mediation, which avoids lengthy and potentially expensive litigation.

Some companies may have specific incentive programs designed to provide financial incentives for the key employees to build value in the company. Common programs include stock appreciation rights, phantom stock, stock options, and deferred compensation. The various incentive programs have tax attributes that should be understood before such agreements are executed.

Leases—Real Estate and Other Assets

Often the controlling shareholder owns assets that are leased to the company. One of the most frequently encountered assets is real estate leased to the company. In a perfect world the terms of the lease are at arm's length but that is only periodically the case in my experience. The lease rate is most often either a bargain rate (too low) or well above the market. The bargain rate is often that way because the lease was structured originally to be in an amount to repay the mortgage, and the lease is simply paid monthly over the years. With time the owner has neglected to keep the lease at a market rate.

The reverse of the bargain rate is a rate in excess of the market. This scenario develops when the business owner is converting cash flow in the operating company into passive income in the real estate company. Tax planning may be driving the decision to favor the aggressive lease rate. Whatever the reason, it is best to establish a market-justified lease rate. This arm's-length lease is a protection for both parties. Such a lease is establishing a reasonable rent for the assets used in the company. The buyer should insist on a long-term lease (perhaps with option periods) with negotiated rent-escalator clauses. As the buyer you hate to acquire the company only to have the rent of the facility increased without proper justification. Such a scenario has occurred when there is a misunderstanding or dispute between the buyer and the seller.

Rental agreements or leases on other assets may also be an integral part of the transaction environment. Such agreements should be arm's length understandings. In Chapter 15, embracing the strategy of employing parallel companies, the use of leases, rental agreements, employment contracts, and consulting agreements is discussed as critical to the success of the transaction.

SUMMARY

This chapter is only a sampler on this important topic of due diligence. Through the use of examples and explanations I have attempted to emphasize that the details are critical to a successful transition. This is an area where decisions typically are committing the parties to years of effort. The chance for misunderstandings with terrible financial and economic consequences is significant if the parties are not prepared to engage in a circumspect analysis of the transaction. Having experienced many successful transactions, the effort to "get it right" is well worth the time and expense.

CHAPTER **8**

Short Course on Taxes

Taxation with representation ain't so hot either.

—Gerald Barzan

T he topic of transaction-related taxes is of course vast, and this chapter is intended to provide some oversight observations regarding the most commonly encountered taxes. Taxes will be considered in the context of those that are likely to be paid. The legal structure of the company will have a profound impact on the exposure to taxes.

This chapter will consider the tax environment from both the seller's and the buyer's perspective. Those two perspectives may be adverse to one another due to the net (after-tax) proceeds to the seller and the ability to deduct the purchase price by the buyer. We will begin with a consideration of commonly encountered taxes to the seller first, followed by a consideration of taxes from the buyer's vantage.

TAX ISSUES FOR THE SELLER

Clearly, if a seller is exiting his company, the intent is to have the transaction taxed as capital gain because the Federal and state taxes' rates are lower than personal income tax rates. This assumes that the company is being sold for some form of gain. The sale of stock by a business owner, once a satisfactory holding period is met, will be taxed as capital gain. The stock is considered as a capital asset by the tax code and is subject to favorable and lower tax rates. One thing to keep in mind is that most transactions are subject to taxes at the Federal level, and again at the state and local level. State and local taxes are typically deductible expenses before Federal taxes are computed, so there is some tax benefit or savings having the state and local taxes as deductions (the amount of the state and local taxes multiplied by the effective Federal tax rate is the tax saving). Technically there could be a tax preference reorganization under IRC Section 368 whereby taxes are deferred, but that is beyond the scope of this book. For discussion purposes we assume there is a taxable event.

If the transaction is not a stock sale it will be an asset sale subject to different tax rules. The sale of assets may in part be subject to capital gain taxes and in part subject to ordinary income taxes. The extent of exposure to income taxes is a function of the company's tax status as either a C corporation or an S corporation (or some other form of pass-through tax entity such as a Limited Liability Company).

C Corporations and S Corporations

We will use the designation of an S corporation as a generic reference for pass-through tax entities, whereby the income of the entity is "passed through on a prorated basis" to the various stakeholders. The income is then taxed to the stakeholders at their income tax rates. This pass-through tax status is especially important for the stakeholders because it means the income is taxed only once to the investors. All of the taxable income is reported to the stakeholders typically as ordinary income and is reported on individual tax returns. It is customary but not required for the company to make a cash disbursement to the stakeholders in an amount at least sufficient for the stakeholders to pay their prorated income taxes. Sometimes the company is in a position to distribute all or substantially all of its earnings to the stakeholders; then they will receive a real financial benefit.

C Corporations   The C corporation is a legal entity that pays income taxes at the corporate level. All public operating companies are C corporations. The income is taxable to the corporation, and if income is eventually distributed to the shareholders, it is in the form of a dividend payment. The bad news for the C corporation shareholders is that dividend payments are taxed again to the recipients. While the current tax rates on C corporation dividends are at an historic low, typically only 15%, that tax rate is set to increase dramatically by January 1, 2013 as explained shortly. In effect there are two layers of income taxes on C corporation dividends; one at the corporate level and a second at the individual level.

The sale of stock in either an S or C corporation is the sale of a capital asset and it is clear such a sale will usually be capital gain. The amount of the taxable gain will be a function of the basis the investor has in the asset. The basis of the stock in a C corporation is typically only what the investor paid for the stock (and typically with after-tax dollars). Retained earnings in a C corporation do not increase the basis of the stock.

S Corporations   The situation is much different for S corporations. The earnings of the corporation are taxable each year to the shareholders, and the shareholders pay ordinary income taxes on their prorated percentage of ownership. Once the current-year taxes are paid, funds that are left inside the S corporation are now part of the accumulated adjustment account (AAA) and that balance is allocated to the shareholders and their stock basis is increased by the amount of the increase in the AAA. Generally, the retained earnings in an S corporation increase the basis of the stock. If the subject S corporation has a long history of retaining its earnings, when investors sell their stock that stock's basis may have increased dramatically from the original investment.

In summary, a stock sale is preferred for the seller of either an S or C corporation because there is typically only one layer of capital gain taxes (but that layer may be comprised of both Federal and state taxes).

Asset Sales and Stock Sales

Asset sales are more complex than stock sales. They are almost universally less tax-advantageous than stock sales. Let's consider the case of the C corporation first. We will assume that all the assets of the business are being sold. When the assets of a C corporation are sold, the entire gain on the sale of such assets is taxable first to the corporation. The gain or loss on each asset is computed and the net tax is a liability to the corporation. When all the assets are sold and paid, the corporation has converted its assets to cash, and the investors will want to have the cash. The problem is that the payment of the cash to the investors is typically classified as a liquidating distribution, and the proceeds are taxable to the investors as capital gain. Unfortunately there are taxes at the entity level (the corporation) and the individual shareholder level. This double layer of taxes may almost be confiscatory when the combined Federal and state taxes are considered at the corporate and individual levels.

An asset sale of an S corporation results in a single layer of taxes, but some of the taxes may be at ordinary income tax rates for the individual investors and some will be capital gain. For example, ordinary income taxes will be paid on the gain related to the sale of accounts receivable, inventory, items held for resale, and depreciation recapture on assets used in the business. Capital gain taxes will be paid on the sale of capital assets such as goodwill and certain other IRC Section 197 capital assets. Common examples of additional capital assets are the gain on equipment once depreciation has been recaptured, and other intangible assets such as patents and copyrights net of amortization.

The following example illustrates the basic concepts with an asset sale and a stock sale. The example is simplified to illustrate the importance in proper tax panning from the seller's perspective.

STOCK AND ASSET SALE

Exhibits 8.1 and 8.2 will illustrate key tax principles when computing the tax impact on the sale of a business to the owner. This example will consider an asset sale and a stock sale of the same company as both a C corporation and as an S corporation. There are four scenarios. We are assuming the same company.

EXHIBIT 8.1   Example Assumptions

ASSUMPTIONS (all amounts $000)		
Sale price and taxable to seller		$10,000
Ordinary income to seller as an S corporation		
	Depreciation recovery	$ 4,000
	Accounts receivable and inventory	$ 2,000
Stock basis		
	C corporation	$ 500
	S corporation (AAA account increases basis)*	$ 2,000
Tax rates		
	C corporation Federal and state combined	35%
	Personal income tax Federal and state combined	40%
	Capital gain tax Federal and state combined	20%

EXHIBIT 8.2 Stock and Asset Sales Illustration

ASSUMPTIONS (all amounts $000)

Total taxable gain	10,000
Ordinary income to S/H S corporation	
Depreciation recovery	4,000
Accounts receivable and inventory	2,000
Stock Basis	
C corporation	500
S corporation (Basis increased by AAA)	2,000
Tax Rates	
C Corporation state and Federal tax combined	35%
Personal income tax state and Federal combined	40%
Capital gain tax state and Federal combined	20%

	C Asset	C Stock	S Asset	S Stock
Taxable gain	10,000	10,000	10,000	10,000
Less corp tax (35%)	3,500	0	0	0
Gain to S/H	6,500	10,000	10,000	10,000
Ordinary income				
Depreciation recovery	0	0	4,000	0
A/R and inventory	0	0	2,000	0
Subtotal			6,000	
Ordinary income tax @ 40%			2,400	
Taxable capital gain to S/H	6,500	10,000	4,000	10,000
Less: Basis	500	500	2,000	2,000
Taxable capital gain	6,000	9,500	2,000	8,000
Capital gain tax @ 20%	1,200	1,900	400	1,600
Corporate taxes @ 35%	3,500	0	0	0
Ordinary income tax to S/H @ 40%	0	0	2,400	0
Capital gain tax to S/H @ 20%	1,200	1,900	400	1,600
Total taxes	4,700	1,900	2,800	1,600
Taxes as % of total 10,000 gain	47.00%	19.00%	28.00%	16.00%

Scenario 1—C Corporation Asset Sale   The gain on the sale of the assets is taxable first to the C corporation at the C corporation combined Federal and state tax rate of 35%. Once taxed at the corporate level, the remaining cash is distributed to the shareholders in a liquidating dividend. The gain will be taxed to the shareholders at the combined Federal and state capital gain tax rate. The basis in the C corporation stock is $500, the original investment. Unlike an S corporation, retained earnings in a C corporation do not increase

the basis of the stock for taxation purposes. This asset sale is a tax disaster for the sellers because they are exposed to two levels of combined Federal and state taxes, first at the corporation level and second individually to the shareholders. In this case the combined taxes are computed to be 47% of the sale price.

> The sale of assets in the C corporation is perhaps the most hostile tax environment for the seller. One option for the seller confronted with this dire tax environment is to reclassify a portion of the assets as "personal goodwill." The personal goodwill is a capital asset and subject to capital gain taxes. The personal goodwill that is identified is removed from the company and is not subject to double taxation. Classifying goodwill as a personal asset is a challenging valuation assignment properly left for an independent valuation firm to determine. The IRS may likely challenge the personal goodwill allocation so it is best to have an appraiser with experience in this arena defending the work. Another option is to impose on the company a significant deferred-compensation obligation just prior to the sale of the assets. We assume the deferred compensation will be deducted from the asset price. The deferred compensation will be taxable to the seller as ordinary income (in our example 40%), but it is taxed only once.

Scenario 2—C Corporation Stock Sale   The gain on the sale of the stock is taxable only once to the seller. The combined Federal and state capital gain tax is just 19% of the sale price of $10,000. This is a tremendous advantage to the seller and it becomes apparent why the seller will insist on a stock sale. Unfortunately many buyers will refuse to acquire stock and will only purchase assets with negative results for the seller.

Scenario 3—S Corporation Asset Sale   The gain on the sale of the S corporation assets is subject to a single layer of taxes to the selling shareholders, but some of the taxes will be at the combined Federal and state ordinary income tax rate of 40% (including such things as depreciation recapture, accounts receivable, and inventory). Other taxes will be at the combined Federal and state capital gain tax rate, 20%. Unlike the C corporation, in this case the company has been an S corporation since inception and the retained earnings are all part of the AAA. The AAA in this example adds to the basis of the stock, which is now $2,000. Our example indicates that the combined Federal and state ordinary income taxes and capital gain taxes amount to 19% of the sale price.

Scenario 4—S Corporation Stock Sale   The net results to the seller in an S corporation stock sale are very attractive. The original basis of the stock, assumed to be $500, increases with time as the previously taxed earnings of the company are retained in the corporation. The retained earnings (AAA) increase the basis of the stock for this example. Due to a higher basis, the taxes to the seller are only 16% of the sale price.

The clear conclusion from this simplified example is that stock sales result in more net proceeds to the seller because they are subject only to combined capital gain taxes. From a pragmatic standpoint, if a stock sale can be negotiated, it is common for the offering price to be lower than a comparable asset sale because the stock is acquired with after tax dollars and the buyer will not get a stepped up basis.

Transaction Terms to the Seller

The material tax differences between the asset sale and the stock sale are demonstrated. The timing of the receipt of the payment is the next major concern for the seller. As mentioned in Chapter 4 on valuations, it is unlikely today that the seller will receive an all-cash offer. The common agenda for the buyer is to insure the seller still has a significant amount of "skin in the game" following the close. This is accomplished by employing a variety of techniques such as an escrow account (an arbitrary amount that is withheld from the sale proceeds for a period of time); seller finance notes that are paid over a number of years; contingent payments comprising an earn-out; consulting and non-solicitation agreements.

Generally, the deferral of taxable gains into the future is communicated as a worthwhile goal. This suggests that the transaction taxes may be deferred in part into future years. The theory is that the overall tax rates for the seller may be lower in future years. Future taxable gains may be subject to installment sale treatment. That is until the 2013 proposed tax increases are considered. There are major tax increases that will automatically take hold on January 1, 2013 as previously mentioned. Deferring taxes to years with significantly higher marginal tax rates may not be in the best interests of the seller.

The seller may opt out of the installment sale election, but that means the entire taxable gain burden is subject to applicable taxes in the year of the transaction. The tax rates may be lower today, but the seller may not have much cash at closing to pay those taxes. Remember the buyer will want to defer payments into the future as long as practicable to have some cash flow that is used as an offset should unknown liabilities be discovered a year or two after the transaction.

A recommended best practice is for the seller to have a professional prepare a pro forma cash flow closing schedule with several scenarios. One scenario assumes the installment sale opt out election, another scenario should include the tax liability by year if taxes are paid after January 1, 2013. This analysis will help the seller in negotiations with the buyer over the terms of the transaction.

Remember that installment sales for larger transactions have a provision that effectively nullifies any possible tax-deferral advantage when the deferred tax is $5,000,000 for an individual ($10,000,000 for a married couple). In such circumstances the installment sale tax considerations are moot.

TAX ISSUES FOR THE BUYER

The buyer wants the transaction to be as favorable as possible from a tax perspective. This generally means the buyer will want to have a tax deduction for the purchase price. With a stock sale the buyer typically must acquire the company with after-tax dollars. The purchase price is added to the buyer's tax basis in the stock. If the buyer is long term in his/her thinking, the buyer will receive literally no benefit by being able to recoup a portion of the purchase through depreciation and amortization. While the seller may want a stock sale, the buyer will resist the structure because of the unfavorable tax treatment.

The buyer will often favor an asset sale for two reasons. First, an asset acquisition enables the buyer to recover his purchase price over time with depreciation and amortization. Second, an asset purchase will generally isolate any contingent liabilities with the seller. The contingent liabilities often accrue to the stock owner. For this reason many buyers insist on an asset sale to avoid the liabilities associated with the stock.

Reporting an Asset Sale—IRS Form 8594

If the buyer is acquiring assets, it is in the buyer's best interests to insure that the seller and the buyer agree on the allocation of the purchase price in a consistent manner. The buyer and the seller will have to report the transaction on IRS Form 8594. Under IRC Section 1060, the proceeds of the asset sale must be allocated to one of seven asset categories according to the residual method of allocation. Generally the purchase price is first allocated to Category 1 assets, mostly cash and cash equivalents (often there is no allocation to this category). Next the residual assets are allocated to Category 2 including actively traded personal assets such as investments, foreign currency, and certificates of deposit. Residual assets are next allocated to Category 3, mark-to-market assets including primarily accounts receivable. The method is applied in a manner similar to Category 4, inventories; Category 5, assets subject to depreciation such as machinery and equipment; and Category 6, most IRC Section 197 intangible assets such as patents and copyrights. Finally, if there is any residual amount remaining it is allocated to Category 7, goodwill and going concern.

Most buyers will insure that the seller allocated the purchase price in a similar manner as the buyer, by having a stipulation in the sale agreement mandating this compliance.

The reason this compliance is so important to the buyer is that certain assets provide a much faster purchase price recovery. For example, the buyer will typically recover the purchase price allocated to the inventory in a few weeks as the inventory is sold (turned over). The seller will be less enthusiastic with an optimal allocation to the inventory because any gain will be taxed as ordinary income. Correspondingly the buyer will favor the optimal allocation of the purchase price to assets with the shortest depreciation schedule such as furniture and equipment (three to five years in many cases). If the buyer fails to allocate optimal amounts to the faster cost recovery assets, the residual method of allocation results in the balance going toward company goodwill in Category 7. Goodwill is an intangible asset amortized over 15 years for tax purposes. This is a long cost-recovery period for the buyer.

The seller on the other hand will favor the allocation to goodwill because goodwill is a capital asset and subject to capital gain tax treatment. The buyer and seller will likely have adverse tax agendas in an asset sale. If the two sides do not have a common understanding of the allocation, they must state that disagreement on IRS Form 8594. This disagreement is an invitation to the IRS to audit the transaction. This is a potential contingent liability not desirable to the buyer, therefore we typically see the buyer leading the allocation discussion.

Stock Sales

While there is a predisposition in many cases for the buyer to favor an asset sale, there are a significant number of situations where the buyer will agree to a stock acquisition. One of the first instances where such a transaction frequently occurs is when there are licensing requirements that have taken a considerable period of time to acquire. This is frequently the case with healthcare providers that have qualified for Federal reimbursement programs such as Medicare and Medicaid. It may take months to have the reimbursement process approved, and until that is obtained the buyer may not be able to stay in business. The solution is to acquire the target companies' stock. In other instances a professional license may be required for ownership, such as may be the case with certain medical and healthcare companies.

Stock sales are also common when private equity groups (PEGs) invest in companies for a short-term investment, with the intent of exiting within say three to four years. The PEG is focused most commonly on maximizing growth and profitability during that time and not on repaying acquisition related debt. The business model is to have the cash flow service interest obligations, but debt principal is mostly repaid when the company is sold.

Stock transactions are common with the sales to Employee Stock Ownership Plans and Trust (ESOP)s. ESOPs are only permitted to acquire the stock of the plan sponsor (the company). Unlike the other buyers, an ESOP is able to acquire the stock with tax deductible dollars (pre-tax) due to special tax incentives provided by the Federal government. All other buyers acquire stock with after tax dollars. The tax benefits regarding ESOPs are discussed in Chapters 12 and 13.

Stock transactions are common in family companies. Families may employ gifting strategies with stock transfers because such mechanics may involve relatively smaller blocks of stock. This scalable attribute is particularly useful when families are transitioning ownership and control slowly over time. The stock may be of further benefit because there may be different attributes to the stock such as voting shares and non-voting shares. Family tax issues are considered in Chapter 16.

Transaction Terms to the Buyer

The buyer has a vested interest in avoiding stock sales because the purchase price must be paid with after-tax dollars. As asset transaction is often much better from the buyer's tax perspective because there is the cost recovery over time through depreciation and amortization. The buyer really has an incentive to structure as much of the transaction as possible as payments deductible in full to the corporation in the year when paid. Examples of this strategy include consulting agreements, deferred compensation, salary continuation, and employment agreements. Such payments are considered expenses to the company, and they are deductible when paid. In this case the obligations are paid with pre-tax dollars and not after-tax dollars. Depending on the effective tax rate of the corporation this is a considerable benefit to the company.

This is an excellent tax strategy for the buyer, but it is typically less optimal for the seller because those payments are ordinary income, and worse, many are subject to Federal Insurance Contributions Act (FICA) withholding. Ordinary income tax rates combined with FICA exposure makes such agreements undesirable to the seller. The combined tax rates on such payments are typically much higher than capital gain rates on capital assets.

IRC Section 338 Stock Sales Taxed as Asset Sales   This section is included because someone may have heard that the buyer can take a stock purchase and treat it as an asset purchase. The principal benefit of this structure is to enable the buyer to receive a tax deduction over time for the acquisition of stock. It is beyond the scope of this book to provide anything more than a few passing comments on the strategy. For the buyer to qualify for the asset sale, there must be a "deemed" sale of the previously acquired stock to itself. The deemed sale is for an amount significantly larger than the stock acquisition price, and there is a taxable gain on the deemed sale to the buyer. The taxable gain is the price paid to be able to qualify for an asset sale and the corresponding depreciation and amortization. There are narrow circumstances where this may be applicable. There are provisions in the tax code permitting certain narrowly defined losses to be offset against the gain from the deemed sale, and if those rare circumstances exist then this is a tax-efficient strategy. Such circumstances are more likely when larger companies that are part of control groups are making acquisitions.

Tax Legislation   At the end of calendar-year 2010 Congress passed a two year extension of the Bush administration tax cuts as previously mentioned. The legislation is the Tax Relief, Unemployment Insurance Reauthorization and Job Creation Act of 2010 (2010 Tax Relief Act). The 2010 Tax Relief Act also contains significant tax enhancements relating to gift and estate taxes. While most transactions are not impacted by gift and estate tax issues, Chapter 16 on buyouts with families contains a discussion of this significant development. Congress elected to include the favorable gift and estate tax provisions for only a 24-month period, and after that time it is anyone's guess what will happen.

SUMMARY

We have explored the tax world of proceeds to the seller either being subject to combined capital gain taxes, or combined ordinary income taxes, or perhaps some combination of both. The results may be dramatic to the seller with an effective tax rate as high as approximately 50% or a low as 15%. The buyer will be concerned about the tax deductibility of the purchase. If the buyer is acquiring stock, the stock is purchased with after-tax dollars and the only depreciation and amortization available is typically from assets already part of the acquired company. There is typically no step up in the basis. The buyer will prefer to acquire assets because of the ability to allocate the price to assets with the fastest depreciable lives. The buyer may also favor a portion of the consideration to be in the form of tax-deductible expenses such as a consulting agreement or a deferred compensation agreement. This assumes that the consulting agreement is in effect subtracted in part or in whole from the purchase price.

Once the parameters of a transaction are known, attention is typically focused on making the transaction as tax efficient as possible.

CHAPTER 9

Buyouts—Non-Sponsored Management

You don't deserve to be called an entrepreneur unless you have
mortgaged your house to the business.

—Ted Rogers

This chapter is focused on the circumstances where the management of the company is intending to acquire the business from its founder. In this case we have a privately held company with a shareholder that is ready to begin the succession-planning process. For consistency we will generally refer to the seller as a single shareholder, when in fact the seller may be several shareholders. We assume that there is an energetic management team (one or several individuals) that has an interest in acquiring the company. This is a "non-sponsored" management buyout; which means for the purposes of this book the management does not have the assistance of a private equity group (sponsor) or a similarly well funded partner as part of the succession structure. The ability of the management to acquire the business generally means that assets or the stock will be purchased. The cash flows of the business and the personal assets of the managers will likely be the financial foundation for the acquisition, which means the size of the transactions in dollars will be limited.

Typically, this privately held company was established by one or two founders (there could be multiple partners but that are less common) and the company has consumed most of their adult working careers. After a success-ful run as business owners, the shareholders are at the point where succession planning is appropriate. If the shareholders have been wise, they have grown the business and along the way they have built a management team capable of running the company into the future. In many cases the management team is competent and loyal. Candidly, the management team often has not migrated to starting their own competing company because of the high risk involved and the capital required to begin a new venture. These common attributes are an integral part of the approach to the buyout strategy.

These buyouts are typically an advantageous development for the sellers and the buyers because of a long working relationship. Typically, the parties know one another, share similar values, respect the contributions each has made to the company, and share a vision of the future of the company. This common baseline of concern and skills is typically the springboard for a successful buyout, but by no means a guarantee of a satisfactory result.

Even if there is alignment with regard to the goals and values between the seller and the buyer, there is often the sheer element of economic scale. As we will see, attempting to pass the ownership of a closely held company to a next generation of stakeholders given the current tax environment is very challenging. The task is even more daunting when the scale of the transaction suggests an overall valuation of millions of dollars. The larger the value of the business, the more difficult the transition will be because the parties will almost certainly begin to approach the limits of debt financing from all sources.

FINANCING ISSUE

ADVANTAGES

The management buyout may be highly successful when a number of essential elements exist. First, there is an owner that recognizes the merit of succession planning and acknowledges that the management as a team is a viable candidate to acquire the company. The owner should recognize the practical aspects of succession planning and realize that if the current management is to be involved the process will take time—often many years—for the company to fully transfer to the successor team. Second, there is a competent management team embracing the critical skills with the energy and drive to buy out the owners. Third, there has to be a strong degree of trust that the seller and the buyer will be negotiating in good faith to reach a deal. If the seller and the buyer have been working closely with one another for many years, there is less likelihood of misunderstandings during the transition process. This element of trust is important because early in the succession process, the buyers will know the total compensation to the seller including benefits. Years of experience leads me to advise the seller to run the business in an ethical manner and keep total compensation before discretionary bonuses and distributions within a reasonable range.

Confidentiality is typically a paramount concern. Where years of working together exist, the requirement for confidentiality is easily attained. The sensitive subject of succession planning is something to remain with only a limited number of trusted managers. Due to the nature of the topic and the substantial financial commitment being asked of the successor management, spouses are also brought into the planning process. The wider the circle of involved individuals, the harder it will be to maintain confidentiality, and all the more important to insure that there are no breaches during the planning process.

> Behavioral issues may often be the most important. Knowing sensitive subjects and properly introducing them increases the likelihood of success. Insensitive and poorly considered actions are deal killers.

Larger transactions involving middle market companies will require the financial help of the sellers. The management team will unlikely be able to provide the necessary capital and debt to acquire the company. It is beneficial when the parties to the transaction know one another. The seller will often have a reasonable idea of the financial wherewithal of the candidate managers. Early in the process it is highly recommended that the owner contact experienced professionals with a transaction history of dealing with succession issues. Such advisors will have the requisite skills to identify strategies of passing value to the seller, and doing so on a tax-efficient basis for the buyer and seller.

NEED ADVISORS WHERE & WHO?

CAUTIONS

In many cases the managers do not possess substantial ready liquidity for the purchase of the company. In today's economic reality younger managers (often married) have the pressures of servicing a home mortgage, raising children, providing spousal support, paying for transportation, and saving for retirement. Even in two-income households, it is very difficult to attain significant savings for investment on an after-tax basis because the combined marginal income tax rates for state and Federal obligations are severe.

Seller Assistance

Often, if management is to acquire the company, it is very likely that considerable financial assistance is extended by the seller. The seller is in a position to extend such help as seller financing for the purchase of the company, taking such things as deferred compensation, or a long term consulting relationship, or authorizing company debt to assist the managers with the purchase. It typically takes years for the buyout to be completed. Accepting a longer-term horizon is often the pragmatic reality of many management buyouts. There is no correct answer for the amount of time it takes to complete a successful transition plan, but a minimum of three years and often many more with larger companies. Some plans are intended to take many years so that the seller maintains effective control until all or substantially all of the terms of the purchase have been fulfilled. In such cases it is common to see planning horizons of five years or more, even approaching 10 years in unusual circumstances. 5 - 10 YEAR PLANS

Buyer Commitment

If there is a buyout team, the seller appropriately wants to see a substantial commitment from the buyers in the form of capital, personal debt, and possibly guarantees. The metrics of the transaction may become very complex with the involvement of the principals but also the spouses where applicable. Spousal consent is often mandatory in community property states for example. Communication is paramount in the more complex environments, and the various goals and agendas will typically be revealed during the negotiations.

There must be a reality check on the valuation of the company. The transaction will typically be a varied agreement combining a wide array of elements such as cash at closing, debt, employment contracts, earn-outs, guarantees, representations, warranties, and other aspects. When the totality of the plan is examined, the seller is likely to realize some defensible multiple of cash flows; in many cases the overall price is similar to fair market value (FMV). There is an art in designing the transition process to be as tax efficient as practicable so that the net proceeds to the seller are within expectations. The terms of the transaction will likely contain a range of variables that are exposed to different tax rates.

Transaction Size

There is likely to be a practical limit on the size of the transaction. Due to the relatively hostile tax environment, it is increasingly difficult to transition a significant amount of wealth to the successor team because purchases are made with after-tax dollars. When a more substantial amount of value is being sold, it will just take longer for the obligations to be serviced. For example, as an arbitrary dollar amount, a transaction in excess of $5 million

PAID BACK W/ AFTER TAX DOLLARS

is a substantial amount of wealth. It will take years for that acquisition-related debt to be repaid with after-tax dollars. Higher amounts typically require longer periods.

The operations of the company are an indicator of the flexibility that is available in structuring an acceptable plan. If the company has a balance sheet that is not loaded with debt, there is a strong likelihood that the assets will support some amount of bank debt that may be used to acquire the ownership interest on the part of the buyers. Stable and reasonably predictable cash flows are predictors of debt capacity for the company. If the balance sheet is already leveraged and the cash flow and profitability of the company are volatile, getting meaningful financial assistance from a bank is not likely. In such circumstances, the seller will almost certainly have to provide most if not all of the financial support for the management team.

SELLER MOST IF NOT ALL SUPPORT

VALUATION INSIGHTS

In today's challenging financial markets, finding substantial readily available cash for a buyout is more unusual than the norm. There is the high likelihood that the transaction will be influenced by the terms extended by the seller.

In these circumstances the overall "value" will be negotiated by the seller and the buyer. There really is no commonly understood standard of value that applies. The parties to the transaction may seek the opinion of an objective resource to provide guidance on the valuation analysis of the company. For cost reasons the parties may agree on a single valuation provider. In other instances the seller may have done sufficient research to know the approximate value of the company, and will be setting the value expectations during discussions. If the seller is providing significant financial assistance, the buyout team should be aware of this vital assistance.

Valuation Assistance

Assuming the seller is setting the valuation expectation, it is highly recommended that the buyer retain the services of an independent and objective appraiser to review the proposed transaction. This step addresses any appearance of favoritism on the part of the advisor selected by the seller. Yes, this often means the buyer should fund the analysis from his/her own resources. This is a best practice in my experience because the buyer will listen more closely when he/she is paying for the advice. If the advice is contrary to what the seller wants to hear, the buyer always has the option of "voting with their feet" and walking away from a bad deal. This commitment by the buyer shows a serious focus by committing some personal resources into the process with no guarantee of success. If the planning results in a successful transaction, the fees may be recovered in the future from the company.

It is highly recommended that the buyer possesses the skills to model the likely cash flows of the company and the new shareholders following the transaction. If such skills are not within the successor management team, they may be found at most experienced certified public accountant (CPA) firms. This is a sanity check to determine if the transaction actually has cash flows following a consideration of taxes, varying operating results, and loan-covenant compliance. It is much better to anticipate potential problems on the front end and have a good contingency "Plan B" if something inadvertently unravels.

> Before discussing any pricing be prepared to address the "law of selective memory." In this case the seller will retain the highest value as an absolute even if it is expressed as a range, and similarly the buyer will remember the lowest value.

It is important to obtain credible valuation advice so that both sides develop a respectful buy-in of the process. There are many objective valuation professionals that can provide the service. Clearly, the larger the transaction, the more appropriate it is to have a professional versed in valuations, getting deals completed, and familiar with the industry.

There is no correct valuation of the company, particularly in today's economic environment. Any amount negotiated will almost certainly have expansive terms to compensate for the lack of cash at closing. A quick summary of options regarding the major types of terms follows.

Practical Considerations

Stock sales have the benefit of being scalable in that the seller does not have to sell the entire ownership interest at one time. Minority position blocks of stock may be sold enabling the seller to retain control. At some point the controlling block of stock may be sold and the seller is often interested in selling the remaining balance. The problem with selling stock from the buyer's perspective is that the stock is acquired with after-tax dollars. Since stock purchases are hostile from a tax standpoint to the buyer, a more flexible approach is often required. Such an approach often embraces a number of cash flows to the seller that may include deferred compensation, consulting, salary continuation, and other common payments that are tax deductible to the company, but ordinary income to the seller. The relative tax benefits of the buyer and seller are considered in structuring the eventual plan.7

Typically, smaller companies with an overall modest valuation are appraised in some relation to industry methodology or industry rules of thumb. Such data is generally available from resources such as transaction databases, industry databases, or reference books. Larger companies may retain a valuation professional to estimate the value for planning purposes. Often a range of value is offered to provide some flexibility is structuring a total package including terms.

In summary, the valuation for a management buyout will be a negotiated package between the seller and the buyer. The eventual total consideration is typically reasonable and has some relation to the cash flows of the company over a period of time often in the four-to-seven-year time frame. It is highly unlikely that a seller will achieve a synergistic strategic value for the business. With planning and communications, the seller should be able to attain a total consideration that is reasonable and doable from a cash flow standpoint.

VIEWPOINT OF THE SELLER

The seller is often the founder of the business, and represents traditional entrepreneurial skills and orientation. There is typically a self reliance on personal skills to accomplish goals. Often the business provides the seller with a wonderful degree of financial independence though a stream of economic resources such as cash compensation, strong benefits, and possibly rental income from a facility leased to the company. The cumulative effect of the resources is often substantial, and some business owners really have no idea what they are taking from the business. In the seller's mind, every benefit is justified individually, but there is little consideration for the total call of the resources of the company. Often the expectation is that a standard of living will be maintained following the sale of the company to the management.

The reality in many cases is that the business is not worth what the seller imagines. There will be an acceptance of what the business will support. Often the seller has maintained strict confidentiality over what is taken from the company, and there may be personal embarrassment with the bright light of disclosure focused on the financial results by the buyer. Heading into a sales mode, it is best for the seller to be realistic about the finances of the company and be prepared to offer a glimpse of economic operating results to the buyer so appropriate planning may be done.

The seller may realize that the unfettered control of the business is coming to an end. The coming transition of the company may mean there is conceptually "one last bite at the apple." Some business owners will behave foolishly and take from the business the optimal amount while leaving as little as possible in the way of assets (e.g. distributing all the cash so that there is virtually no working capital cushion). If this is the case, the seller is already being paid in part for the company as the buyer will notice this depletion of the company and will adjust the price accordingly. The informed business owner will realize that the transition process has to be appropriately scrutinized by the buyer before a reasonable process of orderly transition commences.

Assuming the seller is facilitating the transaction with financial support, it is likely the seller's legal representation will be preparing the key transaction documents. This is to be expected. The buyer should anticipate some legal expense to have the documents reviewed. Trust, but verify.

Have a Plan to Exit the Business

The seller should have a plan for retirement that takes into account reasonably anticipated living expenses. The owner is often not really aware of how much in the way of resources the company provides. A vast array of benefits are often taken for granted, but have a real cost to the company and a very real cost to the owner if they were no longer paid. Negotiating a package of benefits (such as healthcare), combined with selling stock or assets, and in conjunction with other payouts (deferred compensation, accelerated retirement benefits) is a likely scenario to be considered. The total net proceeds should be estimated and compared against the standard of living requirements the seller wishes to maintain.

> I cannot think of a more important topic than the lifestyle of the seller in his senior years. This topic is best addressed with an experienced financial planner and family members.

Time Is an Ally

In spite of the challenges facing the seller, it is important to begin the planning process and make commitments to the successor team. One common mistake is to simply delay addressing the subject and wait too long. Failure to begin a consideration of the succession planning is in fact a decision and it is a very negative signal to your key employees. They want to know: What is their future with the company? If the key employees possess highly portable skills, the risk to the seller is that they will grow frustrated at the lack of career progress and leave. If key employees leave this is a terrible development for the seller and it will diminish succession options. My advice to business owners is to simply "get started." There may never be a perfect time to do the planning, but unreasonable delays will cause uncertainty among your key employees and may reduce flexibility and options in crafting an acceptable package.

VIEWPOINT OF THE BUYER

The buyer team may feel that they will have to acquire the business, and will not typically have the luxury of allowing the business to compound in value with time (patient equity) for years like the seller. There is the requirement to identify and obtain the financing to acquire the company. There may be an element of sweat equity in the structure with the use of such vehicles as stock options, stock appreciation rights, or any other number of methods to permit the acquisition of equity in the company, but the buyer will have to negotiate an overall package acceptable to the seller.

The advisors to the buyer will or should advise on an overall package that allows the company to deduct as much of the transaction consideration as possible. This likely entails such strategies as a deferred compensation agreement (taxable as ordinary income to the seller when received but perhaps more importantly it is tax deductible to the company when paid). This enables the acquisition in part to be accomplished on favorable tax terms to the buyer, but not as favorably taxed to the seller. Other strategies include such items as: granting an employment agreement to the seller, offering a paid board position, installing a non-qualified plan with accelerated benefits, or possibly a non-solicitation and non-competition agreement.

Management Leadership

If there is a management team, leadership will be required. The team will have to decide who is to lead and be the successor president, the number two and so on. The team will also have to determine what will be their exit plan. They should have a shareholder agreement that stipulates the process by which their ownership interests will be redeemed when their employment ends or is terminated. If managers have guaranteed acquisition debt and they subsequently leave before the debt is repaid, some release mechanism should be anticipated.

Compensation to the buyers following the agreement is a sensitive subject. The buyers may feel they should be rewarded for taking on the risk of the obligations associated with acquiring the company. Perhaps compensation is adjusted so that such things as debt obligations or insurance are provided by the company. Generally, the buyers will need to spend a period of time if not a few years making sacrifices in the short term to acquire the company so that long-term financial benefits will be realized once the purchase is complete. That is the nature of sweat equity, particularly where the seller is providing substantial financial assistance. There will be a delicate balance between the time of sacrifice and the time when the benefits of a significant ownership interest begin to pay tangible financial gain. As a rule of thumb, any plan that is in excess of five years needs to be reviewed very carefully for reasonable expectations on the part of the seller.

> Think about the price of leadership. Make sure as a seller you are extending a competitive total compensation package to those responsible for making the transition successful. Securing a trustworthy compensation survey is a first step.

PROFESSIONAL ADVISORS

In the preponderance of cases in my experience, the advisors are selected by the seller and compensated by the company. This certainly makes sense because professional advice is costly and if the advisors are selected by the seller, the cost is typically a deductible event to the company within IRS regulations. This may make efficient tax-planning sense, but my admonition is to have the buyers appoint their own advisors to review the proposed transaction. Regardless of best intentions, the parties to the transaction may at some point become adversarial if something goes terribly wrong. The buyers should be serious enough about the transaction that a modest investment in professional advisors with their best interests at heart should be a standard practice.

Legal Counsel

Most commonly the legal advice is the central issue. Counsel for the seller will have an interest in structuring the transaction to favor his client. The buyer needs to feel that sufficient due diligence on their part is done to feel comfortable that the transaction is arm's length and fair to all parties. Keep in mind that attorneys are trained to be advocates for the best interest of their clients; they do not have to be objective or independent. An attorney for the seller will be guarding the financial interests of his client. Since it is likely the seller is providing significant financial support, this is a reasonable perspective. The buyers are advised to have separate legal counsel for such critical matters such as guaranteeing performance on notes to the seller and a bank (if appropriate), and honoring the terms of the transaction. It is important that the transaction have balanced representation since so much is at stake financially and from a career viewpoint.

Financial Advisors

If a CPA firm has been retained by the company for a period of years prior to the sale, there is a strong likelihood that the firm is well known by both parties. CPAs do have an obligation to be objective and independent when preparing reports related to the company financial statements. This mindset often prevails in providing general consulting to the company. Most CPA firms will be in a strong position to provide objective advice because they are typically engaged by the company, and transitioning the company between the seller and the successor management is most often in the best interests of the parties. The seller appropriately needs assistance in planning for retirement. The CPA firm is often in a strong position to offer help in cash flow planning and estimating retirement income requirements. The seller may also actively solicit the help of an investment and wealth advisor to assist with retirement planning. The best wealth advisors will help with the planning and also implement the investment strategy to realize the desired outcome. Planning for future cash flows to support a standard of living in retirement is an essential function to be addressed by the seller.

Other service providers may be called upon. If there is significant seller financing for example, it is appropriate for the company to carry insurance on the life of the seller. In the event of an untimely death, the insurance proceeds will be used to redeem the seller note. There may be other risks perceived by the seller and some form of insurance protection may be advisable.

Family Members

Family members are helpful in setting goals in a post-sale environment for both the seller and the buyer. There are many psychological issues with selling the business and then standing on the sidelines watching others run the company. This is a particularly daunting challenge if the seller is providing significant seller financing. While the seller has a vested interest in making sure the seller notes are repaid in full, there is a fine balance between interfering with the operations of the company and watching over your financial interests.

RISK ENVIRONMENT

Generally, the economic and financial risks of the business are well known by the key parties since they have worked together for years. We know that potentially bad things can happen even under these circumstances. If the seller is extending financial support to the successor management, there is always the possibility that the successor management will not be able to honor the debt obligations. The seller may not collect on the notes. While this is often a remote concern, if it ever happens a significant portion of the seller's wealth may be gone with little recourse.

If the company is financially stressed, the management may want the opportunity to acquire the business if the pricing reflects the challenges ahead. The degree of financial stress on the business will almost certainly be reflected in the total consideration paid. In some cases the problems confronting the company are the seller's making, and removing the seller from the operations equation may be the best event for the business. In such circumstances, the successor management may relish the opportunity to acquire the business once certain impediments are removed. When the problems with the seller are significant, the removal of the individual results in a rapid turnaround of results. This often occurs when the successor management has the opportunity to work for their own accounts, and the improved operating results accrue to those responsible for the improvements.

Management buyouts between parties that know one another indicate that they may be applied to almost any industry. Since the parties are knowledgeable about the industry, it is assumed that the successor management is satisfied that subject to the overall terms of the transition process, staying within the industry is a viable consideration. Other types of buyouts are often more limited in applications because they assume consistent profitability and the potential for growth. This is particularly the case when third parties are introduced into the transition process, such as a private equity firm.

Financing the Transaction

The acquiring management should anticipate being asked to commit substantial personal resources toward the buyout. The seller will want to see this commitment, and any third-party financial institution or a bank will insist on this. To the successor management the risk of failure may be devastating if the venture eventually fails. Such a failure typically puts domestic relationships at high stress, stress between partners, and even a degree of anxiety between the seller and the buyer. Of course, the financial upside potential is also greatest under these circumstances. The range of documents accompanying a typical management buyout with substantial debt is intimidating. Notes have to be signed by the borrower, and personal guarantees are often mandatory. Often acquisition capital is raised by leveraging such things as a home with a home equity loan. When all of this leverage is being assumed, a spouse and family members may be exceedingly intimidated by the prospect of so much debt (especially when the kids are looking at college). A best practice is to make sure the principals are on sound footing with their marriages entering into the buyout. A healthy domestic relationship is a plus during a period of high stress such as a buyout.

If there is significant seller financing, most likely the good news on the risk front is that the seller is likely to be far more tolerant of the business environment than a third-party lender. Typically, even negotiated loan covenants will not be exercised against the company or called unless the circumstances are egregious. The seller financing typically does not have a "workout" division found in banks, so they are more likely to be patient and work on a longer-term solution to the problems.

TECHNICAL MATTERS

This section is intended to provide a strategic overview of transaction mechanics and major issues. Major items are considered as a reminder that the totality of the proposed transaction needs to be considered.

Records and Financial Reporting

The seller should insure that legal documents are current such as the articles of incorporation, bylaws, stock ownership ledger, and title to applicable assets are confirmed. Additionally, operating agreements such as employment contracts, non-solicitation agreements, leases, and incentive plans should be current.

It is suggested that accounting records be accurate and personal items purged from the system. It is best to write off obsolete assets and purge the business of non-operating assets as such matters will only serve to make the valuation of the company more complex. Having reviewed financial statements at a minimum by a CPA firm is a solid step to help insure that the financial statements are properly prepared on an accrual basis and that some cursory review by a third party is completed. Having reliable financial information is a solid first step in negotiating a mutually respected transaction.

Determine Financial Resources

The debt capacity of the company to a bank or another third party should be quantified. This critical step will indicate how much cash may be available to the seller on the closing date. The financial resources of the successor management committed to the buyout needs to be determined. This will be a soul-searching exercise for the successor managers. As employees of the company and without access to independent wealth, there is likely to be only modest financial resources available for the buyout.

The balance between outside financial resources available and the anticipated transaction price will be filled by the seller. Seller financing is complex and is accompanied by a host of issues including obvious considerations as the term on the note and the interest rate. Additionally, it may be appropriate to consider financial covenants such as operating ratios and payment of management bonuses while the note principal is outstanding. Life insurance by the company on the life of the seller may be a consideration to help insure that the selling family will realize the value of the business in the case of a tragedy. Operational control and the governance of company may also be an issue while the note principal is outstanding. Remedies in the case of default also will be considered. Remember, that the seller note must be repaid with after-tax dollars by the debtor. Depending on the tax rate of the debtor, individuals or the company, the true costs of the debt principal repayment are burdensome.

Assuming that there is seller financing, insurance may be considered as a safety measure to make certain that debt obligations will be honored. The insurance may contain a number of trigger events that cause the insurance to be paid. Trigger events include such items as death, disability, retirement, termination of agreements, and more.

Facilities

When the company requires dedicated facilities such as a manufacturing or distribution firm, the company may be leasing the facilities from the controlling shareholder. A common situation is to find the company leasing the facilities from a Limited Liability Company (LLC) or some other tax advantaged entity. In such circumstances, the operating company should have a long-term lease with the real estate company to protect the interest of both the buyer and the seller. It is recommended that the lease represent an arm's-length transaction, which is typically easily verified with a commercial real estate broker.

The separation of the real estate company from the operating company is a favorable situation in that it allows for the negotiations to span two entities over time without the successor team necessarily having to acquire everything immediately. The seller may work with the successor team on transitioning the operating company first, and leasing the facilities during that time. Once the operating company acquisition obligations are satisfied or comfortably under control from a loan covenant viewpoint, the resolution of the real estate company may be addressed. Holding the real estate company as a candidate to be acquired longer term by the management may be an excellent retention vehicle to help insure that the operating company acquisition obligations are discharged on a timely basis.

Conceptually, the successor management should look upon the real estate rental as long-term seller financing that is fully deductible. Rental payments are ordinary deductions for income tax purposes, and the operating company has the use of the facilities. Even if the successor management has not negotiated a purchase option on the real estate company, by building a successful operating company the management will have options to acquire their own real estate with time and lease it to the operating company if they elect.

> Separating the operating company from the "asset company" (real estate) will typically result in significantly higher overall consideration to the seller. Extending an offer to acquire the asset company to the successor management over time is a time-honored form of golden handcuffs to help insure the successful transition.

Periodically, the real estate is embedded in the operating company. The reasoning for this situation is often related to consolidating collateral for commercial loans. In such circumstances, we have not often seen where the combined value of the operating company with the real estate is worth as much as the two in separate entities. Separating the real estate from the operating company is something to consider if the tax consequences are not too burdensome. Separation of the two entities typically facilitates greater flexibility in structuring the sale over time.

Valuation

The overall value of the company should be determined for planning purposes. One ongoing theme today is that the seller is not likely to realize as much cash in the transaction as in prior years. One strategy for a seller to consider is to "jump-start" the transition process by authorizing equity stakes in the business. For the purposes here, such equity stakes are clearly intended to be minority interests in the business. Minority interests may be subject to a wide range of restrictions such as non-voting stock, restrictions on the transfer of the stock, restrictions on valuation of the stock, dividend preferences, and limited marketability for the stock. Those restrictions will typically depress the value of the stock. The stock may be subject to both a minority position discount and a lack of marketability discount. The intent of considering such a strategy is to place some initial block of stock into the hands of key managers on a tax-efficient basis. Stock is acquired with after-tax dollars, so strategies and equity attributes that defensibly lower the value means that managers will be able to buy into a percentage of the business on a tax-preferred basis.

Once some starting point for equity participation is initiated, then other strategies for passing the controlling interest of the business over time may be blended together for a comprehensive plan. The value of the stock may be adjusted upward if a controlling block is being acquired by removing a minority position discount and reducing the lack of marketability discount.

Structuring the Transaction—Stock Sale

From a tax standpoint this is the ideal for the seller because the proceeds are subject to capital gain taxes and all liabilities remain with the company. Additionally, the seller may transfer a portion of the stock during the transition phase and retain control of the company until such time as control fully passes to the successor team. This is often an unworkable solution for the entire value of the company because the stock must be purchased with after-tax dollars and the proceeds are taxed to the seller. The effective tax rate in getting one dollar of net proceeds to the seller is often in excess of 50% when taxes to both the buyer and the seller are considered. Stock sales enjoy the benefit typically of slightly simpler legal documents, but that is a small consolation. The purchase price of the stock may be negotiated down by imposing on the shareholders any number of obligations that will reduce the value from a stock purchase standpoint.

Stock sales do have the advantage of providing a smooth transition process because smaller blocks of stock may be transacted. The seller may pass minority blocks of stock to the successor managers giving them an incentive to stay and see the transition process through.

To help overcome the disadvantage of having to buy stock with after tax dollars, there are strategies to combine a stock sale with elements of value to the seller that are tax deductible to the company. Unfortunately, tax-deductible amounts to the company are most often ordinary income to the seller and taxed at much higher rates than capital gains. Some common strategies follow.

Deferred compensation. This is a common strategy to reduce the value of the company for a stock purchase. The theory is that prior to the sale of stock (ideally as much time as possible), the company enters into a deferred compensation agreement with the seller. This is typically justified because the seller/founder often started the company years before and often took little salary in the start-up years. The deferred compensation is really just delayed salary and will be ordinary income to the recipient, but it is tax deductible to the company when paid. The relative tax rates of the seller and the company must be compared to see if this strategy makes financial sense. Often this is a viable option.

Accelerated qualified retirement benefit plans. Provisions in the Employee Retirement Income Security Act of 1974 (ERISA) will permit a degree of flexibility in contributions to qualified retirement plans. In certain cases, contributions to the plan may be weighted according to age knowing that a number of the employees are older and they do not have as many years to build a retirement asset as younger associates. The successor management team may look at such a strategy as a means for reducing the price of the stock by an amount of resources (tax deductible to the company) dedicated to funding the qualified plan.

Non-qualified retirement benefits. These plans do not have all the tax benefits of qualified plans under ERISA, but if they are properly installed the payments from the plan to recipients are tax deductible to the company. The intent here is to impose on the company a significant liability that is taken into consideration when valuing the stock.

Consulting agreements. This is a broadly defined area of planning for our purposes that includes such things as consulting to the company, serving as a member of the board, having a non-solicitation agreement, and other services. If the seller is providing an ongoing service, it is common for the company to provide a range of benefits such as medical health insurance, transportation reimbursement, cell phone, and other items.

The parties may substantially agree to the terms of a deal on a handshake, but a formal purchase agreement is highly recommended. This agreement protects the interest of everyone involved. What is emphasized is the requirement for a successor shareholder agreement. While it is easy enough to have a management team acquiring the company, providing the members of the team with an individual exit vehicle is recommended.

If a stock sale is considered, the successor managers may be acquiring blocks of stock individually. One strategy is to have the successor managers acquire minority blocks of stock on a reduced cost basis as previously mentioned. Once some stock is in the hands of the managers, the balance of the seller's stock may be redeemed into the company treasury. The company has to redeem the stock with after-tax dollars, but it is after-tax dollars to the company. There may be some tax advantages to this strategy because the company stock redemption is not subject to payroll taxes. When the full impact of payroll taxes is considered (both to the employee and the company's matching share), it may be more tax efficient to have the company redeem the stock. Stock redemptions do not automatically qualify for capital gain treatment to the seller. Before this strategy is considered, tax laws must be examined to determine if such redemptions qualify for capital gain treatment.

Structuring the Transaction—Asset Sale

An asset sale offers the advantage of allowing the buyer to recover the purchase price over time through a stepped up basis in the assets to the acquisition price. The stepped-up basis permits the buyer to recapture the purchase price through future depreciation and amortization. The acquisition price is allocated to various asset classes in accordance with IRC Section 1060 requirements. Depending on the asset allocation, the cost recovery period may be sharply reduced, allowing the company to have the available cash flow to service debt principal obligations more tax efficiently. While this is an advantage to the buyer, an asset purchase is often a negative aspect for the seller since assets may be subject to both ordinary income tax rates (depreciation recovery and sale of inventory), and capital gain tax rates assuming an S corporation or another pass-through entity for tax purposes.

One disadvantage to an asset sale is that it is difficult to sell less than 100% of the assets, unlike a stock sale which is scalable. An asset sale may also be subject to the same types of options above for a stock sale in reducing the purchase price to the buyer such as deferred compensation and accelerated retirement benefits.

If the company is a C corporation there is the specter of double taxation of the sale price to the seller. An asset sale is taxed to a C corporation first as ordinary income to the corporation. Assuming the sale occurs and assets of the C corporation have been converted to cash, the seller is subject to another layer of taxes when the cash is distributed from the corporation. Typically the distribution of cash is interpreted as a liquidating dividend for tax purposes and is taxed to the recipient as capital gain. This resulting second tax often means that the effective tax rate on the asset sale considering both Federal and state taxes is often at or in excess of 50%.

If an asset sale is contemplated and the single largest asset is company goodwill, this intangible asset is subject to 15 year amortization for tax purposes. This is a substantial period of time and is often a significant negative development for the buyers. The long amortization period is almost as negative from a cash flow standpoint as acquiring stock. In such instances, the same strategies mentioned in the stock sale may be used to accelerate tax deductible cash flows to the company. The relative tax impact to the seller and the buyer due to timing issues will have to be negotiated.

Successor Management

It is common for the successor management team to have employee contracts to protect them, particularly if they have invested money in the company or if they have personally guaranteed debt. Such employment agreements need to specify such obvious things as duties, compensation, and obligations to the company. The key employee often relies on the employment agreement and subsequent salary designation as the source for repaying acquisition debt principal. In the case of a mutually agreed manager termination, consideration should be given to the best efforts to have the employee released from company obligations, such as the guarantee of company debt. If the termination is initiated by the company for improper performance or cause, the employment agreement should have sufficiently strong provisions to help insure against retaliatory behavior on the part of the dismissed employee.

Assuming that the successor management is a team with at least two individuals and possibly many more than two, it is appropriate for the team to have their own exit plan. The buyout of the initial owner is followed by a succession plan by the successor management. Such a plan should be memorialized with a shareholder agreement that stipulates such things as the exit price, how stock is redeemed from a shareholder, the use of insurance to help guarantee payment on the stock redemption, and other material matters. It is beyond the scope of this chapter to develop a description of successor management exit strategies.

PROFESSIONAL SERVICE COMPANY

This chapter indicates that it is often difficult to sell a larger company to the management because the transfer of a significant amount of wealth to the successor team is very difficult in a reasonable period of time due to our tax structure. Attorney Larry Ferguson with Ferguson & Widmayer in Ann Arbor, Michigan has worked as a strategic advisor with many private company owners on a wide range of options. Mr. Ferguson is familiar with ESOPs, sales to private equity firms, transactions with third party buyers and management buyouts to name a few of the more common transactions. He offers advice on a recent successful management buyout of a professional services firm with 15 employees and four key managers. An ESOP was considered, but management felt the company was too small to spread the equity between all the employees, and due to the limited number of employees it may be difficult to keep the Company away from ESOP anti-abuse regulations (mentioned in Chapter 13). The sole owner and the four managers agreed that a reasonable price for the Company is $2.5 million.

The owner wanted a stock sale for obvious tax reasons, but such a transaction has to be paid with after-tax dollars, and the cash flow of the Company would not have supported such a goal. The owner was flexible in the structure of the succession plan because he had confidence and trust in the four managers to fully execute the plan. Mr. Ferguson provided a number of scenarios and one was eventually adopted that included several elements of funding to the owner.

The Company adopted a defined benefit plan based on the average of the three highest years of compensation accruing over 10 years of service, including past service. All eligible employees participated in the defined benefit plan, but the account balance of the owner was the highest due to his prior compensation. The Company discontinued contributions to a safe harbor 401(k) plan with the adoption of the defined benefit plan. The Company would have the savings from discontinuing the safe harbor 401(k) plan, and discontinuing the salary of the owner. The payout of the owner's participation in the defined benefit plan had the effect of lowering the purchase price of the stock because of this liability.

The Company entered into an agreement to pay the owner a stipulated amount for the next 10 years as a non-solicitation and non-competition agreement. The net present value of the payments over 10 years was computed using a market discount rate, and that amount was deducted from the consideration. Finally, the balance of the value was a stock transaction with the four managers using cross-purchase agreements. The managers committed to acquire the stock of the owner, and each manager negotiated the purchase depending on the individual circumstances. One manager had access to family liquidity and used those funds to acquire the prorated equity interest directly. The other managers obtained some funding by leveraging homes and using limited personal savings. The balance of the transaction price was provided by seller notes with terms ranging from three to five years at a market interest rate. The managers with seller notes will hope to pay the loans with annual bonuses. This is expensive financing for the managers because they must have the bonus declared to them, pay individual taxes on the amount, and then use the net proceeds to repay the principal on the seller notes. Interest on the notes is tax deductible to the managers. As a professional services company, it had limited debt capacity and was not a significant source of bank financing.

This structure accomplished in part the owner's desire for a stock sale, as a percentage of the consideration was the acquisition of his stock. The stock sale was subject to capital gain tax treatment. Other elements of the transaction are tax deductible to the Company, such as the payments under the non-solicitation and non-competition agreement and the contributions to the defined benefit plan. While the latter payments are tax deductible to the Company, they are ordinary income to the seller. Mr. Ferguson notes that this transaction structure has several material elements with varying tax implications to the buyers and the seller. The plan worked because the parties to the transaction worked with one another for years and a fair purchase price was determined and agreed to by everyone.

TOOLING COMPANY

This second illustration represents another privately held company with significant debt capacity because it has substantial operating assets including CNC (Computer Numeric Control) production equipment, a substantial commitment to state-of-art CAD design computers and software, inventories, accounts receivable, and proprietary intellectual property related to the design of components for the military and aerospace industries. The Company lists many publicly held corporations as ongoing customers. The Company is located in a rural location in the upper Midwest and is one of the premiere employers in the region.

The founder of the Company wanted the business to remain locally owned and controlled. The senior management consisted of five key employees including two design engineers that were the essence of the successful relationships the Company enjoyed with its largest accounts. The founder and his spouse own the facility leased by the Company (Family Real Estate, LLP), a 55,000 square foot building located on four acres of land. The land is sufficient to permit the expansion of the building to 120,000 square feet if that ever becomes necessary.

While the owner prefers a stock sale, an asset sale was negotiated because of the ability to use the depreciation on the substantial assets in the business to shelter debt principal repayment. The five managers formed a new corporation (Newco) to acquire the assets of the Company and enter into a long-term lease with Family Real Estate LLC. (a five-year lease with two additional five-year option periods). Newco allocated the purchase price to the various assets according to IRC Section 1060. Most of the purchase price is allocated to production equipment, tooling, inventory, and other sundry assets. Only 20% of the purchase price was allocated to goodwill.

Newco is a high-profile local employer and the area banks were receptive to finance most of the transaction and insure the long-term presence of high paying jobs in the community. Additionally, the future growth prospects for Newco are significant. In a competitive market, one local bank agreed to finance 70% of the asset purchase with the seller providing the balance with a note. The business plan indicates that the bank financing will be substantially repaid in five years, and the seller note repaid within another two years. The seller note will likely be refinanced by the bank once a repayment track record is established by the management of Newco within the next three or four years.

The seller feels secure with the transaction because the operations of the business have been sold to Newco at a fair negotiated price. Most of the transaction price was received by the seller on the closing date (70%), and the balance is a seller note at 2% above the bank rate reflecting the seller's subordinated position to the bank and higher risk. An additional aspect of the transaction was a royalty payment related to the revenue generated from the application of proprietary design software developed by the seller. After verifying an arm's length royalty rate with an independent appraiser, Newco agreed to a royalty payment of 5% on applicable revenue with a deferred payment schedule. Newco deferred royalty payments for 36 months while significant acquisition debt was being repaid. The seller also has an arm's-length long-term lease with Newco for the facility. From a practical standpoint the seller hopes the management of Newco will form their own Limited Liability Company (LLC) to acquire the facility once the acquisition debt for the operations has been repaid.

This management buyout will span several years and only with the material assistance of the seller. The seller knows and trusts the Newco ownership. Due to the close relationship the seller knows he will remain an integral part of Newco since he is one of the board members, and will remain on the board until the seller note is repaid. The Newco management has represented to the seller he is welcome on the Newco board as long as he wishes to have a relationship.

SUMMARY

The management buyouts discussed herein often represent companies with a valuation of less than $10 million and often much smaller than that threshold due to the difficulty in transferring value in our tax environment. Since these transactions typically involve individuals that have a history of working together, there is the likelihood of great flexibility in the eventual structure of the transaction. Virtually any business, in any industry, and at any level of financial success is a candidate for this transaction. The financial health of the business may even be a negotiating point. The conclusion is that there are few limitations on transaction structure with the possible exception of scale. It is very difficult to complete a true management only buyout of a company having a value in excess of the arbitrarily selected threshold of $10 million, without the assistance of a private equity firm or some other viable source of substantial outside funding.

Chapter 10

Buyouts—Sponsored Management

To make money, buy some good stock, hold it until it goes up and then sell it. If it doesn't go up, don't buy it.

—Will Rogers

Never invest in anything that eats or needs painting.

—Billy Rose

This is the first of two chapters on sponsored buyouts. A sponsored buyout for our purposes is one where a private equity resource or a private equity group (PEG) or some other similar source of funding with extensive experience with leveraged buyouts is an integral part of the transaction. Throughout the discussion on sponsored buyouts, the acronym PEG will be used to generically indicate the source of the funding.

This book divides the sponsored buyouts into two general categories for discussion and analysis. This chapter considers sponsored buyouts where the management has been instrumental by inviting the PEG to participate in the buyout, and management is driving the transaction. In this case the management plays an integral role in the transition plans for the company. The next chapter considers buyouts where the seller has invited the PEG to drive the deal structure, and the current management is not often an important determining factor in the transaction. The applications for PEG financing are virtually limitless. For the purposes of this book, the PEG is an integral part of the complete or nearly complete buyout of the candidate company. The seller is intending to divest the company to the management and the PEG. The seller may retain a smaller percentage of ownership going forward, but that percentage for our purposes is minimal, or less than 10%.

The world of transactions involving a PEG is so diverse and flexible that this narrow application of buyouts is the focus.

Intended for middle market transactions, this discussion involves the use of private equity funding on a scale that is appropriate for middle market candidates. This chapter represents a situation whereby the candidate company's prior success is largely attributed to the skills of the successor management. The management has typically established an enviable track record of financial success and arguably is in a strong negotiating position to invite an equity source into the succession process. The management is in a position to literally help insure that the buyout will be a success.

Management in this case is an integral part of the succession equation, but for any number of reasons they may not be in a material position to contribute a significant percentage of the transaction price in equity. Often the very success of the management team in building value in their employer works against them in the buyout process because they have created too much value for them to purchase with their own resources. There is good news for the astute management team that has a passion to acquire their employer but acknowledges such a goal will take the assistance of substantial outside financial resources. The larger the anticipated transaction, typically the smaller the dollar amount or percentage equity participation the management team may retain. All transactions are unique and the amount of management participation is going to depend on such items as: the skills they bring to the transaction, prior history growing the business profitably, ability to commit some financial resources to the transaction, willingness to pledge personal assets to the program, and overall commitment to the plan.

ADVANTAGES

One of the biggest benefits is the high likelihood the current owner and the successor team know one another and have worked together for years. There is often the fact that the current owner favors the successor team within limits. The departing seller is typically motivated to optimize the sale proceeds. While it is possible the sponsored management buyout may not be the absolutely highest offer, it will have to be close. It is really the obligation of management to convince the seller they want the opportunity to acquire the company with the assistance of a PEG or other substantial funding resource. While the interest and the passion to proceed may be present, it is very difficult to know how to proceed if you have no prior experience in such matters. Selecting trusted advisors is paramount to success.

Financial Assistance

Outside financial assistance is understood in this chapter to be an integral part of the process. There is a wide range of PEG options to consider. There are literally hundreds if not thousands of financial sources. Obviously, the list has to be quickly reduced to a few leading candidates as soon as possible. It is simply too difficult to interview a near-endless list of financing candidates. An investment banker or other consultant may provide significant value by paring the potential list of PEGs to ones that are interested in the company's industry or markets. Selecting the PEG with the right interests, goals, investment appetite, industry focus, and any number of other factors contributes to melding a mutually comfortable "chemistry" between the management and the PEG. Going forward, management and the PEG will have to develop a trust and confidence in one another as they settle into the partnership that is envisioned. When this relationship is established and the appropriate amount of due diligence is completed, the end results are often financially very rewarding. The extraordinary effort extended to find the right financial partner is worth the time.

> Determining a mutually rewarding fit is most challenging. If the management team and the PEG are adversarial in the early stages, it is a near certainty that the end result will be filled with ill feelings and resentment.

The future of the company will likely entail significant operating debt. During the recession of 2008 to 2011 the PEGs increasingly found it difficult to attract bank debt for buyouts. Rather, the PEGs had to rely more on their own capital to facilitate deals. Assuming that leverage is a significant component of the structure, the management may not have the expertise or comfort level of running a company laden with debt. Finding the right partner to bring the expertise of managing the business in the new financial environment is essential to attaining success.

In this instance an equity partner is introduced into the transition equation to bolster the successor management. The equity partner will commit its own capital to the project and will arrange for additional debt based on the company's debt capacity and the reputation of the PEG. The PEG will have expectations on the return on investment (ROI). Since the PEG is likely leveraged itself, the ROI may be significant. The target returns are often in the range of 15% to 30% or higher on a compounded basis. This is a very high threshold. While it may seem doable within a short period of time, attaining that type of return on a compounded basis for several years is a challenging task. It is also emphasized that the range of target ROI is the goal, and the actual results achieved by a PEG is likely to be substantially lower. We assume the PEG has a portfolio of investments, and while some of those selections are performing as planned, others may falter so that the blended ROI is much lower than the target. There are few reliable statistics for PEGs serving the middle market so it is very difficult to verify actual returns. One pragmatic guide is the length of time the PEG has been providing funding. Since the most common PEG business template involves going back to the same funding sources over time, it makes sense that only those firms with an established track record have been delivering financial success to their backers.

Carried Interest and Management Fees

It is customary for PEGs to anticipate an acceptable ROI on their investment. The overall financial return may be comprised of several elements. Those elements include such things as a management fee to the investors in the PEG, possibly an administrative fee to the candidate company, and carried interest.

We consider first a fee that is negotiated between the PEG and its investors and referred to as the "carried interest." The total funding capability in the PEG is most often a combination of capital by the PEG's principals, and capital contributed by investors in the PEG (from sources such as pension funds, insurance companies, and university endowments). There are no absolute rules regarding the determination of the service fee. The actual carried interest fee that is charged by the PEG is often a function of negotiations between the PEG and its investors. The carried interest fee is often in the range of 15% to 20% of the gain after repaying the capital to the PEG fund investors and achieving a negotiated hurdle rate (i.e. 8%). The carried interest fee to the PEG is typically realized when the investment in a candidate company is liquidated.

The PEG will also likely have a management fee that is charged to its investors in addition to the carried interest. The PEG will have to meet its own financial obligations such as payroll, rent, marketing and business development expenses, and maintaining relationships with their investors. The PEG will charge its investors a separate 1% to 2% management fee, often paid annually. The PEG may seek a third form of compensation by assessing an administration fee to the company where the investment is made. The fee to the target company may take the form of director's fees for example. The successful PEGs will have a portfolio of companies, and the larger number of investments will provide the critical mass to make the business plan for the PEG viable.

VALUATION

Since this is a transaction between independent parties, we assume it is arm's length. The introduction of a PEG typically means the seller will be able to convert a significant percentage if not all of the investment into cash. We have assumed for the purposes of this analysis the PEG and management are acquiring the total or near total equity in the target company. While it is common for the PEG to be involved in transactions where control is being assumed, that is not always the case. Another common transaction structure is for the PEG and management to acquire a significant percentage of the target company (say 55% to 80%) and the seller retains the balance of the equity. Under this later scenario, the seller, PEG, and management are partners in the company with everyone looking for the next liquidity event that will convert their respective investments into cash.

The seller may seek a strategic third-party buyer that will pay a premium for the company. Prior to the 2008 recession the common hope for many business owners was to find this strategic buyer willing to pay a premium price for the company. The strategic buyer today is typically focused on cash flows, meeting loan covenants, and being far more pragmatic about long-term growth prospects. The current conditions of the economy and market today suggest that acquisition multiples are currently depressed, often as a result of future growth being harder to attain in our challenging environment. As the economy rebounds, transaction multiples will improve. It may take some time for multiples to return to the robust days before 2008.

One bright spot is the cost of debt. To the extent a candidate transaction qualifies for a significant percentage of senior level debt, the pricing on that component of the capital structure of the company is favorable. The cost of senior level and secured debt today is in the range of 4% to 6%. While this component of the transaction is favorable, it is still more challenging to entice major banks to finance buyouts much in excess of the assets offered as collateral. Some of the more progressive commercial banks will still lend based on a multiple of cash flows in companies with a proven track record during the recession.

Independent and financially literate candidate partners such as PEGs will typically price the proposed transaction as a multiple of earnings before interest and tax (EBIT) or earnings before interest, taxes, depreciation, and amortization (EBITDA) in the communication to the seller. Sellers should be aware of trends in multiples when considering a transaction.

VIEWPOINT OF THE SELLER

The seller is typically motivated by realizing substantial liquidity for the company and a favorable price. Prior to the recession beginning in 2008, an attractive company that was providing growing cash flows and profits could reasonably anticipate an offer that consisted substantially of all cash. Depending on the circumstances, the offer may be for the stock of the business, meaning a more favorable capital gain tax treatment. The environment for transactions has changed with the recession. Fewer all cash or mostly cash transactions are being completed. Sellers often have to retain an equity position in the company or provide a significant amount of seller financing.

The seller may have an interest in entertaining an offer from the management, but the burden will be on management to piece together a competitive proposal. If any proposal is forthcoming, it will almost certainly be a function of the management team having at least one strong leader. We assume the goal for the seller is to exit the business, and an acceptable package must be offered to get the transaction closed. Circumstances have changed since the beginning of the recession. If a seller is adamant about attaining the maximum possible price for the company and remembers the transaction environment pre-recession, there will almost certainly be disappointment when anticipated offers do not match prior heights. The seller will have the decision of transacting at an adjusted price reflecting the current market or hold on and anticipate more favorable circumstances. There are likely to be practical limits on how long the seller will wait before deciding to proceed.

Non-Recourse Issues

The seller will have a strong interest in a non-recourse transaction. The seller may decide to be more flexible on the transaction price and holding some portion in equity, but will be looking to walk away from the business without lingering exposure to the company. The seller will be far less likely to accept such things as seller notes, personal guarantees, and other representations that could pose as significant contingent liabilities against the sale proceeds. One key role of utilizing a PEG is to provide liquidity, and the PEG is supposed to have the expertise to evaluate the risk environment of the target company so that a mostly cash investment is possible.

Under the right circumstances, the seller may have an interest in holding a negotiated but minority equity stake in the business. In such circumstances the seller has realized enough from the sale of the company to feel secure with future personal financial security. The residual investment in the company is an opportunity to realize an increase in the value of the businesses over time until a next threshold is realized, typically the exit of the PEG.

Total Transaction Consideration

The total consideration for the business is an opportunity for developing a plan that suits the needs of the seller, the PEG, and management. There may be a host of important attributes to the seller that are perhaps more emotional than economic. Some cherished benefits are candidates for consideration that are often immaterial to the financial scale of the transaction. Such things as medical coverage, retained use of a vehicle, company credit card for approved travel, and board membership will likely be incorporated into the transaction mix. The seller is typically surrendering control of the company to the PEG and management, so retaining some symbolic trappings of involvement may help ease the journey into retirement.

> A recurring theme will be the importance of behavioral and psychological compatibility between the principals. I have seen enough deals turn terribly acrimonious because of personal dislikes and suspicion. One option to consider is engaging a consulting psychologist to industry for key personnel insights. If the conflicts persist it is time to consider a Plan B.

The seller may also favor this alternative for confidential reasons. It will be much easier to maintain confidentiality when only a few inside managers and a select number of professional advisors are participating in the discussions. Many business owners find the process of selling to a third party very distasteful because the due diligence process often takes on the profile of adversarial proceedings.

VIEWPOINT OF THE BUYER

We have one buyer with two partners in this case. While management is a driving force in the transaction, the PEG is providing the financing. Each partner will have his/her own perspective and goals. When the acquisition discussions are being conducted there is likely to be more agreement on a united vision for the company so that the partnership evolves and the transaction closes.

Interests of the Private Equity Group

We will address the PEG first, as their interests are typically more likely to be straightforward and defined in financial terms. The PEG is making an investment in the company for the goal of earning an acceptable return. The PEG is not solely tied to a single industry and will typically not have a vision of the future that blends financial goals with qualitative considerations such as protecting the environment, giving back to the community, creating employment, or making an enduring contribution to the product. The decision to invest is driven primarily by financial considerations. Certainly, there may be a tertiary consideration of the qualitative factors just mentioned, but such objectives will often be addressed once the company is financially performing at projected levels and there is some room for a consideration of other goals. The presumption in this chapter is that the PEG has an investment horizon sufficient to meet financial goals and the reputation of the PEG will not be well served if it espouses an interest only in immediate financial interests to the detriment of the other stakeholders.

The PEG will have a detailed vision of how their investment in the target company will be redeemed at some point in the future. This vision is typically tied to trigger events such as attaining pre-determined revenue thresholds, profitability targets, or debt reduction goals. The exit vehicle options may include selling to an even larger PEG, finding a privately held strategic buyer, selling to a publicly held company, or doing an initial public offering (IPO). Since the PEG is always on the search for the next portfolio investment, protecting its reputation is important to long-term success. Candidate companies will typically ask for referrals and often referrals from the management of companies where investments have been made. While the markets are competitive, earning a reputation of being ruthless at the expense of your partners is a questionable long-term strategy.

The PEG is typically coming to the transaction table prepared to offer liquidity to the seller and assume the responsibility for financing the purchase. The PEG will most typically be guaranteeing the acquisition debt from the banks. The PEG will look to the management to make a significant contribution and commitment to the transaction for the opportunity to materially participate in the equity. A highly motivated management is a time-honored strategy to help insure the success of the buyout. There are different techniques employed to provide incentives to the management.

Envy Ratio

The Envy Ratio is an inventive method of measuring the relative opportunity for management. The Envy Ratio is explained in the following formula:

$$\text{Envy Ratio} = \frac{(\text{Investment by PEG}/\% \text{ of equity})}{(\text{Investment by management}/\% \text{ of equity})}$$

For example if the PEG paid $50,000,000 for 85% of the company's equity, and the management team paid $3,000,000 for the remaining 15% (total purchase price is $50M + $3M = $53M) then the Envy Ratio is computed as follows:

$$\text{Envy Ratio} = (50/85\%)/(3/15\%) = 2.94\times$$

The interpretation of this example Envy Ratio is that the PEG paid for a share 2.94 times more than the managers. This ratio indicates how generous the PEG is to the management team. The higher the ratio, the better is the deal for management. The above example is a very good deal for management, but it is unusual for management to produce $3,000,000 in investment. If we take the same example but management is only able to collectively raise $1,500,000 for a 5% stake in the business (the total purchase price is $51.5M + $1.5M = $53M) the Envy Ratio is only 1.81 ((51.5/95%)/(1.5/5%)).

It is entirely possible that in this example management is not likely to raise $3,000,000 in equity to contribute to the transaction. In such circumstances, the PEG may consider providing a number of sweat equity options in addition to cash actually invested in the company. The amount of actual return to the management will often be when the company is sold at a later date. The PEG may have an agreement that stipulates the division of a sale price based on incentives extended to management including such things a stock appreciation rights, phantom stock, incentive stock options, non-qualified stock options.

The generosity of the PEG toward management will depend on the facts and circumstances for each transaction. The more valuable the management team, the stronger the incentive. Strong professional credentials such as medical degrees and engineering licenses are common examples of high-added-value attributes for the management. Other examples of adding significant value include recognition as a market and thought leader for the industry, and consistently attaining superior financial returns for many years.

Interests of the Management

Management typically has a vested interest in participating in the next stage of the company's growth. Once a certain scale is reached regarding the value of the company, management's ability to acquire the business rapidly declines due to lack of financial resources. The best that management can do is to hope to materially participate in the buyout. Management will typically have operating responsibility for the business, but they will not control the key decisions at the board level.

The PEG will have to get management to respond to the new reporting environment especially if it entails a significant amount of debt. The business will have to be managed by the numbers now more than ever to the satisfaction of the new controlling shareholder. Accuracy of accounting records will be essential.

> Many privately held companies that are candidates for the PEG have not operated with the level of debt that the future is likely to hold. It is essential to have a legitimate chief financial officer (CFO) thoroughly experienced with spreadsheets, budgets, and financial reporting. The good news is that such skills are often readily available. For example the public accounting profession generates far more qualified candidates than required by the accounting firms.

Mutual Commitments

If the PEG has extended an invitation to participate in the equity of the company, a viable strategy for the PEG is to insure management is committed to the long-term success of the business and cannot simply walk away if events become stressful. Having the management team investing personal assets to the point of making a material impact on lifestyle is important. Some PEGs like to see management make highly symbolic actions in support of the buyout, like investing funds by taking a second mortgage on a home. This is a sign of commitment and confidence in the future of the company. Having management making such a commitment becomes an even more sensitive subject when they are married with spousal consent considerations. Using family liquidity for a risky investment in the employer places stress in such things as the home equity, college education funding, and retirement savings. Making a commitment and placing personal assets at risk is something that is a point of demarcation for those managers that will participate in the equity future of the company, and those that are merely custodians of a job responsibility.

Generally, the PEG wants to see some commitment of personal assets as described. The PEG will typically not insist on personal guarantees for the company debt as management had no voice in determining the capital structure of the business. If personal guarantees are requested, management will have to decide if they want that much risk when they are really not in control.

There is also a consideration of lifestyle. The successor management will be expected to make a sacrifice for the opportunity to direct the business and participate in the upside. Many managers may be uncomfortable with perpetually investing in their future and sacrificing material well being they have already made an effort to attain. Key executives may have a commitment to such things as a pleasant home, travel, children's education, and club memberships. It may be very difficult to give up those trappings of success to invest in the business. However, the hallmark of an entrepreneur and reliable partner is to frequently make some sacrifices in the short term for the opportunity to build personal net worth longer term.

The PEG with experience will want the management to be motivated by realistic goals. If the goals are so convoluted and unlikely to be achieved, the management will quickly become discouraged. Additionally, if a manager makes an investment and it is subsequently realized that individual must be let go, there has to be some consideration to release that person from company obligations and a return of the investment. It will not help the reputation of the PEG to be ruthless when there have been employment mistakes.

PROFESSIONAL ADVISORS

The seller will have a strong vested interest in retaining advisors that protect his interests. Often the seller will have significant input into the final structure of the transaction, particularly in today's economy. This point is particularly magnified if the seller will be an ongoing investor in the business, even if a smaller shareholder by percent.

Management will be advised to retain an advisor to assist them with the analysis of whether pursuing the buyout makes sense. While the emphasis in this chapter so far is on having the right PEG as a partner, it is often a daunting task to qualify the PEG and find the best one for the transaction. This is where the commitment to the process is paramount. Management will typically have limited funds available to qualify the PEG, but they will have to invest personal time. Depending on the relationship of the management with the seller, the seller may authorize some funding to engage professional talent to investigate PEGs. This may suggest hiring an investment banker to qualify PEGs. Some consulting firms or the larger accounting firms will have investment banking expertise and may be a consideration. Such a relationship will typically involve a commitment fee with perhaps a success fee attached to the final placement of the relationship with a PEG. In this case the investment banker is being compensated to compress the time to search for a suitable investor. Considering there are hundreds of candidate PEGs, narrowing the search to just a handful of qualified candidates is typically worth the expense with the investment banker.

The PEG will come to the table with their own advisors that will be careful to protect their interests. Additionally, the PEG will be thinking about this buyout, but will also be thinking ahead regarding an exit vehicle at a point in time. The PEG is investing a portion of its own funds and typically relies on investors to comprise the difference in the price to the seller. Those investors may have their own advisors, but they often defer to the PEG if there is an established relationship. The PEG will typically be driving the legal document production. Having experience in such matters will make the production of the documents more efficient from a cost basis. Management and the seller will have to retain counsel to review the documents to insure that representations during the sales presentations are in fact reflected in the documents.

Management may be advised to retain the services of the public accounting firm to verify and review the reasonableness of projections. Management may not have expertise in multiyear forecasting and budgeting at the level required by the PEG. Getting help is a recommended step. Understanding how the company is valued is another discipline that the management may not have expertise in. Most public accounting firms will have the skills to analyze the valuation methodology.

RISK ENVIRONMENT

If a PEG is to be considered, it is important to realize that virtually all of them are going to insist on a few fundamental requirements. Briefly, the candidate company must have profitable results and a reasonable potential for growth. Typically well established companies that have weathered recessions and market challenges are good candidates. The company needs to have an experienced management team that has worked successfully together for a number of years. For example, five years of experience together is a reasonable minimum threshold. Within the management team there must be at least one leader that emerges as the next chief executive.

Success is also a function of a realistic valuation. If the company is simply over leveraged and there are unrealistic revenue and profit expectations the transaction will falter and likely be a failure candidate.

Reasonable Expectations

There are a considerable number of qualitative factors to evaluate. Additionally, the individual PEGs often focus on a select number of industries where they have investment experience. Prior knowledge of an industry will provide the PEG and its investors with a comfort level to proceed with these types of buyouts. Over time, certain industries have demonstrated a track record of success and have attracted the attention of a solid portion of the PEG community. It is important to realize that an integral part of the business model for most PEGs is to locate candidates that promise profitable future growth. The growth over a period representing the investment horizon is a proven method to earn the target ROI that PEGs seek. In this respect the PEG will grow its way into the target ROI through leverage by holding debt steady or repaying modest amounts while the equity component of the investment compounds in value.

Since growth is so important to the PEG template, if growth expectations cannot be realistically attained then this structure is unlikely to meet expectations. This fact alone will serve as a limiting factor to determine if a PEG is likely to have any interest. Clearly, this structure is not a candidate for financially challenged companies. Most PEGs will select successful companies and they want management to direct operations. PEGs are typically not in the turnaround business. Restructuring financially challenged companies is a discipline for seasoned professionals that work in that environment.

Case Study—Martell Construction, Inc. and Generation Growth Capital, Inc. Known for its excellence in concrete construction applications, Martell Construction, Inc. (Martell or the Company) was a candidate to be acquired by its management from the prior ownership group. The Company has an excellent history of being affiliated with many high profile engagements in their primary marketing area in the Wisconsin Fox Valley and Upper Michigan. Martell specializes in the construction of such items as concrete sidewalks, curbs, gutters, and concrete pavement. On larger projects the Company is a subcontractor. Many of the projects are high-profile traffic-related jobs including regional bridges and major highways. Martell has a long history of winning repeat relationships within a broad range of customers including commercial, municipal, industrial, heavy highway, marine, and residential accounts.

The management team led by Mr. Mike Carney, President, was interested in acquiring the Company but needed financial assistance. In the middle of a recession, Mr. Carney was able to coordinate an acceptable acquisition proposal to the Martell owners. That proposal included equity investment by the management and Generation Growth Capital, Inc. (Generation) in Milwaukee, Wisconsin. Martell was in part caught by the downward business cycle in construction during this recession, but still enjoyed a strong market presence in its core disciplines. This strength along with careful operational management and tight financial controls provided the critical mass to complete the acquisition.

The Martell management maintains a significant but non-controlling equity stake in the Company. Generation is an equity partner with a longer-term investment horizon. They provide a flexible approach to the buyout allowing management the option of increasing their equity stake in the business over time. Generation is a partner that wants Martell to grow its revenues and profitability. Martell joins Generation as a portfolio company that enjoys some synergies with another Generation portfolio company in the construction industry.

At some point Generation will want to have an exit vehicle from Martell. There are many options and Generation has not decided on a single selection. Mr. John Reinke, Managing Director at Generation, indicates that they are flexible in the choice of an exit vehicle that a majority of the shareholders would agree upon. Management may embrace a series of staged transactions whereby they acquire a greater percentage of ownership with new ownership partners. The future of Martell will have a significant degree of leverage, but management will be in the best position to direct Company operations.

Generation Growth Capital, Inc. is a private equity firm founded with a vision to provide assistance to businesses in the lower middle market, a niche that is underserved by private equity firms according to founder Mr. Cory Nettles. One primary focus is to provide "double bottom line" assistance to deserving candidates. This means that investments are selected with the potential to provide a positive rate of return to Generation, but also provide financial and social assistance to lower and moderate income (LMI) communities. In this respect, Generation helps communities by encouraging entrepreneurs with best practices, growth financing, and job creation opportunities according to Mr. Nettles. Investments are typically in companies with an enterprise value of less than $20 million. Generation will invest between $1 and $5 million in either equity, subordinated debt, or warrant structures. They have a long-term vision for commercial development and have a patient equity outlook. Their investing track record suggests a value system that combines with their financial resources that will serve them well in the heartland.

DISTRIBUTION COMPANY

This distribution company is a market leader with a national footprint. The primary market is throughout the Midwest and the southeast. They are weakest on the west coast, but still have distribution centers in Los Angeles, San Francisco, and Seattle. The products are generally classified as consumer electronics and computer auxiliary accessories. The secret to the above-average industry margins has been the imagination and creativity of the senior management, a team consisting of five individuals. The senior management has developed proprietary software to manage the distribution centers and help insure that stock-outs of the most popular items are almost nonexistent. Additionally, the senior management has developed strong relationships with the key suppliers to the extent that very favorable multiyear buying relationships have been negotiated. Several suppliers have participated in the new branding program for products carrying a proprietary private label name.

The company was owned by a sole shareholder and it was being shopped to strategic buyers and private equity firms. With a value in excess of $100 million, the purchase price made it beyond the ability of the senior management to acquire the firm. The owner realized that the senior management was instrumental to the success of the business and supported their search for a buyer that would provide material support to them. The senior management benefited from a stock appreciation rights (SAR) benefit program worth approximately 5% of the value of the company on a sale to a third party. The SAR program is in essence only deferred-compensation-taxable to the senior management as ordinary income at the time of closing. The senior management knew that the selection of a private equity firm that was partial to their interests would likely provide the strongest incentive program going forward. After several months of selection, the senior management and the owner were comfortable with one private equity firm, XYZ Capital (for the purposes of this illustration). XYZ Capital demonstrated a long history of successful buyouts where the equity participation of the senior management was material and with reasonable future performance targets. The senior management interviewed a number of the XYZ Capital clients and verified representations that were made. XYZ Capital views the investment as a new platform Company, and retaining the senior management was an integral aspect of their strategy.

XYZ Capital provided 85% of the sale price in cash using a combination of their own capital and funding provided by the current lead bank. XYZ Capital was impressed that the senior management to an individual was willing to roll their SARs into the successor entity. The SARs were reconfigured to provide deferred compensation to the senior team that amounted to their own 5% plus an additional 10% from XYZ Capital subject to vesting over a 5 year period. The balance of the purchase price was provided by a seller note at a competitive market rate. XYZ Capital and the senior management developed a long-term plan to grow the Company and increase profitability. After a period of time in excess of five years XYZ capital would seek an exit vehicle that may include the sale of the Company to a publicly held strategic buyer or a larger private equity firm. For several reasons an initial public offering (IPO) was not a serious consideration.

One attractive aspect of the buyout from the senior management's perspective is that they were treated as an equal equity investor. Their percentage participation was predicated on all of the investors selling at the same time with each receiving a prorated amount of the purchase price. XYZ Capital did not insist on being paid first from sale proceeds with management participating only if certain financial targets had been obtained. This "all-in" approach adopted by XYZ Capital was a lynchpin in being selected by the owner. The owner was satisfied that his senior team would participate in the financial growth of the Company. Assuming the mutually agreed growth forecast is achieved, the senior team could be the eventual recipient of an approximate $25 million SAR program.

TECHNICAL MATTERS

One of the daunting challenges is balancing the interests of multiple parties to the satisfaction of everyone. The more parties to the transaction, the more challenging the task. Once a PEG is introduced into the transaction consideration, it is assumed the company is too large for management to acquire on their own. A limit on the amount of personal debt that may be assumed becomes reality. This fact will limit the participation in the equity of the company subject to the generosity of the PEG.

Tax and Legal Structure of the Company

If the candidate company is a C corporation, the capital structure offers a wide spectrum of options. The C corporation may offer multiple classes of stock, and those various classes may be defined with equity attributes suitable for each class of investors. This flexibility is most helpful for the management because incentive equity programs may be considered, such as incentive stock options and non-qualified stock options. The C corporation offers great flexibility in the capital structure, but it is also subject to high marginal corporate tax rates.

The S corporation offers some benefits as a pass-through entity for tax purposes, but there are sharp restrictions on who may be a shareholder, and generally there is only one class of stock permitted. There may be two classes of stock possible such as voting shares and non-voting shares if all the other attributes are held constant.

There are a myriad of other legal entities that may be considered such as Limited Liability Companies (LLC), and Limited Partnerships. Generally such organizations are pass-through entities for tax purposes. The preference of the PEG for one structure over another will typically be a function of the tax environment. The structure that minimizes taxes both on a yearly operational basis and upon an exit event will be selected. Additionally, individual states will have their own regulations regarding such entities. It is beyond the scope of this book to explore this vast selection of options.

Private Equity Group Funding

The PEG will likely have relationships with a number of investors providing funding for them. The PEG will have its own capital, but that may be a limited amount. The PEG will typically approach other funding sources for capital, such as pension plans, insurance companies, university endowment managers, and other long-term horizon candidates. Generally the agreements provide the PEG with access to a stated amount of capital that may be drawn upon subject to applicable documentation and agreement of terms.

Having access to this level of capital enables the PEG to invest in a candidate company with its own funds, and then leverage that amount with debt financing from other sources, such as a bank. The ROI for the PEG under such circumstances is powerful, but it is clear the business model entails the use of significant amounts of debt. As long as the debt obligations are satisfied, the opportunity for the PEG to be highly profitable is enhanced. If the economy drops into a deep recession and loan obligations are compromised, the business model is in trouble.

Knowing the actual source of the PEG's funding and the blend of its own capital and that of other investors is a key insight into the staying power of the fund. This is a partnership, and locating a partner with that view is often a key component to everyone realizing his/her goals.

Professional Support

It may be unlikely the management has the expertise to adequately model the buyout. Management may have to model a few buyout scenarios as a reality check to determine if it is worth the effort to contact PEGs or investment bankers. This first-pass sanity check may be cost-effectively broached working with the public accounting firm or another consultant familiar with buyouts. At the earliest stages gaining some understanding of the valuation and the cash flow prognosis is critical before interviewing candidate PEGs. A realistic budget should be approved; in most cases this will cost a few thousand dollars. Once the feasibility is successfully passed and it makes sense to proceed, then retaining the services of an investment banker or another qualified resource may be the next step.

SUMMARY

The pragmatic observation is that this type of transaction will be complex and difficult to attain because of the various interests. The complexity need not be an impediment with the right circumstances, but it will require a patient long-term perspective that will almost certainly span a wide range of business conditions. It is essential that the key players are all in agreement with the long-term vision for the company.

CHAPTER 11

Buyouts—Sponsored

The lion and the calf shall lie down together, but the calf won't get much sleep.

—Woody Allen

This is the second chapter on sponsored buyouts. This chapter assumes that the Private Equity Group (PEG) has been invited in by the seller and the management is not a key driver in the transaction. The intent of the sponsor in this chapter is to acquire a controlling interest in the candidate company, and typically apply its ability to raise appropriate capital (debt and equity) to assist the candidate in growth opportunities. The clear intent in such transactions is to build a company's revenue and profitability as quickly as possible all the while planning the exit of said company within a carefully defined window. As in the prior chapter a standard nomenclature is used to represent the equity sponsor, in this case it is a PEG. To the PEG, the management of the company is important but not essential. The goal of passing significant equity to the management is typically not a major consideration. Management may participate in the growth of the value of the business but on a significantly reduced scale compared to Chapter 10.

This is a proven business model with many outstanding financial successes. The basic business template is to identify a candidate company, provide sufficient financial resources to enable the company to attain some significant short term goals and then to craft an exit vehicle to magnify this performance spurt. The exit vehicles may be realized by selling to a strategic buyer (often much larger and publically held) for a substantial premium, selling to a larger PEG, or preparing the company for an initial public offering (IPO).

From a general perspective, many of the candidates are technology and communications companies. There is a broad understanding here of technology companies in that many industries have technology applications. We may find technology-centric core capabilities in a variety of industries such as automotive, manufacturing, and agriculture. What is attractive about technology companies is that their products and services can find a rapidly expanding market because the latest application is making the legacy technology obsolete. The focus on returns is largely driven by product and service obsolescence within a short period of time. Technology changes rapidly, and in many cases today's winners are tomorrow's losers. The casualty rate among such firms can be significant. The old adage of striking while the iron is hot certainly applies in this case.

> Successful sponsored buyouts in this category are really intended for a narrow range of businesses that are poised for substantial upside potential providing they have access to sufficient capital to make the potential a reality. Simply over-leveraging mature companies with untenable amounts of debt is most often a losing situation.

Unquestionably, one of the primary driving aspects of transactions in this chapter is to realize significant growth in the shortest period of time. One of the main attractions to using a PEG where the company has considerable upside revenue and profit potential is access to capital, both debt and equity. The PEG will be aware of the potential calls on resources and is in a position to deliver on a timely basis if goals are being met. The PEGs are very exacting in the qualities they seek in candidate companies. Certain industries have provided a rich source of transactions that have proven to be strong investments. While it's not totally accurate to generalize about the candidate industries, certain industries have offered the best prospects for profitable growth.

ADVANTAGES

The application of this business model is fairly well defined for our purposes. The investment criteria for the PEGs are very demanding. While profitability is always an integral part of the analysis, growth opportunities often dominate the decision of whether or not to invest. Often the one major item missing from the candidate company is the lack of financial resources to take advantage of the vast market for the main product or service. So much energy goes into developing the product or service; building a sales and marketing organization simultaneously places too much stress on the ability to grow internally.

Dedicating substantial financial resources for example to the marketing efforts of a core product or service may be a highly risky environment. Outstanding sales personnel will pay for themselves, as the theory goes. It may take time for those new associates to become highly productive, and while this orientation is occurring they are consuming compensation dollars. Perhaps the effort requires establishing new offices taking the candidate company into the business of managing far-flung branches. Many candidate companies in the technology fields have few assets to stand as collateral to senior lenders. Such senior level sources of funding are always thinking, if something goes wrong, how they are to be repaid. In this case it's accounts receivable primarily. Finding a resource such as a PEG that already understands the industry, both the risks and rewards, is an excellent combination. Traditional financing is supplanted by informed risk capital. Such PEGs typically must have substantial resources to be a player in this field. The risks are substantial, but the rewards may be spectacular, particularly when the timing is perfect.

Depending on the strength of the core products and services, the seller may be in a strong negotiating position to demand a substantial amount of cash at closing with limited contingencies. This was the case during the dot.com transaction feeding frenzy of the late 1990s. Anyone with a sufficient memory of that time will remember the market quickly disintegrating in the financial meltdown of 2000–2001. Technology companies for a period of time lost their investment aura as a result of the speculative buying binge on the part of many PEGs and failed IPOs. The broader financial markets will always be eventually interested in yields and returns on investment (ROIs). The discredited companies and investment theories of a decade ago may come back into favor one day because the technology market does promise one of the golden attributes for investors, namely growth.

When investment criteria are matched with candidate companies, the resulting transaction may result in spectacular, albeit often short term, financial gains. The PEG will be thinking ahead to the time of exiting the company once carefully defined goals are attained.

CAUTIONS

Clearly, this is a higher risk endeavor. The financial exposure is often very great because the returns are predicated on such things as intellectual property, rapid technology obsolescence, and talented individuals; but not the hard production assets as in manufacturing and distribution. The next twist in technology development may render the candidate company obsolete, and the investment is quickly diminished. The candidate investment industries are in rapid motion and timing the investment is critical for success.

The PEGs in such cases are often strategic analysts and typically have substantial industry expertise. This is often a driving factor in how generous the sponsor may be toward the existing management. The existing management must be guarded about their financial security and try to negotiate financial or equity participation in the business when the decision to exit or "flip" the company is made. If the business is in fact sold within a reasonable time after the investment, the legacy management may be at serious risk if a new buyer is introduced. Perhaps a select few managers may participate in the venture, particularly if they are "impact" or key employees due to education or experience that is highly valued. Many other less critical managers will typically be replaced or found to be redundant if the successor company or owner decides to move operations in the interests of greater efficiencies.

Management may or may not be able to negotiate a significant percentage of the financial rewards when the company is resold. The ability to negotiate a package is a function of important attributes such as contribution to product and services development, key customer contacts, industry knowledge, and similar concerns. The risk of losing a key manager to a competitor at a sensitive time in the product development may also contribute to negotiating strength. Often the window of opportunity when the individual's skills are paramount may be reduced because technology changes so rapidly.

These types of transactions are often substantial commitments of resources by a PEG. Keeping in mind there is often a race to grow the business, one tremendous attribute of the PEG is to be able to fuel opportunity with financial resources. Such financial strength may come at a cost to the company since the resources required are often considered investment and more speculative endeavors and come at a significant cost. Management participation percentages and amounts are typically carefully limited by the PEG.

VALUATION

In most cases timing an investment is exceedingly important, particularly with technology-centric companies. If the product or service is rising rapidly, the market value of the company is often subject to the imagination of the beholder. Traditional financial models predicated on such things as the cost of capital and long-term sustainable growth rates are not germane to the analysis. There may be an innate "feel" for the value of the business. PEGs are often proactive in looking for investment opportunities. To entice owners to be interested in selling, the PEG may have to champion a valuation that is attractive. Such a valuation may have to be aggressive and on the upper end of the current range of multiples in the market. Investments are typically intended to be short term with the intention of realizing growth and profit projections and then exiting the business. Anyone with a memory of the dot.com hysteria in the late 1990s knows that the multiples of publicly held technology companies defied the laws of traditional finance. Price earnings multiples were often in the 30s, 40s, and above. In some cases the pricing was almost arbitrary because the internet company had little or no earnings but was a concept with a spectacular future in theory.

This is one section of this book where traditional valuation theory did not often apply prior to 2008. The new reality with the recession is that PEGs are more realistic in the amount that they can afford. Candidate companies will have to demonstrate they survived the recession in reasonably good shape financially. You may have read in the newspapers about all the money that is held by PEGs waiting for investment opportunities, but there are fewer investments that look attractive in a recession.

Auction Environment

One key point to emphasize is the negotiating and communication ability of the PEG principals. There needs to be an understanding of why the business is for sale and what a PEG brings to the table. If a company is a candidate for a PEG investment, the wise seller will aggressively shop the business and may try to establish an auction environment. The auction environment is typically managed by an investment bank with experience in such procedures. The investment bank will often assist the seller in the production of an offering memorandum that casts the company in a positive but realistic light. The investment bank knows the offering memorandum will be aggressively circulated to PEGs and other candidate investors in the hope of garnering interest in the business. In the case of particularly promising companies, it is not unusual to have 6 to 12 interested parties.

In a controlled auction, candidate buyers are given a set period to respond with a serious letter of interest. The seller may select a few of the most promising offers for further discussion in the hope of raising the price by playing one buyer against another. At some point the seller will have to select one investor and pursue the transaction to a close. Even with all this preparation and qualification, an auction environment may still result in the second- or third-best bidders prevailing. In some cases the company may not get sold even with a number of candidate buyers. There may be instances when the auction process results in only a limited number of possible investors, one or two. In this case the negotiating leverage on the part of the seller is greatly reduced, but it still may provide some benefits.

If a bidding environment really develops then the seller may expect a substantial premium. This was more often the case prior to 2008. Of course, the amount of cash at closing may be an issue in addition to performance clauses. At some point the market for more speculative PEG investments may return, but that is likely to be a few years away.

> The involvement of an investment banker or a similarly skilled intermediary experienced in managing an auction environment has a history of gaining the best consideration and terms for a seller. The investment banker will have a cost, but that will typically pale in return to the value that is added.

In today's environment, there is a great caution among PEGs. We are in the midst of a terrible recession, and there are a limited number of candidate companies that have weathered the downturn in reasonable shape. While some deals are being completed, the investment criteria today are exceedingly demanding. PEGs that have experienced losses in their investment portfolios have to answer to their investors. In many cases the PEGs renew funding relationships annually or sooner when draws on capital are made. PEG's are wary of making an investment in an economic environment that could lose money and further erode the relationship with major investors. Another concern is that the market for IPOs is currently depressed, closing one potential avenue for exit.

VIEWPOINT OF THE SELLER

Since the preponderance of these candidates are clustered in the technology fields there is a strong correlation and likelihood that the candidate sellers are "younger." For our purposes they are often in their 30s and 40s, but this is only a generalization. What we often do not find are sellers in their mid to late 60s that have spent a career with the same company. Long careers in a single technology-oriented company are not that common. Owners and key managers often have experience with a number of technology-based firms.

The seller needs a credible reason for placing the company for sale when age does not suggest a time for retirement. There are a number of solid reasons. A few more common reasons include transacting now because the financial resources of the sellers are not sufficient to take advantage of market opportunities, there is concern that financial assistance is required to keep the company current in technology developments, and in some cases burnout because of the intense pressures. The burnout is not a retirement consideration, it is a need to move on to something else. It is important to spend time on this factor because the reasons for the availability of the businesses are not traditional concerns of more established and stable firms. Because the candidate business is likely to be larger, the financial gains to the sellers are often enough to promise a life of future financial independence regardless of the next career or job. Often there is not a sense of loyalty to the business.

The technology world is often ruthless and companies grow, stagnate, and fail at significant rates. Technology companies may only have a useful life of a relatively short number of years before they must be reconfigured, sold, or merged into another entity. Finding an interested buyer with ample financial resources at the right moment is often the dream of technology-based entrepreneurs. For the right price the company is for sale, and historically, the right price was often a substantial number promising a degree of financial independence to the seller. Under such circumstances the sellers will simply move on to the next opportunity.

VIEWPOINT OF THE BUYER

The buyer is a PEG looking to earn an appropriate return for its investors. We have assumed in this book that most of the buyouts are for the control of the subject company. This may not be the case. If the goals of the seller and the PEG are openly communicated on the front of discussions, the PEG may be assisting with an investment to grow the business with an exit plan for all the investors within an anticipated period of time. The buyer is focused on the business aspects of the candidate and making a return on the investment. When the time horizon is more immediate, the PEG may be making the investment in a "bolt-on" company, or a company that is very complementary to other portfolio investments. The PEG is investing in an industry where they already have significant operating experience. Due to the risky nature of the industry, the focus is on maximizing gains in the shortest period of time. There is more limited concern about the long-term prospects for the business. The successful companies of today may enjoy fleeting gains before competitors react to the products and services and drive them into obsolescence or offer more sophisticated alternatives.

Before 2008 there was often a sense of urgency to develop a fast growth business plan, execute the plan, and capitalize on the upward trajectory of results. Investments were often accompanied with a significant degree of speculative outlook. In today's depressed economy, the mood among PEGs is far more reserved. The potential IPO option is greatly reduced today. While it may come back, industry IPO statistics are a cause for alarm. The U.S. market for IPOs (mostly technology companies) is very limited save a few blockbuster deals. Smaller IPOs are not as common due in part to the higher costs of disclosure, reporting, and compliance.

Sellers benefit from an auction environment and having a number of potential suitors bidding up the value of the company. Many PEGs rail at such an environment and refuse to get involved in a bidding war as they have an investment philosophy that precludes such a ruthless beginning. There is often merit to the position, but the seller will have to decide on what values are most important.

As a result of the recession, the business model of the PEGs just prior to 2008 is being challenged. Growth prospects by necessity have to be more reasonable. The PEGs have a blend of their own capital and the capital of other investors seeking higher returns than the promise of public company returns. In essence since 2000 public company indices of value have not significantly increased in value. Yes, some companies have paid dividends, but equity returns have been depressed by two major recessions. PEGs have to be careful about over-representing investment capabilities to their investors because history will catch up with them. You can mislead investors only for a brief time and then your reputation is compromised. Once outside investors turn against a PEG it is a challenging task to find new stakeholders. Investors may be somewhat more tolerant of financial underperformance because most publicly held investments have been challenging during the recession.

The PEG will consider a limited amount of equity participation to the management team if they have highly desirable skills. Said differently, there may be an opportunity for a very limited number of key employees that can make an impact on the performance of the candidate company. The limited amount of participation is often a percentage point or two of the transaction value. Since the PEG is controlling the process, they are not typically seeking to have management investing in the business with their own funds.

PROFESSIONAL ADVISORS

The transaction details will most likely be driven by legal counsel for the PEG. This is close to the sale of the business to a third party. For our purposes the PEG will typically be purchasing control. Great care will be taken in the drafting of the documents to protect the interests of the buyer. Historically, sellers of the candidate companies could interest several PEGs thereby extracting favorable terms. In most cases, a large percentage of the transaction was in cash. That was before 2008. Today, there are fewer transactions, and the percentage of cash that is tendered is an item subject to negotiation.

Looking ahead, the PEG will typically have a law firm that is widely experienced in the sophisticated types of exit options including an IPO, mergers and acquisitions, or selling to a public company. To optimize the total value of the investment, PEGs will carefully consider exit options. Typically a PEG knows what attributes potential buyers want to see for the next transaction. The company will be groomed with an eye to the exit, and a skillful PEG will have a few years to work on the relative appeal of the business. PEGs also realize when it is time to count losses, recoup the investment as best as possible, and move on to the next opportunity.

Sellers should engage a financial advisor that is practiced in asset protection. In many cases the seller has made substantial bets on the business and pledged all manner of assets (including home) to the company. In many cases the seller is entrepreneurial and building the company has consumed personal assets. Finding traditional sources of financing prior to a sale to a PEG is very difficult because the business has few items of interest to a bank seeking collateral. If a sale to a PEG results, the seller is advised to have a financial advisor literate at investing for the long term. This longer-term horizon is often antithetical to the entrepreneurial spirit in technology disciplines due to short product life cycles and the need to continually reinvent.

RISK ENVIRONMENT

Literally by definition, these transactions are often programmed to be leveraged. The intent on the part of the PEG is typically not to repay a significant amount of the debt, but to merely service the obligations for a period of time until the next planned stage for the business, likely a sale to a strategic buyer or an IPO.

The business model is typically predicated on finding both a profitable company and one with strong growth potential. The profitability is required to service the debt obligations, and the growth is the leverage required by the PEG to realize the targeted return. Due to the reliance on debt, one of the biggest risks is the unplanned recession that hurts cash flow and puts growth in question. An evolving change in the market or technology may also put a damper on the plans to sell the business within the targeted time frame. The current recession beginning in 2008 has lasted several years; during that time the number of PEG transactions in the middle market has dropped significantly.

Today's Reality

Sponsored buyouts that were initiated just prior to the beginning of the 2007 recession have generally not done well as a result of the broad economic problems in the country. By today's standards many of the leveraged transactions are risky and many have fallen into default provisions of the loan agreements. The loans cannot be called in many cases, but many are placed in "workout" teams with the end goal of ending the relationship. That frequently means the loans have to be refinanced, a difficult set of circumstances if the candidate company is not performing. My reason for mentioning the high default rates is that few saw the depth of the recession and did not think such a plunge would happen.

Unfortunately it did happen, and the global economy is sufficiently interconnected that a similar catastrophe could happen again. Such risks as material uncertainties in the Middle East, a disruption in energy resources, or a "hot" exchange of weaponry between major powers could easily tip the balance. Heavily leveraged buyouts will continue to be perceived as risky and perhaps prohibitively risky for middle market companies in the future.

Many of these recent buyouts are financially disappointing for the PEGs because anticipated returns are not realized. The target company may be successful, but not as successful as planned by the PEG. An underperforming company will be sold if possible by the PEG in order to free the committed capital which may be reinvested elsewhere. The PEG will have a number of plans to exit the business on a sliding scale of relative likelihood. Often the underlying core company is a viable business but due to any number of factors, it is not meeting the financial expectations of the PEG. The PEG will want to get its investment back, and is not in a position to accept a fire-sale price if avoidable. The PEG may be forced to hold the investment until the market returns.

COMPUTER SUPPORT SERVICES COMPANY

Computer Support Services Company (Company) is well established in a four-state area on the eastern seaboard of the United States. Founded in 1980, it has steadily grown and has witnessed an increasing amount of growth as the population ages. The Company had done a credible job of justifying price increases, but such increases had been just barely keeping up with inflation and rising costs. The founder and his wife were both in their late 60s and wanted a rapid exit vehicle as most of their net worth was committed to the Company. Selling the business for an optimal price was paramount and several interested prospects were bidding on the Company. After an analysis of competing proposals the owners selected ABC Equity, a private equity firm with several similar portfolio companies in different regions of the country. The overall price was approximately $40 million with 90% of the price paid in cash at closing. Management did not have the resources to make an offer and an ESOP required too much seller financing.

ABC Equity may be perceived as a strategic buyer adding a "bolt-on" company and willing to pay a premium price for the Company because of prior experience and the fact they own four other similar companies in different geographic regions. On a combined basis ABC has computer support services in 15 states including this acquisition. ABC Equity is proactively looking to expand its reach. Eventually its exit plan may be to combine all of the related portfolio companies into one large consolidated enterprise that is taken public or sold to a large national computer services provider. The senior team at the Company has been together for a number of years and they work well as a unit, but none of the managers has unique skills. ABC Equity has a strong management team at the corporate level that is focused on growing the in-home care business quickly.

While the senior management was a contributor to the success of the Company, their skills were recognized as competent but not essential to operations. ABC Equity will appoint a general manager from the senior management that reports to its Group President overseeing the in-home portfolio of companies. The senior team was provided modest incentives subject to the Company attaining specified operating results. The management incentives will be paid only upon the sale of the Company to a next owner, and only after ABC Equity has obtained its targeted return. Management is at risk for nominal equity participation or even no participation if ABC Equity fails to meet its targets. Additionally, the management incentive program is subject to forfeiture if a senior manager's employment is terminated before a liquidity event. Senior management is reviewed by ABC Equity, and failure on their part to meet expectations will likely result in employment being terminated. ABC Equity will replace an underperforming individual from the existing stock of other managers in their portfolio.

TECHNICAL MATTERS

The PEG is clearly driving this transaction structure, but will typically require some assistance on the part of the management. While management input may be helpful, they will not be asked to make a meaningful investment in the company, and their equity upside potential is limited.

The PEG may consider a range of managerial incentives that provide economic worth to the managers but cap their participation in the capital appreciation. This is often the key consideration because management typically is not asked to be at significant risk if the transaction turns sour. The primary risk is with the PEG, and it is reasonable to assume they will stand to gain substantially all of the upside potential. There are a range of incentives that may be considered, but they depend on the legal structure of the acquiring company.

Capital Structure

The PEG has its own sources of capital that it invests in the business. For the most established PEGs they have a considerable capital base that is their own funds. This capital base may be supplemented by commitments from other sources of capital such as insurance companies, pensions, and educational endowments. The intent of the PEG under this business model is to invest and provide a target return to the investors when an exit strategy is implemented. The PEG will typically negotiate a program with its major investors that considers how funding is drawn and how the funding is repaid. The investment by the PEG is conceptually considered to be capital, since it will be subordinated to the debt that may be part of the overall buyout including senior debt or mezzanine debt as appropriate.

The overall capital structure for the candidate company after the sale will include debt as part of the investment by the PEG, and it will almost certainly include debt from more traditional sources of financing. The senior level debt will be secured by the assets of the candidate company and the PEG investment. Mezzanine debt for example may also be employed to fill in the gap between the transaction price and all the resources deployed by the PEG. The mix of debt placed on the company may result in debt service obligations that are substantial.

Carried Interest and Management Fees

It is customary for PEGs to anticipate an acceptable ROI on their investment. The overall financial return may be comprised of several elements. This topic has already been considered in Chapter 10, and it is only briefly mentioned again. The PEG typically charges its investors a management fee of 1% to 2% and carried interest up to 20%. The carried interest fee is often in the range of 15% to 20% of the gain on the sale of the portfolio company after the return of capital to the investors and after achieving a hurdle rate (i.e. 8%).

The PEG is investing funds and will still have to meet its own financial obligations such as payroll, rent, and marketing and business development expenses, while maintaining relationships with their investors. These expenses are covered by the management fee that the PEG charges its investors, however, the PEG may also seek to have portfolio companies contribute to these costs via director fees, preferred stock dividends, or administrative fees. The successful PEGs will have a portfolio of companies, and the larger number of investments will provide the critical mass to make the business plan for the PEG viable.

SUMMARY

This structure comes closest to the sale of the business to a third party. The PEG is the controlling party in this structure and typically looks to maximize financial gains. There is little emotional attachment to the business and the employees. There have been a number of notable successes, but those often reflect technology firms that hit the jackpot due to strong growth, thorough analysis, and a healthy dose of good timing. A few stellar investments often will counter a much larger number of lackluster transactions.

This investment strategy is risky with high costs and in some cases very high returns. PEGs must thoroughly understand the market dynamics and brace for the viability of the fund or time with outside investors.

CHAPTER 12

Buyouts—Management and Employee Stock Ownership Plans and Trust

The man who waits for roast duck to fly into mouth waits very very long time.

—Chinese Proverb

This is the first of two chapters focused on the applications of using an Employee Stock Ownership Plan and Trust (ESOP). This chapter addresses an inside buyout whereby the management, possibly the founders and an ESOP, are used to acquire the ownership interest of exiting shareholders. This represents a consortium of stakeholders including individual investors along with the ESOP. The next chapter is dedicated to situations where the ESOP is the sole shareholder going forward, and the primary reason for this singularity is largely driven by overwhelmingly positive tax and cash flow attributes. The next two chapters are organized to provide an overview of ESOPs in a readable narrative followed by illustrations of how an ESOP works and a discussion of the major applicable rules and regulations.

This chapter concentrates on circumstances where the successor management of the business (or successor shareholders including investors and family members) is an integral part of the buyout. We assume that individual managers and key employees will have an actual equity stake in the business. For a wide range of reasons, an ESOP is also employed to be part of the buyout. In most cases the ESOP is in part used because of the strong tax attributes it brings to the transaction environment.

Buyouts embracing the use of an ESOP enjoy great flexibility as to structure and the ability to meet the goals of both the sellers and the buyers. While

ESOPs have an earned reputation for tremendous flexibility, they are also subject to an array of applicable Federal rules and regulations largely due to the tremendous tax advantages they enjoy. One key aspect of the chapters on ESOPs is that they exist in a rigorous regulatory environment, and the major aspects of the regulations will be addressed later in the respective chapters. This is done so as to make the concepts of an ESOP understandable, with the caveat that this overview must be considered in light of the regulatory environment for a successful application.

ADVANTAGES

ESOPs are often perceived as a "win-win" development because of the tax benefits accruing to the sellers, and the economic and tax benefits to the buyer, the ESOP. ESOPs, however, enjoy a range of applications in addition to making a market for the stock of selling shareholders.

Traditional Uses of an Employee Stock Ownership Plan and Trust

- One of the most publicized applications for an ESOP is to make a market for the stock of a shareholder wishing to leave the business. The reasons for leaving may be retirement, failing health, diversification of finances, or a wide range of personal issues. The ESOP may acquire the stock from a departing shareholder with pre-tax dollars and the sale of the stock is typically a favorably taxed event for the seller.
- An ESOP may also be used as a strategy to raise capital. Contributions to an ESOP are tax deductible within payroll limits. The company may contribute authorized but unissued stock to the ESOP at its fair market value (FMV). The company obtains a valuable tax deduction for the contribution of the new issue stock to the ESOP without an offsetting cash outflow. The tax savings to the company represents a source of capital. For example we assume the company is in a 40% tax bracket, and the company contributes the FMV of $100,000 of new issue stock to the ESOP. The company receives a tax deduction of $100,000, and the tax savings are $40,000 ($100,000 × 40% rate = $40,000 tax savings). The tax savings in this case represents cash that is not going to Washington; rather it is retained in the company, hence a source of capital. This strategy is a source of capital to acquire equipment, facilities, or another company. This strategy is also dilution to existing shareholders since new stock is being issued. The relative dilution to existing shareholders is offset against the contribution of capital.

- The ESOP is an employee benefit provided by the company. Many companies adopt the ESOP as an incentive for the employees to stay, and make contributions to the financial success. The employees are provided the opportunity to share in the financial success of the company thereby aligning the interests of all of the "owners." Employee productivity is typically increased when the installation of the ESOP is accompanied with ongoing communications.
- When an ESOP is used in conjunction with ownership interests on the part of other investors, this signals to all stakeholders in the company that there is a succession plan. This is an important communication because the universe of stakeholders includes customers, vendors, banks, employees, and the community. The wider community of stakeholders will often be relieved if there is a succession plan. This is particularly the case with a major employer in a more rural region where the loss of that company to a third-party buyer may have a highly negative impact on the region.

Selling Stock to the Employee Stock Ownership Plan and Trust

Employing the use of an ESOP as part of the buyout strategy means that the exchange is contemplated only as a stock-based transaction. An ESOP may only purchase the stock of a selling shareholder, and by default managers and key employees will also be acquiring stock.

Typically, a stock-based transaction is highly favored by the seller because it means the sale is likely a capital gain taxable event. With ESOPs the gain on the sale of stock is a function of the company being an S corporation or a C corporation (only corporations may have an ESOP). As an S corporation, the gain on the sale subject to the applicable holding period is taxable to the selling shareholders as capital gain. As a C corporation, the gain on the sale subject to applicable holding periods may be taxable as either capital gain or there is a special election available only to individual shareholders in a C corporation to have the gain fully deferred ("tax free") under IRC Section 1042. The IRC Section 1042 election will be illustrated later in the chapter, but it essentially enables the selling shareholder to defer all taxes on the sale of stock to the C corporation ESOP once qualifying regulations are satisfied. The key regulations include selling at least 30% of the value of the corporation to the ESOP, and investing the sale proceeds into qualified replacement property (QRP) within one year of the transaction date. Compliance issues are strict if the IRC Section 1042 election is made.

Purchase of Stock with Pre-Tax or After-Tax Dollars

Management has the opportunity to acquire a direct equity stake in the business, but as previously indicated this equity stake must be acquired with after-tax dollars. Even if the company assists management with loans or extended terms, the stock will still be acquired with after-tax dollars. Management, having acquired its stake in a hard-earned manner, may appreciate the ownership interest and work harder to insure the investment grows. Management enjoys the appreciation of the investment until such time as the employment in the company ends, and the investment is redeemed or sold to a successor owner. In many cases management also serves as the directors, key officers of the business, and as trustees of the ESOP. Management typically serves in many corporate governance roles, and while it is common in many privately held companies, this is not recommended. Conflicts of interest may arise with the duties and obligations of the various positions and the same individual serving in conflicted roles is placed in a potentially litigious situation.

While managers and investors acquire an equity interest with after-tax dollars, the ESOP is distinctive in its ability to acquire the same equity interest with tax-deductible dollars. The advantage of this attribute will be illustrated in our examples. The clear advantage of this tax benefit is easy to see if the effective income tax rate is 40%. The outside investor must produce $100 in after-tax dollars to acquire stock in the company. The ESOP on the other hand only has to produce $60 for the same investment ($100 less the 40% tax savings or $40).

> Making a tax-deductible contribution to an ESOP is the only area in the tax code I have seen where the debt principal is also tax deductible. The higher the effective marginal tax rates on the parties of interest, the more valuable this unique attribute.

Employee Stock Ownership Plan and Trust as a Shareholder

Employees of the company become "owners" though their participation and eligibility in the ESOP. The ESOP is actually a trust that owns the stock for the beneficial interest of the plan participants. The employees gain a tangible and viable economic interest represented by the value of the stock that is allocated to their account. Employees will receive a statement of account listing at a minimum: the shares of ESOP stock, its value per share, additional assets in the account (cash or cash equivalent), and the vesting percentage. With time this account will grow in value providing a significant sense of ownership in the business. Many employees will understand the significance of this benefit immediately; other employees may come to realize this benefit with time as the account grows. In most cases the company exclusively provides the financial benefit of the ESOP through contributions or dividends with no employee contributions. ESOP participants have a right to minimal disclosure regarding the plan sponsor, the company. Most companies will not permit employees to make contributions to the ESOP because such a direct investment will require extensive financial disclosure about the company including financial statements and results of operations.

CAUTIONS

Most management and ESOP installations involve the use of debt as leverage to acquire stock. The application of debt must be carefully applied so that the company is not so overly burdened with acquisition obligations as to threaten its survival. In these types of buyouts, the transaction is typically accomplished over time. The company is literally buying itself by the application of its earnings to the transition process in a highly tax efficient manner.

ESOPs are qualified plans under Federal regulations (the Employee Retirement Income Security Act—ERISA). Every ERISA qualified plan is really a trust that requires the designation of a trustee with fiduciary responsibilities. Fiduciary responsibilities are very strict requirements regarding the conduct of overseeing the assets of the ESOP. The trustee obligations are to be taken very seriously and it is highly recommended that only fiduciary obligation–literate candidates serve as a trustee.

The size of the proposed transaction may be a consideration. While there are few size limitations in a management buyout, the application of an ESOP changes the metrics. The ESOP requires ongoing valuations, record keeping, and often the engagement of an outside trustee. These services have a cost, and that cost may be beyond the benefit that small companies see in such a structure.

Federal regulations inhibit the concentration of too much equity into the ESOP account balances of a few employees for S corporations only. Business owners and their advisors must be aware of S corporation ESOP anti-abuse statutes, discussed in detail shortly. If this buyout strategy is to be viable a working rule of thumb is that the company needs approximately 20 full-time employees to stay compliant with the anti-abuse statutes and the potentially ruinous excise taxes that may be imposed.

Repurchase Obligation

There are a myriad of benefits to using an ESOP, but there is an overriding financial consideration longer term. Once the ESOP acquires the stock, the stock is allocated to the accounts of the employees according to Federal regulations. With time the stock allocated to the employee accounts becomes vested, and account balances compound in value until the amount is distributed to the participant. When distributions are made, these payments are generally referred to as the repurchase obligation. This repurchase obligation is a Federally mandated obligation of the company, and the company must redeem the stock of the ESOP participants. Correspondingly, the ESOP participants have an automatic "put" of their stock back to the company for cash, and the company must redeem the stock. The stock may be redeemed by the company back into its treasury (redeemed with after-tax dollars and the stock is retired); or the company may authorize the ESOP to redeem the stock with tax-deductible dollars and the stock remains outstanding. Most companies will authorize the ESOP to redeem the stock and the stock is "recycled" or reallocated to the accounts of the active participants.

The repurchase obligation is a binding commitment to the company. The higher the percentage of outstanding stock owned by the ESOP, the larger the repurchase obligation in dollars. When the ESOP ownership percentage is relatively modest (say under 50%), the repurchase obligation is easily discharged by the company because the amount of stock to be redeemed in any one year is often nominal. The higher the percentage of stock owned by the ESOP, the more care should be taken by company management to address this obligation and to plan for the redemption.

The repurchase obligation may be addressed by companies each year on a "pay-as-you-go" program, or a more comprehensive recycling plan of repurchase and diversification may be adopted. Having a repurchase obligation analysis is recommended when the ESOP-related stock approaches a substantial percentage of the company ownership. This repurchase obligation study is particularly important when the employment of the company is substantial and the financial exposure of a pay-as-you-go may catch a company off guard in a sudden financial downturn.

The repurchase obligation is a signature attribute of ESOPs. While it is a serious consideration, this obligation may also be discharged with tax-deductible dollars. In smaller companies the repurchase obligation may be addressed with a thoughtful spreadsheet listing the major individual account balances and the likely redemption or diversification dates. Larger companies have the option of acquiring third party software that is actuarially centered and analyzes the re-purchase obligation in detail.

Funding the repurchase obligation is accomplished by embracing any number of financial strategies. During good years, the company may contribute extra resources to the ESOP conceptually as a rainy-day fund. The company may have a tacit sinking fund for segregated resources on its balance sheet. The company may maintain debt capacity at a bank, in the event the repurchase obligation is severe debt may be used to secure the cash to meet the obligation. The ESOP documents often permit the company to have the flexibility to redeem stock on an installment basis over several years, thereby spreading the redemption cost into succeeding years.

VALUATION INSIGHTS

This buyout contemplates multiple investors in the process. Managers, investors, family members, and key employees are candidates on one side of the investment register and an ESOP as another investor. As mentioned in Chapter 4, the standard of value of the ESOP is derived by both the IRS and the Department of Labor (DOL). For ease of understanding we will assume the standard is FMV. A different price may exist for the other investors. For example, a defensible discount may apply to the stock price of the shares purchased by outside investors because they are investing after-tax cash and they do not enjoy the statutory protections conferred on the stock owned by the ESOP. Outside investors typically do not have the advantage of a tax-preference buyer willing to make a market for their stock if they leave the company (remember the ESOP may acquire the stock with tax-deductible or pre-tax dollars). If the outside shareholders have a shareholder agreement at all, the redemption options are often limited and hostile from a tax standpoint.

Under the FMV standard of value for ESOPs, the hypothetical buyer will be a C corporation. While there are court cases suggesting S corporation attributes should be considered when determining FMV, those cases involved gift and estate taxes as reviewed only by the IRS and do not include ESOPs. Remember the IRS and the DOL have oversight on ESOP valuations.

Typically the overall value of the company's stock in this instance is likely to be at or near FMV for all the investors. This is often the case for equitable relations between the investors. The point is that the stock will not represent the value of the business to a strategic buyer. While a strategic buyer sounds attractive to the seller because of the implied higher price that is being tendered, it is important to consider the net impact of the transaction after all taxes have been paid and all goals have been considered. For example, the ESOP acquires the stock of selling shareholders with favorable tax consequences for the sellers, whereas an outside buyer may be acquiring the assets with potentially very hostile tax consequences to the seller.

VIEWPOINT OF THE SELLER

One of the most pronounced benefits of this buyout is that the seller is in control of the process. The seller determines the extent to which stock is sold to the investor group, when it is sold, and often the terms of the transaction are largely driven by the seller. This is in sharp distinction to when an outside buyer is acquiring the business, and that buyer is in control of the decision to proceed or not.

Selling to the Associates that Made the Company Successful

Many business owners have an emotional predisposition to sell the company to people they know and trust. In most cases we start with the predisposition to sell to family members. Absent family members interested in the business, the next most commonly mentioned group is key employees and managers. While often very deserving of the ownership opportunity, there typically is a limited ability to purchase and finance the transaction. One of the pronounced limitations is the requirement that such investors must acquire the equity with after-tax dollars. The ESOP is attractive because the "employees" will be owners in the company, including the managers and key associates. The employees are typically an integral part of the financial success of the company. Key employees and managers are often disproportionately responsible for that success.

This buyout is scalable in that the seller determines when stock will be sold, how much stock, and to whom the stock will be sold. If the buyer elects, smaller blocks of stock may be sold to the investors at the outset to get the process started. Beginning modestly enables selling shareholders to retain control of the company while testing the skills and interest on the part of management and employees to assume the responsibilities of ownership.

This is a time-honored consideration to see who will step forward to be the leaders of the company.

The seller may wish to stretch the transition process as he may not be ready to relinquish full control of the company. One substantial advantage of this buyout is that the seller may craft exactly the degree of involvement that suits the individual's goals. Common goals may include establishing ongoing normalized cash compensation, benefits, eligibility for bonuses, and terms on financing if seller notes are provided. One item to note is that shareholders considering selling a partial interest in the business to other investors including management and the ESOP need to allow the new stakeholders to participate on a somewhat prorated basis in the success of the company.

The transaction will be a sale of stock. In most cases this will be a taxable event to the sellers, but it will be taxable at prevailing capital gain tax rates. In narrowly construed circumstances, if the company is a C corporation, selling shareholders may sell their stock "tax free" providing that all regulatory requirements are met (the IRC Section 1042 sale discussed shortly).

Financing Considerations

In this era of closely watched loans, it is very difficult to have traditional sources of funding from banks providing the financing for the transaction. Banks may provide small amounts of funding if modest blocks of stock are being sold. Individual investors may be expected to buy the stock with their own resources (with savings or funding provided by leveraging personal assets). An ESOP has no ready inherent liquidity unless the company contributes cash to the Plan prior to the purchase of stock, an action often called prefunding. Any shortfall in funding between the stock purchase price and the ability to fund with other resources will almost always mean there will be seller financing.

Sellers often object to the very concept of providing the financing, but with today's challenging financial markets the prospects are not as adverse as they may first appear. However, investment return opportunities for sellers with newfound cash are typically not attractive, particularly if "safe" investments are desired (like treasury certificates). Sellers may be compensated for the risks they are assuming by providing financing. Interest compensation for risks may be referenced to commercial loan rates extended by secured lenders, and commercial rates for unsecured loans. Unsecured loans represent the class of transactions where the note is typically not fully collateralized by the assets of the company. Such a position is often perceived to be mezzanine financing, and it carries a much different interest rate than secured lending.

VIEWPOINT OF THE BUYER

The buyer in this instance may be composed of individual investors, such as key employees, and the ESOP. We will consider the viewpoint of individual investors first. Management and key employees are often delighted to have the opportunity to acquire an equity stake in the company. It is important among this group that leadership is demonstrated by at least one or more individuals. Typically, the management team has unequal financial resources or the ability and interest in owning stock. The leadership of the management group is often favored with attractive purchasing terms as a reward for their direction. Managers will be expected to have a tangible investment in the company and not just acquire stock with loans from the company or loans from the seller. It is important to keep spouses informed of the intent to purchase stock. The specter of personal guarantees is an intimidating aspect of this process and spouses may dread pledging personal assets toward the purchase of something as risky as the business.

The upside potential of the purchase may be enormous. Certainly the case can be made that the managers will prosper in the future as a result of their efforts. The focus and dedication of the managers will go a long way to insure the successful outcome of the investment. There are no guarantees with buyouts and with some frequency the best of intentions ends up failing. Sometimes the failure is a personal and financial catastrophe. Our market-based economy permits failure as an integral feature of our society. With the cost of failure so high, people with something at risk will typically strive for success with extraordinary effort.

This structure is typically an outstanding opportunity for the ESOP. The ESOP trust actually owns the stock, and the trustee will make the decision to purchase the stock. The ESOP has no stand-alone ability to pay for the stock and is entirely dependent on contributions or dividends from the company to meet the acquisition obligations. Virtually all ESOPs are 100% funded by the company. The ESOP will allocate the stock into the account balances of the eligible employees over time.

Employee Stock Ownership Plan and Trust Attributes

Conceptually, all employees enjoy the same percentage benefit as a function of their qualifying compensation. Higher compensated employees will enjoy a higher benefit. For example, if the ESOP contribution is 10% of qualifying payroll, the employee earning $100,000 will receive a $10,000 contribution, and the employee earning $30,000 will receive a benefit of $3,000. Contrary to common belief, the ESOP will reward higher-income employees with a greater allocation subject to qualifying limits. The ESOP also rewards loyal employees through vesting and the ability to gain allocations of assets though departing employee forfeitures and stock redemptions. The ESOP participants also gain because the assets in the account are free to compound without taxes until the assets are withdrawn from the plan. Like all other qualified plans, the distributions from a plan are taxed as ordinary income to the individuals, but individuals typically have the election of taking a lump sum distribution or some other extended payout option.

> The ESOP rewards employees according to their contribution to the company (typically expressed in terms of compensation), and it also rewards commitment or tenure. With time the ESOP bestows the greatest participation to those employees that are driving the creation of value.

PROFESSIONAL ADVISORS

The existence of the ESOP will drive the requirement for ERISA- and ESOP-literate advisors. The other investors and the seller may also have a requirement for separate advisors. Due to the close nature of the buyers and the sellers, some advisors may be serving the interests of multiple parties for expediency, particularly in smaller transactions for cost considerations.

Employee Stock Ownership Plan and Trust Trustee

The transaction involving an ESOP must have an ESOP trustee by legal definition. The trustee has the duty to adhere to fiduciary standards and must act prudently in discharging the duties of the position. Anyone may serve as the trustee, but this general statement is accompanied with a great number of practical considerations. The trustee has fiduciary obligations, and the breach of those obligations may subject the trustee to substantial financial penalties. It is a best practice for the trustee to have prior ERISA, and preferably ESOP, experience. The trustee will actually determine the value of the stock; this is exemplified by the process of the trustee engaging an independent financial advisor to compute the FMV of the stock. The trustee may rely on the financial advisor's determination of FMV, but it is the obligation of the trustee to understand the assumptions in the valuation report. The trustee will have to approve the report, and in this approval process the trustee in effect determines the value of the stock. An overview of the trustee and fiduciary responsibilities are considered in more detail later in this chapter.

Employee Stock Ownership Plan and Trust–Literate Counsel

Legal counsel that is experienced with ESOPs and ERISA is very important in these transactions. Initially, the ESOP requires a trustee, and the trustee is advised to have separate legal representation distinct from the other parties to the transactions (e.g. the sellers, the company, and other investors). In smaller transactions, it is common (but not necessarily recommended) for the various parties to share legal representation. Multiple parties may rely on the advice of a lead attorney that is ESOP-literate. The company may engage legal counsel and the sellers may rely on that assistance for insights into the transaction. Outside investors are advised to retain their own advisors to inform them of their interests and legal exposure if something goes wrong. Clearly, in smaller transactions professional advisors are often shared, but legal counsel will certainly advise the various parties that such reliance is not a best practice and if something goes wrong the legal relationships will be acknowledged.

Independent Appraiser

The valuation of the stock acquired by the ESOP must be provided by an independent financial advisor to the trustee. The trustee engages the independent financial advisor, and the trustee has the obligation to act prudently in discharging this obligation. It is appropriate for the trustee to interview candidate advisors to inquire about their overall valuation experience, specific ESOP valuation expertise, experience with the IRS and DOL, any courtroom testimony and experience, and a host of other germane issues. There are a number of highly qualified valuation firms with substantial ESOP experience providing this service and finding a competent firm for the valuation is an important obligation of the trustee. Most ESOP valuations will have a qualifying statement that the value determined in the report is only for ESOP purposes. For the sake of expedience, costs, and understanding, the stock acquired by the management is often valued using the ESOP report. If this is contemplated, the valuation firm should be notified of the multiple uses so that the report adequately covers this point in the analysis. The largest companies may have separate valuations for the ESOP and the managers, particularly when the stock pricing is different for the various investor classes.

Other Advisors

The selling shareholders may have personal financial advisors regarding the transaction. Often the company will retain a CPA firm for accounting services and taxes. The CPA firm typically has earned the status and stature of a trusted advisor over time. It will be a valuable resource on the tax attributes of the transactions related to all sides of the transactions: sellers, management, and the ESOP. The CPA firm often assists in feasibility analysis particularly in such critical areas as cash flow analysis related to servicing acquisition related debt. There are specific financial reporting requirements under generally accepted accounting principles (GAAP) that apply to ESOPs. The primary reporting standard is from the American Institute of Certified Public Accountants Statement of Position 93-6, *Employer's Accounting for Employee Stock Ownership Plans*.

The ESOP will require a record-keeping resource, or an administrator. If the company already maintains a qualified plan such as profit sharing, 401(k), or a pension, a good first contact is to determine if the current record keeper has ESOP experience. ESOP record keeping is often complex and fundamentally different from other types of qualified plans. Most ESOPs have debt, and stock is allocated according to the repayment of acquisition debt determined by a range of contributions, dividends, or S corporation distributions made to the plan. As just represented there are a number of mechanics to allocate stock to account balances, and those methods are very technical. It is a best practice to engage a firm with considerable ESOP administration expertise as the costs of restating incorrectly computed employee balances are very burdensome.

RISK ENVIRONMENT

In most cases these buyouts are not excessively leveraged as all the parties typically wish to have a successful outcome. Excessive leverage may place the company at a high degree of risk if there is a default on the notes. The parties are not adverse in their goals. Taking the succession process in manageable stages is a solid practice. Time is a pronounced ally of this buyout. It permits an orderly transition process with an allowance for the management to earn equity with time and effort.

There is one favorable study recently conducted by the National Center for Employee Ownership (NCEO) that focused on the default rate of buyouts involving an ESOP and buyouts without the use of an ESOP; often sales of the company to an outside third party. In the NCEO *Ownership Update Newsletter* from September 30, 2010 their findings are discussed. The results are not surprising to those close to the employee ownership community, but they may be a very pleasant development for business owners and financial institutions. The incidence of acquisition loan default when an ESOP is involved is a small fraction of normal commercial loan defaults. According to the study, generally between only 1% and 2% of the ESOP Companies were in default during the period 2009 and 2010. The data was provided by ESOP consulting firms. A comparable default rate for non-ESOP companies is substantially higher during the same period, approaching 20% in the worst cases. The non-ESOP company data is based on information regarding publicly held companies. The NCEO indicates that a true comparison is difficult, but the data clearly indicates that the default rates for ESOP debt is much lower.

There are many logical reasons for this favorable ESOP result. The more obvious reasons include not over-leveraging the company, and if the company is facing trying circumstances it is generally a defensible communication to all the employees that costs have to be closely monitored or even reduced to avoid default on the note. The ESOP notes certainly appear to be a more secure risk by a substantial margin.

While most buyouts are carefully negotiated and structured, there is always the risk that in spite of good intentions, there may be a default or company failure. The ESOP trustee may be open to a charge of breach of fiduciary responsibilities if procedures were not documented, followed, or wantonly ignored. The ESOP trustee may be sued in Federal Court for breach of duty, and the potential liability is significant. The fiduciary liability accrues to the individual acting as the trustee. If litigation is commenced against a trustee, the case will be heard in Federal Court where the rules of engagement are strict and expensive because the financial stakes are often exceedingly high. While the potential liability is substantial, following recommended procedures and using an independent ESOP trustee is cost effective and greatly reduces the risks.

Standards for Likely Success

This book is written in an era following one of the most severe recessions in memory. While there is a risk of a company failing, that risk is greatly reduced by adopting a longer-term time horizon to accomplish the buyout. The longer term is intended to reduce the amount of debt that is required to redeem the stock of the exiting shareholders, but it also is an integral part of typically responsible ESOP installations.

The best ESOP candidates are companies with an established history of financial success and with reasonably stable cash flows. Another key ingredient for success is a proven management with years of working together.

Indeed, a management team that has been together for many years often provides the degree of confidence the sellers want to see before agreeing to help finance the transaction.

An open company culture with ongoing communications is one of the best indicators of future success. Companies that already communicate openly with their employees on such matters as customer service, quality production, watching costs, and tracking indices of quality service such as six sigma mechanics are strong candidates for an ESOP. The incidence of a well educated workforce is also a distinct positive as those associates will quickly understand the tax benefits of the ESOP and the philosophy of working together in a common financial interest.

Today there are several scholarly studies linking successful financial performance with employee ownership being effectively communicated to company associates. One of the best resources is *Shared Capitalism at Work Employee Ownership, Profit and Gain Sharing, and Broad-Based Stock Options:* Edited by Douglas L. Krause, Richard B. Freemen, and Joseph R. Blasi (University of Chicago Press, 2010). One takeaway from the studies is that communication combined with employee ownership is a powerful combination. Effective and ongoing communication developing an "ownership culture" may also be positive in non–employee owned companies.

SAMPLE TRANSACTION

Assumed facts—Professional Services Company ("Company"; computer consulting). There are two selling shareholders, 60 employees, S corporation, and a history of consistent profitability supporting the FMV of the Company. There are three key managers buying 30%, 15%, and 15% ownership stakes. The ESOP will purchase the remaining 40%. When the stock is purchased the three managers will retain 60% of the stock and have control of the Company. The FMV of the Company on a minority position basis is $5 million and bank financing was secured for the ESOP purchase of $2,000,000 ($5,000,000 × 40%). The two selling shareholders provided most of the financing for the managers, but that part of the transaction is not pertinent for the ESOP analysis. The senior team was eligible to earn significant

bonuses if the company financially meets its targets, and the bonuses
will help them service their acquisition notes. The senior managers
are provided employment contracts with stated duties. They also receive a shareholder agreement that stipulated how their stock will be
redeemed if their employment is terminated or if they retire.

Exhibit 12.1 indicates the traditional structure of this buyout.

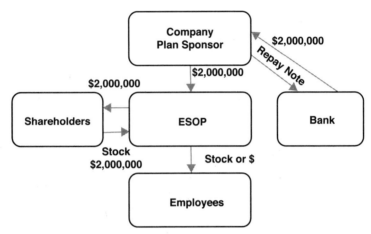

EXHIBIT 12.1   Sample ESOP Transaction

The flow of the transaction is illustrated in the following steps.

- The two retiring shareholders are selling 40% of the stock to the
  newly created ESOP for a total of $2,000,000.
- The Company has arranged financing from a bank for the entire
  ESOP purchase amount. The bank lends $2,000,000 to the Com-
  pany in order to gain a secured position on all the assets of the
  business ("outside loan").
- The Company advances the $2,000,000 to the ESOP ("inside
  loan").
- The ESOP buys the 40% block of stock from the retiring shareholders with the $2,000,000 in cash. The 40% block stock is held
  as collateral by the ESOP.
- Selling shareholders receive the cash. Since this is a stock sale, any
  gain will be taxed at capital gain rates.

- As the ESOP acquisition debt is repaid according to the "inside note," a prorated portion of the stock held as collateral is released to the ESOP participants. The stock is allocated to the accounts of the ESOP participants according to the eligible payroll; generally each employee's reported W-2 earnings.

- For planning purposes, the Company will often want to pre-pay the "outside" note and remove the debt from the balance sheet. Having a separate "inside" note allows the repayment of the outside note as soon as cash flow permits without accelerating the release of stock from collateral and also accelerating the repurchase obligation.

Case Study—Woodman's Food Market, Inc. Woodman's Food Market, Inc. (Woodman's or the Company) is a leading regional retail grocery chain featuring an extensive line of products including: bakery, dairy, meat, produce, frozen foods, and other complementary offerings. Today Woodman's is noteworthy for embracing super stores with the newest additions to the 13-store chain ranging in size from 200,000 to 250,000 square feet. The most recent stores feature expansive retail space and are joined by dedicated warehouse facilities. Due to its size and smart purchasing protocols, the Company buys a material percentage of its inventory directly from major national producers and stores the products in the dedicated warehouse space it controls. Woodman's offers in total over 67,000 different items dwarfing the number of products offered in most other retail grocers. The dedicated focus of serving customers has produced enviable revenue results. Woodman's passed $1 billion in sales in 2009.

The Company has not always been the modern-day success demonstrated recently. The business started on a roadside corner in 1919 by the then farmer and entrepreneur John Daniel Woodman (first generation). He was joined in the business by son Willard John Woodman (second generation) and in 1921 founded a food store in Janesville, Wisconsin. The family remained dedicated to retail food sales over the years. Phil Woodman (third generation), son of Willard John Woodman, joined the Company upon graduation from college in 1966. Phil Woodman is the current President. The first superstore covering 90,000 square feet was built in Madison, Wisconsin in 1979, followed by another superstore in the same city in 1984 that covers 210,000 square feet (over 4 acres). Today, all of the locations are considered superstores with attached warehouse space. Clint Woodman (fourth generation) continues the family dedication to excellence and began his tenure with the Company on the retail floor sweeping aisles, arranging produce, taking direction, listening, and learning the businesses from the ground floor. Clint Woodman has already logged over 20 years with the Company and is currently a Vice President.

The Company has consistently experienced growth opportunities during its history. Expanding the Company in the earliest years was always a financial challenge. According to current President Phil Woodman, during the 1970s the highest marginal income tax rates on the Company approached 50%. He studied the tax benefits of recently enacted ESOPs, and discovered that authorized but unissued stock in Woodman's could be contributed to an ESOP at its FMV. By way of a stock contribution, the Company receives a tax deduction in full and within contribution limits for the FMV of the stock. The Company receives a valuable tax deduction with no outlay of cash. Conceptually, this application of an ESOP is a capital creation plan. Capital is created by the tax savings for the Company by gaining a tax deduction with no cash expense. Using the prevailing math of the day, a share of stock contributed to the ESOP at a hypothetical value of $2.00 per share is worth almost $1.00 in tax savings (investment capital). More shares are outstanding as a result of the new issue stock contribution, and there is some equity dilution to the existing shareholders.

According to Phil Woodman, "The potential dilution of the shareholder's equity has to be analyzed in relation to the financial benefit of the capital creation. We were able to invest the tax savings generated by the ESOP into the growth of the Company. Additionally, we communicated with our employees they have a piece of the equity in the business." Discretionary Company contributions to the ESOP continued for a number of years. In 1998 the family sold a sizable block of stock to the ESOP.

When you drive past a Woodman's superstore you are impressed with the size of the facility. You cannot miss the wording prominently featured that says "Employee Owned." Clint Woodman states, "Our ongoing commitment to employees and the communities we serve are testimony to the long-term vision we have taken in building Woodman's into a regional leader." The Company continually reinforces the fact it is employee owned and has worked diligently to build a culture of ownership and community pride throughout the organization. It is an ongoing feature at Woodman's among its 9,000 satisfied employees. During the time the Company has been contributing to the ESOP, employees have come to recognize the special culture of ownership and involvement that has been created. Clint Woodman offers, "Our employees make a significant difference in our approach to customer service, and having them as our partners in the Company is a tremendous benefit."

One can only imagine the smile on John Daniel Woodman's face if he could witness the Company he started at a crossroads almost 100 years ago.

Case Study—Molded Dimensions, Inc. Originally founded in 1954, Molded Dimensions, Inc. (MDI, or the Company) has migrated to a firm that engineers and molds custom rubber and polyurethane mechanical parts for original equipment manufacturers (OEM) and aftermarket industries. The company is fully integrated with capabilities from material and tool development through full production including worldwide manufacturing resources as needed. MDI has served major accounts in a wide range of industries including healthcare, construction, waste management, marine, automotive, high speed packaging, electronics, and capital equipment. Located near Milwaukee, MDI services companies primarily located in the heartland.

Mike and his wife Linda (from the area) Katz are alumni from larger publically held corporations and they were looking to acquire a company in the Milwaukee area. Both were fascinated with the metrics of smaller privately held businesses. The process of making contacts and networking over several months began. This often frustrating experience led to numerous dead ends, but one such contact produced a viable lead. Having looked at several other prospects, Mike and Linda gained some level of expertise in asking questions to qualify the candidate company. If the right circumstances prevail Mike and Linda would make an offer (the "stars in alignment theory of acquisitions" according to Mike). This time patience paid off and Mike and Linda found a suitable business owner interested in selling his company.

Getting the Deal Closed The good news is that the business owner was interested in selling. The less good news is that the asking price was beyond the financial capability of Mike and Linda. Mike and Linda talked to the owner and said they could only afford an amount that was still at least 10% below a reasonable expectation of value. The asking price gap was bridged with the introduction of an ESOP. As part of the acquisition, the ESOP would become an investor (minority position) along with Mike and Linda. The owner was captivated by the idea of having his employees participating in the sale; he agreed to provide a subordinated note on behalf of the ESOP so that the transaction could close at an acceptable number. The note to the ESOP was repaid with tax deductible dollars, whereas the investment by Mike and Linda had to be made with after-tax dollars. In April 2001 the new owners of MDI gathered on the production floor just in time for serious participation in the recession. Mike and Linda know nothing about ESOPs prior to acquiring MDI, but once the mechanics were explained they embraced having the employees as their partners.

Following the handshakes and good wishes, the task of getting to work on the production floor began. Mike says: "The jeans and steel pointed shoes seem like a long way from the public company environment." From the outset, information was shared with the employees. Ongoing communications regarding the ESOP were commenced and in time the concept of shared goals became an accepted fact. The recession was taking its toll on the leveraged Company. Watching the cash very closely, MDI survived the first few critical years and began to experience profitable growth. Mike and Linda have shared the overall responsibilities of managing the business along with a number of key managers. This partnership has enabled Mike and Linda the flexibility to have an enviable private and family life coexistent with the challenges of directing a growing closely held company.

Today the Company has prospered and continues to grow even through a second major recession since the acquisition. Continuous improvements in production have been implemented and information is routinely shared with the employees. The commitment to processes and controls is ongoing and near legendary with MDI producing yearend financial statements within days of the closing. No small task with job shop and manufacturing accounting. Not surprisingly, MDI has communicated routinely with its bankers and has always met commitments. When the time to expand presented itself, the financing was already in place.

The MDI future looks to be very positive. A loyal and motivated workforce is ready to assist in the product development and service evolution. Mike works well in small groups noting: "We have ongoing meetings with the employees on such matters as financial literacy and the impact of costs on MDI. I like to have more frequent meetings with eight employees or less so their voices may be heard and input acknowledged." MDI has developed a culture of ownership with everyone thinking about costs and their impact on the Company. Having engaged employees has made the MDI financial rewards substantially larger than on the date of purchase and that is a winning situation for everyone.

Case Study—Oconomowoc Residential Programs, Inc. Oconomowoc Residential Programs, Inc. (ORP or the Company) has been under the current management since 1984. ORP has a highly developed and defined mission: ORP's vision is to be the provider of choice for people with disabilities. For over 25 years the Company has provided an array of services within a continuum of care for children, adolescents, and adults with a variety of disabilities. Those services include capabilities in therapeutic care, residential support, day care, community based programs, and in-home services for people with developmental, behavioral, medical, and emotional needs.

The values of ORP are endemic throughout the organization and include such items as:

- Commitment to social justice for people with disabilities
- Their work as a vocation makes a difference in the lives of people with disabilities
- Honesty, integrity and constancy of purpose
- Employee ownership, sound financial management and a commitment to growth and development

The commitment to growth embraces the building of an ever more professional organization, but also a focus on training and development of the ORP team.

ORP manages over 100 separate different care facilities located in Indiana and the home state of Wisconsin. As championed, ORP is a family of employee owned companies. Those facilities become mainstays in the communities where they are located and a beacon of hope and promise for the people that come to rely on their helping and sensitive assistance. The Company has grown over time to the point where it currently encompasses in excess of 2,000 employee owners. ORP established an ESOP in 2002. The ESOP owns 30% of Company's stock. According to Chief Executive Officer Jim Balestrieri, "Having our employees as partners and stakeholders in the Company helps us fulfill the vision of ORP by instilling the values essential for a healthcare service organization." Through ongoing internal communication and training programs, employees have embraced the sense of alignment between the interests of the owners and the mission to be of service in the community.

The Company is largely dependent on government funding and government reimbursement programs. The outlook for the services provided by ORP is positive with an aging population. Getting the government to recognize the essential services provided by companies like ORP and continuing to provide funding at necessary levels will be an ongoing challenge.

The current ownership enjoys the freedom to establish goals, values, and policies consistent with the ORP vision. Having the ESOP is always an option for the current outside investors seeking ready liquidity. Financial literacy training has been accelerating at ORP since the ESOP has been on the scene. David Nagy, Chief Financial Officer, states, "The financial acumen gained through being an employee-owner gives ORP's staff a competitive edge in negotiating rates and contracts with customers." ORP prides itself on its employee ownership as a mark of distinction in the healthcare community. The management of the Company in concert with its employees decides on the level of care and support offered to individuals, not a distant and removed corporate office of some larger enterprise.

While it is beyond the scope of this overview to discuss each of the ORP operating units, specific mention is made of the Oconomowoc Developmental Training Center (ODTC). Located on 160 acres of wooded countryside, the facility symbolized the ORP commitment to ongoing state-of-art education for the entire community served. The facility offers a full complement of training capabilities backed by a professional staff of experienced caregivers. Within the ODTC the Genesee Lake School offers comprehensive services for students age 4–21 with a variety of behavioral, social, emotional, and academic needs. The goal of Genesee Lake School is to prepare students to return to their home school and succeed in the least restrictive environment possible. The educational capabilities are extensive at ODTC, but the point to emphasize is the Company has the resources and the caring staff to fulfill its vision. The educational commitment has been extended to the supervisors and managers at all of the facilities. According to Jim Balestrieri, "The ESOP has been instrumental in helping our managers understand the financial administration of the business and justify rates and reimbursement programs before applicable regulatory agencies."

The ORP family of employee-owned companies is structured to grow in resources and grow in the number of individuals served. Providing the highest standard of care is not possible without the commitment of all the employees. The senior management team has taken extensive steps to be stewards of an organization by meeting its needs across the spectrum of human resource capabilities and the physical facilities needed to be of service. ORP is on the right path to provide the care of the Company vision today, tomorrow, and well into the future.

TECHNICAL MATTERS

This section is provided for those business owners and their advisors seriously considering an ESOP. This will have appropriate code citations and references to applicable procedures in anticipation of a sale of stock to the management and the ESOP. ESOPs are Federally regulated and this section is intended to consider the major provisions of such regulations. Clearly, if an ESOP is being considered appropriate legal and professional counsel should be consulted to insure compliance with all regulations.

The sellers and management may negotiate an almost limitless variety of transaction structures. There is great flexibility in such matters regarding a wide range of issues such as classes of stock, dividend preferences and other matters. Only a corporation may have an ESOP.

Employee Stock Ownership Plan and Trust and Qualifying Stock

An ESOP is a tax-qualified defined contribution deferred compensation employee benefit plan intended to be primarily invested in the securities of the employer (or the plan sponsor) that meets the requirements of IRC Section 401(a) and IRC Section 4975(e)(7). The ESOP is "tax qualified" which means that certain rules have been adopted by the plan to protect the interests of the plan participants. In return for adoption of protective rules, the ESOP receives certain tax benefits. The legal entity that actually owns the stock is the trust (employee stock ownership trust). The trust owns the stock for the beneficial interest of the plan participants. Before cash or stock is contributed to the ESOP, a legal trust must be first created. The employees do not own stock, but the economic value of the stock is allocated to employee account balances subject to applicable rules of ERISA.

The ESOP must own only the class of stock with the highest voting, dividend and liquidation rights. From a practical standpoint, most ESOPs own only the common stock of the employer. Today, most ESOPs are in S corporations, which only permits a single class of stock. When the employer is a C corporation, the ESOP may own preferred stock or super common stock with specifically stated dividend rights IRC Section 409(1).

Employee Stock Ownership Plan and Trust Trustee

The trust actually owns the stock in the ESOP, and the trust will have a trustee with fiduciary responsibilities. General ERISA fiduciary rules are contained in ERISA Sections 401 to 408. It is beyond the scope to describe the extent of fiduciary responsibilities, but an overview of the most important provisions is listed.

- Anyone may become a trustee including company officers or company employees. The fiduciary standard of conduct is very high, and company officers and employees may have conflicts of interest relating to the fiduciary obligations. Companies will often engage an independent outside trustee for the ESOP. Another frequently observed scenario is for the company to maintain an ESOP trust committee comprised of company officers and key employees in concert with an outside trustee. There is no single best structure, but whoever agrees to serve in this capacity is advised to be well versed and literate in the obligations of serving as an ESOP trustee.
- The major provisions of fiduciary obligations are briefly considered. The fiduciary must act for the sole and exclusive benefit of plan participants. This is often referred to as the "exclusive benefit rule" or the "duty of

loyalty," ERISA Section 404(a). This is a high standard of behavior, and any company officer, director, employee, or shareholder may have a conflict of interest with time.

- The fiduciary must discharge duties "with the care, skill, prudence, and diligence under circumstances then prevailing that a prudent man acting in a like capacity and familiar with such matter would use in the conduct of an enterprise of a like character and like aims," ERISA Section 404(a). The fiduciary may rely on the advice and reports of other advisors, but must still perform an independent investigation into matters and should understand the work of other advisors in sufficient detail to reach a personal conclusion. This is generally referred to as the "prudent man" obligation.
- The fiduciary is required to consider the interests of the plan participants only in their position as participants in a qualified retirement plan, ERISA Section 404(a). Other interests are not to be considered. This requirement may place a fiduciary in an exceedingly difficult position when the interests of the ESOP are in conflict with the interests of individual employees. For example, the fiduciary should not consider the impact on employment at the company when making decisions regarding the ESOP.
- The fiduciary is expected to act only in a manner permitted by the plan documents and ERISA, ERISA Section 404(a). The fiduciary must read and understand plan documents, keep the ESOP in compliance with changing statutes, file all applicable reports in a timely manner, have the ESOP stock valued at least annually, and reposed to other duties as detailed in the plan documents.
- The fiduciary is to guard against prohibited transactions as defined in ERISA Section 406(a)(1). Generally, prohibited transactions are those where conflicts of interest and self dealing are in evidence.

The obligations of being an ESOP trustee with fiduciary responsibilities are a high standard of conduct. Such obligations must be taken seriously as the penalties for the breach of fiduciary duties is very substantial. Such penalties may include the financial exposure for losses suffered by the plan, possible excise taxes and other equitable relief determined by a court, ERISA Section 409(a).

While the obligations of being a trustee are significant, there are thousands of ESOPs in closely held companies with no litigation or overt issues. A best practice if you have agreed to be a trustee is to act responsibly, know your obligations, and have the name of a good ERISA attorney in your Rolodex™ for those instances when questions arise. Know when to ask for assistance.

Funding Methods and Contribution Limits

Once the legal entity is created, assets are contributed to the ESOP from a number of common sources including cash, company stock, or debt. The sources of company stock may be newly issued stock, treasury stock, or outstanding stock typically owed by a shareholder.

An ESOP is authorized to borrow money for the purpose of purchasing employer stock. An ESOP is specifically exempted from the general ERISA rules barring a qualified retirement plan from borrowing money to purchase the stock of the employer.

Employers rarely allow employees to acquire stock in an ESOP through direct investment of their own funds. Direct investment of employee funds will require extensive financial disclosure, which most companies are unwilling to make. As participants in an ESOP, the company provides all of the funding in most cases, and as participants in a qualified benefit plan the disclosure requirements are sharply reduced. Employers do not have to disclose financial information about the company or how the stock is valued, for example.

Periodic contributions to the ESOP are tax deductible within established limits set by statutes. Contribution levels are subject to such things as specified payroll limitations and contributions allocated to the accounts of the highly compensated employees under certain circumstances. When contributions to the ESOP are made to repay acquisition-related debt principal and interest, now the debt principal payments become tax deductible if the payments are within the qualifying payroll percentage limitations. Generally interest expense is tax deductible to the company and the debt principal payment is not tax deductible. With an ESOP the interest expense and the principal payments are obligations of the company, and the entire amount is tax deductible within payroll limitations. While the percentage of qualifying payroll that is deductible for tax purposes is generally the same for both C and S corporations, there are a few differences in how the deduction is computed for tax purposes. Those differences are explained in the following paragraphs.

- C corporations have slightly different payroll contribution limits than S corporations. In a C corporation, for years after 2001 the maximum deductible contribution is 25% of IRC Section 404 qualifying annual payroll subject to a number of limitations. The 25% limit will not apply to a participant's deferral contributions to a 401(k) plan for purposes of IRC Section 404, but will apply for IRC Section 415. The cap on participant compensation that may be included for all qualified plan purposes is $250,000 for 2012, and is indexed in $5,000 increments.

The total annual addition limit (including such things as forfeitures) is the lesser of 100% of qualifying pay or $50,000 for 2012, and this amount is indexed in increments of $1,000, IRC Section 415(c)(1). The contribution limit does not include interest expense on ESOP-related obligations if no more than one-third of the plan sponsor's contributions are allocated to the accounts of highly compensated employees within the meaning of IRC Section 414(q).

- In an S corporation, the contribution limits are similar to C corporations with one significant exception. The 25% contribution limit in an S corporation includes the interest expense on ESOP-related debt. This is a significant distinction, especially if an S corporation ESOP is heavily leveraged. In an S corporation, for years after 2001 the maximum deductible contribution is 25% of IRC Section 404 qualifying annual payroll subject to a number of limitations. The 25% limit will not apply to a participant's deferral contributions to a 401(k) plan for purposes of IRC Section 404, but will apply for IRC Section 415. The cap on participant compensation that may be included for all qualified plan purposes is $250,000 for 2012, and indexes the cap in $5,000 increments. The total annual addition limit (including such things as forfeitures) is the lesser of 100% of qualifying pay or $50,000 for 2012, and this amount is indexed in increments of $1,000, IRC Section 415(c)(1).

Multiple Qualified Benefit Plans

Today, companies that sponsor ESOPs often also sponsor other qualified benefit plans such as profit sharing and 401(k). Employer contributions to qualified plans are limited by statute. When multiple plans are maintained, the employer contribution limits are primarily reserved for the ESOP (often the ESOP-required debt repayments). However, self-directed investments by employees (deductions from the employee's compensation) to other benefit plans generally do not count against ESOP contribution percentage. In this manner, the company offers an ESOP, which is primarily invested in the stock of the employer, and also a 401(k) that offers investment diversification. The ability to offer multiple benefit plans is a decided plus for many employers because retirement assets are not exclusively invested in the stock of the plan sponsor.

Employee Stock Ownership Plan and Trust Tax Issues and Incentives

The tax incentives are slightly different for C and S corporations. Generally, when an individual shareholder sells stock to an ESOP, that sale will qualify for capital gain tax treatment. There are special incentives, however related specifically to C corporations.

- *C corporation attributes:* Multiple class of stock are permitted which enhances planning flexibility. There may be an unlimited number of shareholders. There are no limitations on the types of shareholders. The corporation may pay reasonable dividends to the ESOP that are tax deductible (within statutes) and may be used to repay acquisition debt. The corporation pays income taxes. Selling shareholders typically qualify for capital gain tax treatment on the sale of stock. If at least 30% of the value of stock is sold to the ESOP, the selling shareholder may elect the IRC Section 1042 tax-free rollover. Assets contributed to the ESOP compound free of taxes until such time as the assets are distributed to plan participants.
- *S corporation attributes:* Typically a limit to a single class of stock (only voting rights may vary). All shareholders are treated similarly with regard to such things as S corporation "distributions." Total shareholders are limited to 100 (the ESOP counts as a single shareholder). There are many restrictions on the types of shareholders and care that must be taken to avoid the termination of the S election by inadvertently allowing an unauthorized shareholder. The company may make distributions to its shareholders, but care must be made to insure that distributions to the ESOP are allocated properly between allocated accounts and unallocated account balances. The S corporation pays no income taxes; income is passed through to the shareholders. Selling shareholders typically qualify for capital gain tax treatment on the sale of stock. Selling shareholders are not eligible for the IRC Section 1042 tax-free rollover. The income passed through to the ESOP stock is not subject to income taxes, therefore the ESOP does not require a cash distribution to pay income taxes. In practice, S corporations typically make a distribution to shareholders so they have cash to pay income taxes. If this is the case, the cash distributed to the stock in the ESOP is not subject to income tax, and it remains in the ESOP and may be used to repay debt within regulatory limits.

IRC Section 1042 Tax-Free Rollover

This election is available only to C corporation shareholders if they have met ownership holding period requirements (three years). The IRC Section 1042 election is available to the shares sold to the ESOP that takes the ownership percentage to 30% of the outstanding value of all the stock. The proceeds from the sale of the stock will not be subject to transaction taxes (capital gain taxes) if the proceeds are invested in QRP during the period including three months before the sale and twelve months after the sale.

- QRP generally includes securities of all domestic (U.S.) operating companies both public and private where 50% or more of the assets must be used in the active conduct of a trade or business. QRP includes individual securities such as stocks, bonds, notes, and debentures. The company issuing QRP may not have passive investment income in excess of 25% of gross receipts in the preceding year in which the purchase occurs. QRP does not include mutual funds, real estate, government securities, and municipal bonds, foreign securities, partnerships, and limited liability companies (LLCs).
- Taxes on QRP are deferred until such time as the QRP is sold. Once sold, the QRP is taxed and it inherits the tax basis of the original employer stock. If the QRP is held until the death of the selling shareholder, the investments are subject to estate taxes and will receive a stepped-up basis. Significantly, the QRP will not pay capital gain taxes in this event, and the sale of stock to the ESOP really becomes "tax free." The investment strategy of QRP is typically "buy and hold." The tax deferral applies as long as the QRP remains with the seller. A seller note is an inappropriate choice for the QRP because as the debt principal is repaid, it becomes a taxable event.
- Selling shareholders wishing to make the IRC Section 1042 election have to be aware of the rules of attribution relating to relatives that are employed by the company. If there are relatives of the selling shareholder employed by the company as defined in IRC Section 409(n)(3)(a), rules of attribution prevent those relations from participating in the ESOP. Additionally, any 25% shareholders in the company are ineligible to participate in the ESOP. These restrictions may seem arbitrary and unfair, but they exist. If there are relatives or 25% shareholders that are ineligible to participate in the ESOP, such individuals are often provided a non-qualified retirement plan to amend for the restriction.

The IRC Section 1042 tax-free rollover has tax benefits, but the restrictions on QRP to optimize the tax deferral are cumbersome. Interest in this tax benefit has been tepid recently because capital gain rates have been at historically low levels since 2003 and most sellers elect to pay the tax. Higher capital gain tax rates will increase the attractiveness of this benefit. With the specter of capital gain tax rates increasing significantly by January 1, 2013, I anticipate greater interest in this incentive.

The IRC Section 1042 tax-free rollover is a strong tax benefit, but it is similar in concept to an entire class of corporate transactions under IRC Section 368: tax preference reorganizations. The IRC Section 368 statutes have been an outstanding acquisition tool often embraced by public companies permitting combinations and mergers without the immediate impact of taxes that an actual sale would incur. IRC Section 1042 places ESOPs in C corporations on a level footing that the mergers and acquisitions industry has enjoyed for many years.

Repurchase Obligation

The company is required to make a market for the stock that is owned by the ESOP. This is the repurchase obligation. This is a compelling advantage to ESOP participants because it guarantees that there is a market for their stock. The company may elect to redeem the stock of a departing ESOP participant into either the company treasury (repaid with after-tax dollars), or it may redeem the stock into the ESOP (repaid with tax-deductible dollars).

The employee technically has the option of placing a "put" of the stock back to the company, and directing the company to redeem the stock, or the employee may elect to keep the stock. Since companies do not wish departing employees to have the option of becoming an actual shareholder by retaining the stock, corporate bylaws are typically amended to prevent this event from happening.

Anti-Abuse Provisions—S Corporations

Congress addressed a growing abuse of S corporation ESOPs in 2001 with the passage of the Economic Growth Tax Reconciliation and Recovery Act. Generally, the abuse is related to single-employee S corporations being established as 100% ESOP owned. Such an entity is literally income tax free with all the tax benefits accruing to a single employee. This structure was viewed as tax manipulation and was outlawed. The Federal Legislation was written with the assistance of the ESOP community to eliminate unintended enrichment within an ESOP.

There is a two-part test developed in the regulations to determine if the S corporation ESOP is subject to the anti-abuse penalties. If the corporation is found to violate the regulation, IRC Section 409(p)(4), it will be subject to severe excise taxes. The rules relating to this provision are very complex and major provisions are briefly mentioned.

Under the regulations, first all "disqualified persons" are identified. A disqualified person is someone who owns more than 10% of the deemed owned shares or certain family members under rules of attribution that own more than 20% of the deemed owned shares. Deemed owned shares include stock allocated to the individual account balance in the ESOP and "synthetic equity" owned by the individual (such as stock appreciation rights, phantom stock, warrants, restricted stock, and other interests that give the holder the right to acquire or receive stock in an S corporation). The concept of deemed owned stock is very complex and beyond the scope of this discussion. In addition, the stock that is deemed owned by disqualified persons is measured, and if disqualified persons own more than 50% of the stock a non-allocation year results. If a non-allocation year is determined, then exceedingly punitive penalties apply. Due to the complexity of the anti-abuse regulations, it is essential that qualified professionals be consulted in such matters.

As a result of the anti-abuse provisions, more employees in a candidate ESOP company is preferred. From a practical standpoint, an S corporation should have a minimum of 15 to 20 employees to stand a good chance of staying above the penalties of a non-allocation year. In the next chapter, the financial and tax power of 100% S corporation ESOPs will be discussed, and the importance of this regulation will become more apparent.

Exhibit 12.2 summarizes the primary tax and technical aspects of ESOPs in C and S corporations. This guide is included to provide an overview of many of the technical regulations impacting ESOPs.

Other Shareholders and the Employee Stock Ownership Plan and Trust

In this section on technical matters, an overview of major ESOP-related regulations has been considered so far. As this chapter suggests, ESOPs may be only one of several investors in a privately held company. This sub-heading is intended to provide a consideration of major issues relating to the company that has multiple shareholders.

- The ESOP is valued on the FMV standard and subject to a rigorous analysis by an independent appraiser that reports to the Trustee. Other shareholders in the firm may have their stock valued on a different standard depending on the attributes of their stock. ESOP stock enjoys

EXHIBIT 12.2 Comparison Between C and S Corporation ESOPs

Description	C Corporation	S Corporation
Typical applications	Sell minimum 30% for IRC Section 1042 tax deferral, migrate to S corporation over time	Sell any percentage, eventual goal is often 100% ESOP for tax benefits
Tax status of sale of stock to ESOP	Capital gain	Capital gain
IRC Section 1042 Tax Deferral	Applies only to C Corporations, subject to 30% test and QRP	Does not apply
Annual employer payroll contribution limits	25% qualifying payroll for all qualified plans	25% qualifying payroll for all qualified plans
Application of the contribution limit to interest and principal	25% applies to principal, interest is deducted separately	25% includes interest and principal
Self-directed employee contributions to qualified plans	Does not count against employer 25%	Does not count against employer 25%
Employee contributions	Not generally recommended, it is an employer-provided plan	Not generally recommended, it is an employer-provided plan
Maximum eligible individual payroll	$250,000 and indexed for inflation	$250,000 and indexed for inflation
Annual additions limit to all qualified plans	$50,000 and indexed for inflation	$50,000 and indexed for inflation
Dividends C corporation	May be tax deductible, must be reasonable, does not count against 25% contribution limit, subject to corporate alternative minimum tax	Does not apply
Distributions S corporation	Does not apply	May be paid directly to all shareholders, unlimited, does not count against 25% contribution limit
Income taxes	Subject to C corporation income taxes	ESOP not subject to income taxes, outside shareholders pay prorated taxes
Anti-abuse provisions	Does not apply	Possible severe penalties
Classes of stock	Multiple classes permitted	Only one class permitted
Number of shareholders	Unlimited	100 (ESOP counts as one)

a Federally mandated market: the repurchase obligation as discussed. Other shareholders may not have the advantage of this protection, and correspondingly their stock may be subject to additional discounts, such as a significant lack of marketability discount. From a practical viewpoint, if there is a material differential between the ESOP stock value per share and other shareholder value per share, that differential must be defensible. It is highly recommended that any differential that is stipulated be documented to avoid misunderstandings in the future.

- The ESOP may be valued on a minority-position basis or a control-position basis if the requirements for control as proposed by the DOL are met. Other shareholders will have their ownership stakes valued typically by the attributes of their block of stock. For example, certain shares of stock may be subject to voting rights and dividend preferences that will create pricing differentials.
- The ESOP may not be compelled to acquire the stock of other shareholders by prior agreement. The ESOP Trustee may have the option of acquiring stock subject to a prudent investigation and a consideration of all applicable relevant facts.
- If there are multiple shareholders, an appropriate observation on guidance is to treat all investors equitably. Litigation has evolved when shareholders have not been treated fairly, and the oppressed shareholders have the election of pressing litigation against the oppressor.

SUMMARY

The buyout involving a variety of ownership interests including management, family, other investors, and the ESOP is infinitely flexible in design attributes. The ESOP enjoys certain tax advantages that few other shareholders have, but tax advantages are often insufficient reasons to have only the ESOP as a single shareholder. There are tax and regulatory differences between C and S corporations relating to ESOPs. The ESOP has many applications within the corporate ownership structure.

Many companies start with an ESOP that is in a limited role and percentage of stock ownership. With time the tax attributes of the ESOP are realized and more companies migrate to the ESOP owning a progressively higher percentage of the outstanding stock. Frequently, the ESOP evolves into the 100% shareholder in the company, which is the subject of the following chapter.

CHAPTER 13

Buyouts—100% Employee Stock Ownership Plan and Trust

We are confronted by insurmountable opportunities.
—Pogo (Walt Kelly)

T his is a separate chapter by design because the metrics of a 100% em-ployee stock ownership plan and trust (ESOP) are virtually unique in the business world. Certainly this chapter is complementary and builds upon Chapter 12 on buyouts with management and ESOPs. With this 100% buy-out, the longer-term destination is to have a company that is owned entirely by the ESOP. It is a certainty that the company is an S corporation, or it is a C corporation on its way to becoming an S corporation.

The advent of the 100% ESOP company is a relatively recent phe-nomenon. The highly favorable tax legislation permitting S corporations to sponsor ESOPs has been in existence in its present form a relatively few years. Until 1999 virtually all privately owned ESOP companies were C corporations by Federal statute. Today it is estimated that over 80% of all privately held companies with ESOPs are S corporations, and the preponder-ance of them are 100% employee owned. The dramatic financial success of these employee—owned companies has only become apparent for all prac-tical purposes in the past few years. For business owners, my advice for you is to ask your professional advisors how many ESOPs they have actively installed or consulted on the past five years. If that number is less than 20 as an example, it is likely your professional advisors have no idea just how successful and effective the 100% ESOP is.

One powerful attraction to this corporate structure is largely concen-trated on the attributes of S corporations under our IRC regulations. Basi-cally, no S corporation is subject to either Federal or state income taxes (they may be subject to other state imposed taxes). In tax nomenclature, S corporations are "pass-through" entities for income taxes. The S corporation shareholders will have the taxable income of the S corporation "passed-through" to them, and that income is typically taxed to the individual shareholders at their effective tax rates. The income from the S corporation is most often reported to shareholders on IRS Form 1099. The income is taxed to shareholders at their highest marginal income tax rate, which may approach 50% when both Federal and state taxes are considered. The S corporation typically distributes sufficient cash to the shareholders to enable them to pay personal income taxes (although the S corporation is not required to make the cash distribution unless commanded by legal documents such as company bylaws or shareholder agreements).

When all of the company stock is owned by a qualified plan, in this case the ESOP, it is important to emphasize the ESOP does not pay income taxes. The ESOP is a qualified plan holding assets for the beneficial interest of the eligible employees. The income of the S corporation is in essence reported to the single shareholder, the ESOP, but the ESOP has no income tax liability. This has the practical effect of making the company an income tax–free entity. I am selecting my words very carefully here; while the company has no exposure to income taxes (because no S corporation pays income taxes), the 100% ESOP company does have a significant future stock repurchase obligation. When the ESOP ownership percentage rises to 100%, the repurchase obligation is a substantial amount that must be planned. Since the company is not subject to income taxes, planning for and funding the future repurchase obligation is a manageable task.

While a 100% ESOP S corporation offers tremendous tax benefits, there is the issue of who is managing the company if everyone is an ESOP participant. While all the eligible employees are participants in the ESOP, the senior management of the company must still manage and make the hard decisions to insure that market competitiveness is maintained.

This chapter is complementary to the preceding chapter on ESOPs, and many of the observations apply equally to situations where the ESOP is both the only shareholder (100%) and where the ESOP is one of perhaps several shareholders. On matters of similarities, I will briefly mention those attributes and observations in this chapter to emphasize those same items.

ADVANTAGES

From the prior chapter the advantages of the ESOP are briefly repeated. While the traditional uses of an ESOP still apply, the 100% S corporation ESOP is notable for the overwhelmingly positive tax attributes.

Traditional Uses of an Employee Stock Ownership Plan and Trust

- One of the most publicized applications for an ESOP is to make a market for the stock of a shareholder wishing to leave the business. The reasons for leaving may be retirement, failing health, diversification of finances, or a wide range of personal issues. The ESOP may acquire the stock from a departing shareholder with pre-tax dollars and the sale of the stock is typically a favorably taxed event for the seller.
- An ESOP may also be used as a strategy to raise capital. Contributions to an ESOP are tax deductible within payroll limits. The company may contribute authorized but unissued stock to the ESOP at its fair market value (FMV). The company obtains a valuable tax deduction for the contribution of the new issue stock to the ESOP without an offsetting cash outflow. The tax savings to the company represent a source of capital.
- The ESOP is an employee benefit provided by the company. Many companies adopt the ESOP as an incentive for the employees to stay, and make contributions to the financial success. The employees are provided the opportunity to share in the financial success of the company thereby aligning the interests of all of the "owners." Employee productivity is typically increased when the installation of the ESOP is accompanied with ongoing communications.
- When the company is being sold in its entirety to an ESOP, this signals to all stakeholders of the company that there is a succession plan. This is an important communication because the community of stakeholders includes customers, vendors, banks, employees, and the community. The wider community of stakeholders will often be relieved if there is a succession plan. This is particularly the case with a major employer in a more rural region where the loss of that company to a third party buyer may have a highly negative impact on the community.

Selling Stock to the Employee Stock Ownership Plan and Trust

Installing an ESOP as the buyer results in the acquisition of stock by the plan. This transaction is typically subject to more favorable capital gain treatment of any gain on the sale of stock. We assume that the company is already an S corporation, and selling stock to the ESOP while maintaining the S corporation status is the likely result. This is certainly the case while the Federal capital gain tax rate is at an historic low rate of 15%.

It is technically possible that a longstanding S corporation may convert to a C corporation just before the sale of stock to the ESOP so that the transaction qualifies for the IRC Section 1042 tax-free rollover, which is available only to shareholders in a C corporation. The metrics of the IRC Section 1042 election have been previously considered, but it is highly unusual to see this strategy when the clear intention is to become a 100% ESOP.

The qualifying employees become participants in the ESOP as stock purchased by the plan is eventually allocated into the accounts of the individuals. The plan participants do not actually become shareholders in the company; rather the ESOP holds the stock and allocates shares for the beneficial interest of the participants. Typically, the employee enthusiasm for the ESOP will be much greater once they realize that the ESOP is destined to become the 100% owner of the company. This is a much different scenario than the case where the ESOP is only one of several investors, and there may be questions about the governance and direction of the company.

Most companies will not want the employees to buy stock in the company with their own funds because of financial disclosure requirements. As participants in a qualified retirement plan provided by the company, the employees have very limited access to sensitive and confidential financial information. Once employees actually invest their own funds into company stock, extensive disclosure requirements prevail compelling the business to reveal information often best hidden from the public domain. It may be appropriate to offer select key employees some additional financial and retention incentives to move the company ahead, but those incentives are typically carefully considered to be compatible with the S corporation attributes involving a single class of stock.

S Corporation Attributes

This chapter first emphasizes the income tax–free nature of the 100% ESOP S corporation as a significant benefit. This tax attribute is often sufficiently strong enough to tip the decision to migrate from a company that is owned by the management and the ESOP to a company entirely owned by the ESOP. In the case of the 100% ESOP, I think it is still advisable to have the senior management of the company endowed with powerful financial incentives to grow the value of the business. There are senior management incentives and retention financial programs that are tax and regulation compatible with S corporations. Such programs include stock appreciation rights and phantom stock (these plans are discussed later in this chapter).

When a company adopts this capital structure, all of the eligible employees have a stake in the company. As previously explained, the employees have the same percentage stake as their qualifying payroll (with some consideration to S corporation distributions), but the higher paid participants have a greater absolute dollar participation in the plan. Additionally, the ESOP rewards loyalty to the company by providing benefits that are cumulative and they compound free of taxes until withdrawn from the plan. This participation may become a tremendous advantage if the company conscientiously communicates the employee ownership advantages (and obligations). The previous chapter highlights the financially powerful impact of proper communications and employee ownership. The 100% ESOP company often magnifies this advantage. Revisit Chapter 1 and the story of SRC Holdings Corporation for an example of how powerful the attributes can be.

> When the company is 100% ESOP and an S corporation, there are no corporate income taxes (there is the repurchase obligation, however). This means that all of the debt in the company including ESOP acquisition obligations and preexisting debt are repaid with pre-tax free cash flow. With effective tax rates for non-ESOP S corporations approaching 50% between Federal and state authorities (in such states as California and New York), it means that debt is repaid in approximately half the time.

Longer term, the advantages of the 100% ESOP are pronounced. Since the company pays no current-year income taxes, this often means the company will accumulate cash and liquidity following the repayment of the acquisition-related debt in advance of the eventual repurchase obligation that is building. There is likely to be a significant timing difference in this liquidity availability, an advantage that may be capitalized if the company seeks to grow through acquisitions or reinvesting its liquidity. This ESOP company may acquire candidate targets with pre-tax cash flow; the rest of the business community must acquire the same target company with after-tax cash flow. This financial advantage may be material.

CAUTIONS

Perhaps the one sage comment is to not let the S corporation tax attributes overwhelm sound business logic. The 100% ESOP corporation enjoys an enviable tax environment, but the corporation governance issues are also considerable.

Corporate Governance

Every ESOP must have a trustee with fiduciary obligations. As the ESOP percentage increases and arrives at 100% of the outstanding stock, the role of the trustee in corporate governance is magnified. In this case, following common corporate governance the trustee votes all of the stock at a shareholder meeting (often annually) and elects the board of directors. The board will appoint the officers of the company. Under these circumstances the ESOP trustee wields tremendous long-term power by electing the board. The trustee will (or should) be thinking longer term and being mindful of the fiduciary responsibilities. This often imposes a cautious approach to the management of the business, but it also typically results in a longer-term strategic assessment of the company.

Effective corporate governance is critical for long-term success. The 100% employee-owned company in my opinion should not be managed by committee. It is important that the senior management of the company manage it for optimal results with respect to the financial interest of the shareholder (in this case the ESOP). Typically, the optimal management of the company embraces a longer-term time horizon under the theory that shareholders are not under intense pressure to maximize short returns at the expense of longer-term viability and reputation. Accordingly, the company should be oriented to remaining financially successful and not fall victim to the thinking that the company is in the job protection business at all costs.

Acquisition Debt Analysis

When the ESOP is designed to be the 100% shareholder, there is often the temptation to reach that 100% status as soon as practicable for the tax benefits. This thinking may result in too much acquisition debt being assumed by the company, placing the company at a greater risk of default or even financial collapse if something goes wrong. It is best to arrive at the 100% ESOP destination without over-reliance on a crushing acquisition debt burden. The tax benefits are almost the same if the ESOP acquires the stock in multiple transactions, for example 55% with the first transaction (for a control position valuation), followed by a 45% second transaction. Dividing the acquisition process into two manageable pieces will better enable the company to successfully navigate the responsibilities of the acquisition debt.

The repurchase obligation now represents the full FMV of the company. The need for a repurchase obligation analysis or review is very strong. The Trustee must be aware of the financial significance of the repurchase obligation on the future health of the company. The larger the company by ESOP participant head count; the more compelling the case for a more formal repurchase obligation study. With the larger companies, key attributes such as employee demographics (age distribution), account vesting, and employee turnover are carefully considered.

VALUATION INSIGHTS

The standard of value is FMV (or adequate consideration). There has already been significant discussion about the 100% ESOP company as an S corporation. While the actual tax election of the ESOP company is overwhelmingly tilted to being an S corporation, the FMV standard of value assumes a C corporation. The hypothetical buyer longer term will be a C corporation. There is some confusion about S corporation stock valuations due to a few isolated but high-profile estate tax court cases where S corporation tax attributes were quantified. Those were estate tax cases under review by the IRS and not ESOP valuations under the watchful eye of both the IRS and Department of Labor (DOL).

As mentioned, FMV for an ESOP is a standard of value that is closely watched by both the IRS and the DOL. When the ESOP is the sole shareholder, this determination of value drives the future repurchase obligation of the business. Longer term, the future repurchase obligation will be in competition for the resources the company needs to evolve and grow. A recommended valuation approach is to have an income approach that considers a future or forward projection of operating results. This is not an absolute recommendation as there are circumstances when relying on a projection is an act of substantial guesstimates and assumptions. In some cases it is simply not practicable to provide a defensible forecast. What is right with the future orientation is that it folds into the analysis the long-term requirements of the company, including capital reinvestment.

Paying for Control

When the company is 100% ESOP, in virtually all cases the ESOP is paying a control position price for the stock. This makes intuitive sense because there are no other shareholders.

The DOL has issued proposed regulations in May 1986, 29 CFR Part 2510, *Regulation Relating to the Definition of Adequate Consideration, Notice of Proposed Rulemaking* (Regulation), that defines their understanding of the standard of value for ESOPs that have an impact on an ESOP paying a control premium for stock. The ESOP is permitted to pay a control premium the extent other investors would pay a premium if two conditions are met. First, the ESOP must have control in appearance, which suggests over 50%

of the stock in most cases. Second the ESOP must have control "in fact." To determine if the ESOP has control in fact, the appraiser will have to examine the corporate governance of the company to determine if control has passed from the selling shareholder to the ESOP.

When the ESOP owns all of the stock, the repurchase obligation takes on a heightened importance because this long-term obligation is substantial. As the ESOP ages and all the stock is allocated to the accounts of the employees and participant accounts are vested; it is a recommended practice to have a repurchase obligation study completed. For the largest ESOP companies, dedicated software that is actuarially balanced is available to assist with this often complex analysis. Even in smaller companies a repurchase study is recommended so that management can plan for stock redemptions.

VIEWPOINT OF THE SELLER

Many sellers are fascinated with the prospect of having their company freed from income tax exposure. Yes, there is the stock repurchase obligation, but that is a financial commitment by the company to the employees who are responsible for making the business successful. Many business owners have a bias to their employees and key managers, and this structure addresses that goal. Even if the company is entirely owned by the ESOP, there are senior management incentive and retention programs that are compatible with being an S corporation. Embracing such programs, like stock appreciation rights or phantom stock subject to vesting, provides strong motivation for the key managers to stay with the company, particularly when ESOP-related acquisition debt is being repaid.

Financial Assistance

In today's economy and with the most common sources of buyout financing under conservative clouds, it is a certainty that the sellers will have to provide assistance in the form of seller notes. In some cases the sellers will finance the entire purchase price and earn a commercially defensible rate of return rather than invest sale proceeds in "safe" government treasury bills at a near nominal 1–3%. The informed sellers realize that under this structure the acquisition debt is repaid with pre-tax cash flow, the power of this attribute is illustrated later in this chapter with very attractive results. Sellers are often left with a choice: financing the ESOP buyout and extending credit to the managers and employees that have made the company a financial success, or extend credit to a third-party outside buyer that must repay the seller note with after-tax dollars. The seller in the case of the ESOP buyout is in a strong position to drive the terms of the sale, including the terms of the seller note. In the case of the sale to a third party, the seller is not typically driving the material terms of the transaction.

There are a common number of instances where the candidate company is a major employer in a smaller community (something less than Chicago). The shareholders realize the economic and social impact of the company on the community. The owners often attend the same church as the employees, send children to the same schools, and elect the same local representatives. There is often a strong sense of community, or just "heartland values." The ESOP alternative is a strong consideration in such circumstances since the community retains the company and the economic engine for growth and jobs. Often the shareholders have a strong sense of legacy, and wish to have their name attached to the company that remains a strong reminder of the economic vitality of the region.

ESOP transactions enjoy the advantage of being scalable, whereby the plan may acquire any amount of stock determined by the selling shareholders. For the purposes of this chapter, we assume there is a race to make the company 100% ESOP as soon as possible.

VIEWPOINT OF THE BUYER

Here, the only buyer is the ESOP. The ESOP trustee ultimately is the real decision maker, and subject to compliance with applicable regulations, the ESOP wants to become a shareholder or even the sole shareholder of the company.

Compliance with applicable Federal rules is more magnified with a 100% ESOP. The ESOP trustee will have binding corporate governance issues that need to be balanced with fiduciary responsibilities. There are no outside shareholders beyond the ESOP, and there are no employees or other key stakeholders with a direct equity interest in the company. Leadership for operations will have to come from individuals currently employed as the managers or officers of the company. They will almost certainly also be members of the board of directors, along with other outside directors that may be independent.

Senior Management Issues

Since there are no outside shareholders, there is a strong case to be made that the key senior managers of the company be granted long-term financial incentives to stay and grow the business. The S Corporation ESOP tax benefits are so strong it is suggested that incentive reward programs be adopted to reward the senior management, compatible with S corporation attributes.

Stock Appreciation Rights and Phantom Stock   Reward programs like stock appreciation rights (SAR) and phantom stock are good candidates. These financial incentive programs are not considered a second class of stock and are compatible with the restrictions placed on S corporations. SARs and phantom stock are really just deferred compensation with equity-sounding names. One advantage to these types of incentive programs is that they may be deliberately structured to reward a long-term commitment to the company by stipulating a vesting period.

SARs are often structured as an incentive for the senior management to increase the value of the company. After the installation of a heavily leveraged ESOP, the equity value of the stock typically falls in value because equity is largely replaced with debt. One strategy to consider is granting SARs with an exercise price pegged to the value of the stock following the installation of the ESOP. In this case the value is depressed due to the acquisition debt. As the debt is repaid the value of the SARs should almost certainly increase. The SARs provide an incentive to the senior team to repay the outside acquisition debt as quickly as possible. The repayment of the acquisition debt means less risk to the company and reduced risk to the ESOP participants. This is a worthy objective. Granting the SARs is often related to "units" of stock, without stock actually being issued. The SARs should be subject to vesting and timed to vest when the ESOP-related debt is repaid. The SARs are an accrued expense on the financial statements, and taken as a tax deduction when they are paid to the recipient, and reported as ordinary income to the recipient.

Similarly, phantom stock is typically granted in "units" comparable to common stock without stock being issued. Some defined metric is developed by the board to compute how the units of phantom stock are to be awarded to the senior management. The phantom stock should be subject to vesting. The cost of the phantom stock to the company is usually an accrued expense in the financial statements. The expense is taken as a tax deduction when paid and it is ordinary income to the recipient when received.

Employee Stock Ownership Plan and Trust Trustee

It is strongly recommended where it is contemplated the ESOP will be acquiring the controlling interest block of stock, if not all the stock with the first transaction, that an independent outside trustee be engaged for the transaction. This structure effectively removes the selling shareholders from the possible taint of conflicts by possibly being on the selling side and the buying side of the transaction (if the sellers serve in some manner as the ESOP trustee). There are a number of well qualified independent trustees that have significant ESOP experience and will provide the rigorous representation that the buyer should have. The outside trustee has full authority to negotiate the purchase of the stock for the benefit of the ESOP.

The trustee will negotiate the purchase price of the stock, and typically will be involved in actively negotiating a wide spectrum of additional attributes of the transaction. Candidate additional matters include such items as the terms of seller notes, senior management incentive programs, seller employment agreements, long-term leases related to buildings owned by the seller and leased to the company, and other material matters impacting the transaction. Full buyouts by the ESOP are often very complex transactions with a myriad of details and aspects. The trustee will typically engage an independent valuation firm as the financial advisor to assist in providing the determination of value for the stock, but to provide a fairness opinion regarding the fairness of the transaction in all of its material aspects from a financial perspective. The negotiating skills of the trustee in such transactions becomes important as you can see that this is a world of mergers and acquisitions with a cast set of complex issues. After all, the company in total is being acquired in much the same manner it would be sold to a third party.

PROFESSIONAL ADVISORS

Similarly as in Chapter 12, most of the advisors are the same and have substantially similar roles. The one major difference is that the ESOP is the sole shareholder, and there are no other outside shareholders with interests that may be adverse to the ESOP.

It is essential to have legal representation that is thoroughly vetted and literate on the Employee Retirement Income Security Act (ERISA), ESOPs, and the subtle requirements of a mergers and acquisitions environment. When a 100% buyout by the ESOP is contemplated, it is frequently a situation that the transaction is very complex with a host of ancillary issues related to transferring the ownership of the company to the new shareholder.

Additional advisors include an independent valuation firm that is familiar with ESOPs and also familiar with fairness opinions and has a strong background in business transactions. The trustee must be able to rely on the advice of the valuation firm and if anything goes wrong or is subject to review by a Federal agency it is essential that the processes and procedures embraced to reach the purchase decision be documented and that prudent judgment was used.

Due to the structure of 100% ESOPs, many of them have migrated to the status over time with multiple transactions. Some of those transactions may have been when the company was a C corporation, and some as an S corporation. The record-keeping environment may become exceedingly complex and well beyond the record-keeping skills of other qualified plan administrators. It is advised that an experienced administration firm with extensive ESOP expertise be engaged for the record keeping. In some cases the ESOP administration firm is the most experienced and they often will be able to provide the administration on other qualified plans like 401(k)s.

Acquisition Debt Considerations

There is a strong case to be made for the involvement of an experienced certified public accountant (CPA) firm. Most of the 100% buyouts are with firms that are financially successful; and that is why they are heading to an employee-owned company from the start. This suggests a significant amount of debt, and the ability of the company to service the debt requires a serious analysis of future cash flows and resources to determine if the company can meet its obligations. The existence of the acquisition debt often means that loan covenants will require a financial report from a CPA firm, often a review opinion or an audit opinion. The financial disclosure for an ESOP according to the American Institute of Certified Public Accountants Statement of Position 93-6, *Employers' Accounting for Employee Stock Ownership Plans*, is a must to understand. The genesis of SOP 93-6 is the growing occurrence of ESOPs accompanied by significant amounts of acquisition debt. There are specific financial reporting requirements for leveraged ESOPs.

Once the ESOP has over 100 participants, the plan itself is typically audited according to Federal regulations. The ESOP is audited, not the financial statements of the company. The ESOP audit will typically involve testing of the participants' account balances and footnote disclosure of the salient factors regarding the ESOP.

RISK ENVIRONMENT

Unlike in Chapter 12 where many of the companies with ESOPs are selling stock to a consortium of investors including an ESOP, this chapter is specifically addressing the 100% ESOP. Our experience is that these transactions are typically accompanied with substantial acquisition debt. We note that many but not all companies sell 100% of the stock in a single transaction to gain the substantial tax benefits. Sellers wishing to reduce the risk of such heavy reliance on debt may elect to sell stock to the ESOP in a series of transactions. Given the recent experience of the recession beginning in 2008 and the deep impact it has had on the economy, taking a longer view and selling stock to the ESOP in a series of transactions is a prudent option to consider.

It is a near certainty that the ESOP will require assistance from the sellers to provide financing in one of many forms. The sellers may actually extend shareholder notes to the company, who in turn loan the amount to the ESOP. The sellers may guarantee notes from banks and other financial resources to the company (outside loans) who in turn loan the proceeds to the ESOP (inside loans). This two-loan structure is often preferred by financial institutions because it gives them a collateral position first on all the assets of the company. If the financial institution (or a seller note) loans money directly to the ESOP the only collateral provided is the stock in the company. This collateral position is inferior to being secured by the assets of the business.

As mentioned, many traditional sources of financing provided by banks and other financial institutions are hesitant to make buyout-based loans with a large component of cash flow lending in addition to the collateral provided by the company assets. If the sellers are required to provide assistance or even substantial assistance they may be appropriately compensated for the costs of the risks being assumed. It is beyond the scope of this chapter to address the many options on structuring seller financing, but a few summary observations are appropriate. The seller notes will be repaid with pre-tax dollars, and the sellers will have a substantial hand in structuring this level of debt. The seller notes will be subordinated to the debt of a senior lender that will have a secured position on the assets of the company, if a senior lender is used. Being subordinated to a bank is not typically high on the list of desirable attributes of the sale from the view of the sellers, but they may be compensated for the lack of security their position represents.

In Chapter 12 the National Center for Employee Ownership (NCEO) study on ESOP debt default rates indicated that there is a much less likelihood of default than in non-ESOP companies. This should give some significant level of comfort to parties extending credit to the ESOP company.

The 100% ESOP companies are more likely to have a significant amount of acquisition-related debt, and a few desirable company attributes bear repeating. The best ESOP candidates are companies with an established history of financial success with reasonably stable cash flows. This factor will often limit the candidates for heavy acquisition leverage. Companies in a wide spectrum of industries are 100% ESOP, but if operating results are volatile, reliance on a substantial level of acquisition debt is not recommended. Rather, more volatile operating environments may migrate to the 100% ESOP over time encompassing several smaller transactions so as not to overburden the company. Risks are reduced when the ESOP is accompanied by an ongoing effective communications program. The financial performance of the company is greatly enhanced when a genuine ownership culture is developed and continually reinforced.

SAMPLE TRANSACTION

Assumed facts—Professional Services Company (computer consulting). This is the same example illustration as in Chapter 12 with the distinction that the ESOP is acquiring all the stock in a single transaction (100%). There are two selling shareholders, 60 employees, S corporation, and a history of consistent profitability supporting the FMV of the Company. There are three key managers and they will not have a direct equity stake in the Company with actual stock; they are participating in the financial success by being granted SARs. The SARs are in effect long-term deferred compensation and compatible with an S corporation. The ESOP will purchase all of the outstanding stock in a single transaction. The FMV of the Company on a control position basis is $6 million. This transaction differs from the same example illustration in Chapter 12 in that the value of the Company is on a control basis (Chapter 12 had the Company valued on a minority basis because the ESOP was acquiring only 40% of the stock). The minority value of the Company is $5 million and a $1 million control "premium" has been added to arrive at a FMV of $6 million on a control basis. Bank financing was secured for only 45% of the purchase price, $2,700,000 ($6,000,000 × 45%), and the balance of the debt is provided by shareholder notes, $3,300,000.

Exhibit 13.1 indicates the traditional structure of this buyout.

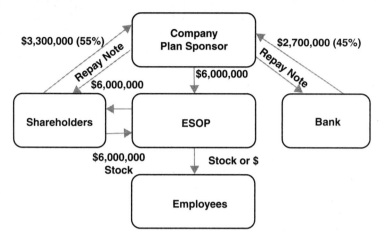

FIGURE 13.1 Sample ESOP Transaction

The flow of the transaction is illustrated in the following steps.

- The two retiring shareholders are selling 100% of the stock to the newly created ESOP for a total of $6,000,000.
- The Company has arranged financing from a bank for 45% of the transaction, $2,700,000, and the selling shareholders provide financing on the balance of the acquisition price, $3,300,000. The bank lends $2,700,000 to the Company in order to gain a secured position on all the assets of the business. The selling shareholders also lend $3,300,000 to the Company and subordinate their position to the bank (together the $6 million is the "outside loan").
- The Company advances the $6,000,000 to the ESOP ("inside loan").
- The ESOP buys the 100% block of stock from the retiring shareholders with the $2,700,000 in cash from the bank and a $3,300,000 note from the selling shareholders. The 100% block of stock is held as collateral by the ESOP.
- Selling shareholders receive the cash from the bank. Since this is a stock sale, any gain will be taxed at capital gain rates. Since there are shareholder notes in the amount $3,300,000, payment on those notes is subject to installment-sale tax treatment if elected.

- As the ESOP acquisition debt is repaid according to the inside note, a prorated portion of the stock held as collateral is released to the ESOP participants. The stock is allocated to the accounts of the ESOP participants according to the eligible payroll; generally each employee's reported W-2 earnings.

- For planning purposes, the Company will often want to pre-pay the outside note and remove the debt from the balance sheet. Having a separate inside note allows the repayment of the outside note as soon as cash flow permits without accelerating the release of stock from collateral and also accelerating the repurchase obligation.

- This is a 100% sale of stock to the ESOP, and the transaction is heavily leveraged. Such a transaction is only recommended when the Company has a demonstrated history of strong cash flows in and out of recessions to help insure that there will not be a default on the acquisition-related debt.

- The tremendous advantage of this structure is having all the debt (outside loan) repaid with pre-tax cash flow. For example the outside debt may be entirely repaid within 10 years, but the inside note may be amortized over 15 years (the release of stock from collateral). This timing difference is helpful to the Company because the repurchase obligation will not materially begin until the inside note is fully amortized. The practical application is that the Company will have a few years to build liquidity to meet the repurchase obligation in the future.

Case Study—Sentry Equipment, Inc.

Started in 1924 as the Henszey Company, it was a supplier of power plant components and milk evaporators to the dairy industry. In 1959 the name was changed to Sentry Equipment, Corp. (Sentry), and targeted the power-generation industry selling sampling products and specialty heat exchangers. Sentry is located in Oconomowoc, Wisconsin (CEO Mike Farrell will gladly pronounce "Oconomowoc" if you contact him personally). Today Sentry provides components and complete systems for power plant steam and water monitoring, and a wide variety of process industries. Sentry offers sampling products including such items as variable pressure reducing elements (VRELs), sample temperature control units, sample coolers, automated sample controls, low emission samplers, sanitary samplers for food products, and composite samplers for liquids and bulk solids. Power plant sampling and analysis systems are typically categorized as capital equipment purchases and sales are often cyclical and dependent on power plant construction. Components and equipment upgrades sold to existing power plants is more recession resistant, and a service sector was recently added to help balance revenues.

The original shareholders adopted an ESOP in 1985, one of the first such plans in the region. By 2000 the last of the outstanding stock was acquired by the ESOP and today Sentry is owned 100% by its employees. Mike Farrell compliments the team at Sentry for their dedication and helping to build a broad product offering that has catapulted them into the international sales arena. According to Mike "Most of the products contain a significant element of design engineering and applications experience, and having the ESOP provides an incentive for our employees to stay with Sentry. With low turnover, we provide an exceptional level of customer support and service."

Sentry recently relocated to a new state-of-art facility that showcases their commitment to product development and world-class support. Since the move to the facility in 2007, Sentry has already expanded the manufacturing capabilities in 2010. When customers visit the plant they are impressed with the commitment to technology, product improvement, and the longevity of the employees.

Once Sentry products are installed customers look for ongoing support and service. Since the products are capital equipment and have wear points, the equipment will have to be serviced and replaced at some point. Chief Financial Officer Brian Baker comments, "Our technical support teams have been with Sentry for many years and know the product line and customers thoroughly. This is invaluable goodwill that we build with our customers since many are repeat buyers and have grown to place great trust in Sentry's ability to honor commitments."

The ESOP has been integral to providing an alignment of interest between the employees and the Company. Shares are redeemed from departing employees and recycled to the other team members. The Company has built an experienced and talented senior management team that is dedicated to the long-term viability of Sentry. Sherry McDermott, Vice President Human Resources, commented, "The Company continues to grow and our future looks promising. Our employees know that a financially successful Company is in everyone's best interest. We make a commitment to our employees and seek to reinforce our culture of ownership." The business model of commitment to quality and employees has worked well for almost 90 years. Congratulations to their team for the vision of the Sentry leadership.

Case Study—Chatsworth Products, Inc.

Chatsworth Products, Inc. (CPI) headquartered in Westlake Village, California was formerly a business unit of publicly owned Harris Corporation. The business unit was focused on providing services and products to the communications and other related industries. When CPI was affiliated with Harris its main products were two-post racks, shelves, and cable runway associated with central office communications applications. The client server revolution was just beginning.

Harris decided that CPI was a non-core business unit and was targeted to be divested in the late 1980s. Mr. Joseph Cabral, Business Unit Manager, was determined to make an attempt to acquire the business unit from its parent. Negotiations with Harris had to be confidential since talking about a possible acquisition while still managing CPI was very challenging. Discussion with any other employees outside the management group was generally prohibited. Negotiations continued for several months as Harris had a duty to maximize the price for its shareholders. The recession of the late 1980s and the fact that the core business of CPI was a lower profile manufacturing company likely dissuaded many potential buyers. The management team, though, knew the inherent value and could see potential easier than unfamiliar third parties. With Joe's leadership, they approached the parent a number of times, but with each proposal meeting some objections were raised, which were sufficient to delay the transaction.

Interested financial resources at the beginning of discussions pulled back after a period of time as the economy entered a recession. Management, who were risking their personal wealth to fund the feasibility investigation, were essentially back to ground zero without a banking resource. With financing options dwindling, the team's advisors put them in contact with the National Cooperative Bank (NCB) in Washington, D.C. NCB was ESOP-literate and had a successful history with employee buyouts. With NCB's help and a leveraged ESOP, the employees acquired CPI in 1991. An interesting aspect of the transaction is that employees added equity by rolling over distributions from Harris's 401(k) plan into self-directed individual retirement accounts (IRAs). They then directed the IRA trustee to invest in the acquisition corporation that had been set up to accomplish the buyout. The funding from the self-directed IRAs was equity in the transaction, lowering the requirement for debt. The employees were making an investment in the Company, which became CPI, so according to securities rules, full financial disclosure was made and a limited-offering circular was presented to all employees. A small number of qualified investors as well as the maximum 35 unaccredited investors agreed to make the investment and the deal was struck. Late in 1998, the self-directed IRAs were rolled into the ESOP allowing CPI to take advantage of legislation authorizing S corporations to have an ESOP, and CPI became a 100% ESOP owned company.

The financial performance of CPI during the 1990s had been admirable. The industries served by CPI were doing well, particularly the communications industry, and the Company prospered accordingly. Many new products were developed to store, secure, and manage PCs and other equipment needed to support the migration from mainframe computing. However, the dot.com bust of 2000–2001 was especially hard on CPI when the Company experienced a pronounced downturn in business volume. Management and the employees gathered and faced the recession on a combined basis acknowledging that costs had to be reduced and the process was going to be painful. Adjustments were made and the cost-cutting pain was shared across all departments. In 2004 company operations were stabilizing and Joe Cabral retired.

The CPI management team and the Company's board of directors stepped up, filling vacated responsibilities. Ultimately, the Company found real stability under the leadership of new president and longtime employee Mr. Larry Renaud. Other members of the senior management team also have many years of service with CPI. As a cohesive group, they are leading CPI to "delight the customer" by providing integrated IT infrastructure solutions for data center applications. Product capabilities have been greatly expanded to include such areas of concentration as: containment systems, power and environmental monitoring systems, keyboard, visual, mouse (KVM) systems, power management systems, along with expanded product lines in cabinets, racking, and cable management. CPI features a Research Development and Training Center (RD&T) that enables visitors to observe real-world data center thermal testing. The RD&T offers state-of-art test facilities in addition to a product showroom and complete training capabilities.

In addition to manufacturing operations in California, Texas, and North Carolina, CPI has expanded internationally with sales offices in Mexico, England, China, Dubai, and Canada. Larry Renaud likes to remind everyone at CPI that "Teamwork, Caring, and Commitment are essential ingredients for a successful ownership culture." As a team the CPI employee-owners at times faced significant financial and business challenges during its first 20 years as a 100% ESOP. The adaptability of the employee-owners and a spirit of "We're All in This Together" have enabled CPI to survive and position itself for further success. CPI will continue to strive for further growth by expanding both its product offerings and markets to address global opportunities. Larry Renaud said: "The business success to date of CPI's employee ownership structure and culture are evidence that with proper nurturing ESOPs can be sustainable long-term organizations."

TECHNICAL MATTERS

Chapter 12 contains a lengthy section on technical considerations regarding key elements of transactions. Please refer to that chapter. There are a few additional considerations mentioned here that relate to specifically to a 100% ESOP company.

Employee Stock Ownership Plan and Trust Trustee

The trust actually owns the stock in the ESOP, and the trust will have a trustee with fiduciary responsibilities. General ERISA fiduciary rules are contained in ERISA Sections 401 to 408. Please refer to Chapter 12 for an expanded discussion of ESOP trustees.

   While trustee obligations are always to be taken seriously, this matter is magnified when the company is 100% ESOP. In this instance there are no other shareholders that must be consulted. The ESOP trustee has the authority to elect the board of directors, and with this election goes tremendous authority.

   This point was not mentioned in Chapter 12, but when the ESOP is 100% there is the issue of having an outside trustee and not relying on inside managers and officers to fill that role. If an outside trustee is a consideration, the trustee may be a "directed trustee" or a full "discretionary trustee." There are significant differences in the designation. The directed trustee, often an independent outside trustee, is typically one member of a trust committee that is composed of other officers and key employees in the company. The directed trustee takes direction from the other members of the ESOP committee. The advantage of the company is that the independent trustee has the experience in corporate governance and may be invaluable when the occasional unusual circumstance arises. A full discretionary trustee in such circumstances will elect the board of directors and will exercise full discretion in the discharge of all fiduciary responsibilities.

Funding Methods and Contribution Limits

Once the legal entity is created, assets are contributed to the ESOP from a number of common sources including cash, company stock, or debt. The sources of company stock may be newly issued stock, treasury stock, or outstanding stock typically owed by a shareholder.

   Since most 100% ESOPs will be S corporations, focus on S corporation contribution limits is appropriate. While there are contribution limits in place for tax purposes, as discussed in Chapter 12, the 100% S corporation ESOP is able to repay acquisition debt entirely with pre-tax cash flow regardless of deductible contribution limits. What is likely to occur is that there will be no debt prepayment penalties or limitations indicating the external debt to the company (the outside loan) will be repaid as fast as practicable. Stock will be allocated to the accounts of the participants typically over a set amortization period in excess of the time required to repay the actual debt (the inside loan amortization). This timing difference is beneficial for the company because the repurchase obligation will be delayed until the inside loan is amortized.

Multiple Qualified Benefit Plans

Today, companies that sponsor ESOPs often also sponsor other qualified benefit plans such as profit sharing and 401(k). Employer contributions to qualified plans are limited by statute. When multiple plans are maintained, the employer contribution limits are primarily reserved for the ESOP (often the ESOP required debt repayments). However, self-directed investments by employees (deductions from employee compensation) to other benefit plans generally do not count against ESOP contribution percentage. In this manner, the company offers an ESOP, which is primarily invested in the stock of the employer, and also a 401(k) that offers investment diversification. The ability to offer multiple benefit plans is a decided plus for many employers because retirement assets are not exclusively invested in the stock of the plan sponsor.

The 100% ESOP company typically offers participants a greatly enhanced retirement benefit. There is the overriding concern that this benefit is concentrated into the stock of the participant's employer. This concentration is intended and unavoidable when the ESOP is acquiring the stock in the employer. Remember the ESOP is most typically an exclusively provided employer benefit. There are strategies to help limit this exposure. One strategy is to have the company support a 401(k) that is funded mostly with employee self-directed contributions. With time the ESOP account balance is also subject to diversification rules as the participant approaches retirement age.

Employee Stock Ownership Plan and Trust Tax Issues and Incentives

The tax incentives are slightly different for C and S corporations. Generally, when an individual shareholder sells stock to an ESOP, that sale will qualify for capital gain tax treatment. There are special incentives, however related specifically to C corporations, which have been discussed in Chapter 12 and are not repeated here.

S corporation attributes: Typically a limit to a single class of stock (only voting rights may vary). All shareholders are treated similarly with regard to such things as S corporation "distributions." Total shareholders are limited to 100 (the ESOP counts as a single shareholder). There are many restrictions on the types of shareholders, and care must be taken to avoid the termination of the S election by inadvertently allowing an unauthorized shareholder. The S corporation pays no income taxes; income is passed through to the shareholders. When there are specific circumstances of a 100% ESOP company, the income is "passed through" to the sole shareholder, the ESOP. The ESOP is a qualified plan and pays no income taxes. Taxes are eventually paid by the plan beneficiaries typically as ordinary income when distributions are made to employees no longer with the plan sponsor. The company is essentially an income tax–free entity, but with a significant deferred repurchase obligation that will have to be funded.

Repurchase Obligation

The company is required to make a market for the stock that is owned by the ESOP, that is, the repurchase obligation. This is a compelling advantage to ESOP participants because it guarantees that there is a market for their stock. The company may elect to redeem the stock of a departing ESOP participant into either the company treasury (repaid with after-tax dollars), or it may redeem the stock into the ESOP (repaid with tax deductible dollars). Remember, even with the attractive tax attribute of a 100% ESOP company, the repurchase obligation will be a financial commitment for the plan sponsor.

Anti-Abuse Provisions—S Corporations

The anti-abuse provisions were discussed in Chapter 12. The tax attributes of a 100% ESOP company are often so attractive that many business owners want to sell all of their stock immediately to the plan. There are practical limits on the size of the company.

As a result of the anti-abuse provisions, more employees in a candidate ESOP company are preferred. From a practical standpoint, an S corporation should have a minimum of 15 to 20 employees to stand a good chance of staying above the penalties of a non-allocation year.

Corporate Governance in the 100% Employee Stock Ownership Plan and Trust Company

The ESOP trustee in this case has tremendous corporate power by electing the directors. Care must be considered in the governance of the company following the sale or the completion of the stock to the ESOP. There is a range of options regarding the trustee function. The most common options are briefly mentioned to provide insights on the most likely encountered scenarios.

The safest and highly recommended option is for the ESOP to have an independent outside trustee with full discretionary authority to appoint the board of directors. The trustee will not serve as a director, but the directors are accountable to the trustee each year at the annual shareholder meeting. The ESOP trustee does not want to be responsible for the daily operations of the company.

Another commonly found option is for the ESOP to have a trust committee comprised of an outside trustee and a number of inside senior employees or outside independent directors. Together this ESOP committee will serve as the trustee. Often the outside trustee is a directed trustee, which means it will be directed by the members of the committee. The advantage to this type of structure is that the ESOP committee will have the input of a professional trustee that typically maintains a portfolio of similar clients. This outside objective expertise on fiduciary matters is enormously beneficial.

Another option is for the company to have a trustee comprised entirely of key employees. This is a common occurrence in many smaller ESOP companies, but this structure may present substantial problems that expose the individuals to great potential liability. In these cases the trustee is current key employees, and the trustee typically appoints those key employees as directors, who in turn appoint the officers of the company. Clearly, the same select number of key employees serves in multiple roles: trustee, director, and corporate officer. There will be times when the duties and responsibilities of those different positions collide or conflict with one another. In such cases it is imperative that conflicts be identified so that individuals may recuse themselves from certain decisions, or an independent outside trustee is engaged for a specific company need.

Since the 100% ESOP is almost certainly an S Corporation, the possible exposure to the S corporation anti-abuse regulations must be closely monitored. While this is not an issue for large companies, the lower the number of employees the more pronounced this will become. For example, an S corporation with 30 employees must be very careful to compute ongoing compliance with the anti-abuse regulations just mentioned. Under the section regarding professional advisors, we recommend an experienced ESOP administration firm thoroughly familiar with the 409(p) testing requirements because the penalties for non-compliance are so severe.

SUMMARY

There are a number of key summary points that are different with the 100% ESOP and companies that have an ESOP but are not 100%. The tax environment is systemically different. The 100% ESOP S corporation does not have exposure to income taxes. While the company is repaying acquisition debt, there is typically a significant build-up of cash within the company over time. The company must have the discipline to deploy the cash in a manner that fulfills the long-term goals of the company.

The company should be looking at long-term strategic planning in a new light. Not having the income tax exposure permits a longer-term planning horizon because resources are building. The company appropriately should be thinking longer term to grow the business and provide for the repurchase obligations.

CHAPTER 14

Buyouts—Professional Firms

Choose a job you love, and you will never work a day in your life.
—Confucius

The secret is not to learn something you don't want to practice.
—Anonymous

This chapter is included because it is common for professional service companies to have a strong requirement for a succession plan in place. For any number of reasons, such a plan often does not exist. The emphasis in this book is on inside buyouts. In the case of professional firms the strategy of embracing an inside buyout may have a powerful appeal among the peer group of professionals.

ARCHITECTURAL AND ENGINEERING, PUBLIC ACCOUNTING, AND MANAGEMENT CONSULTING FIRMS

The emphasis here is on professional firms with a commercial application. A limited subset of professional firms will be considered including: architectural and engineering firms (A&E); public accounting firms (CPA); and management consulting firms. Each of these three categories will be considered. Law firms and medical practices have been consciously excluded because they typically have exacting licensing requirements that sharply restrict ownership eligibility.

The A&E firms are one of the largest professional service provider disciplines. Licensing is a key requirement in architectural firms. Licensing is also a key consideration in engineering firms, but the engineering discipline is exceedingly broad and encompasses many activities. A professional engineering degree and applicable experience is required to sign plans. Engineering activities may be worked upon at the job site by non-licensed employees. A significant amount of work may be completed by staff members in an engineering firm under the supervision of a licensed professional. Typically, engineering firms are populated with professionals with university degrees and substantial technical training. One great challenge for A&E firms today is retaining the younger associates with the most current computer and technical skills. Those skills are highly portable, and the most recently educated with the latest exposure to software and technical applications often have attractive options if the current employer overlooks their contribution. We will examine what progressive A&E firms are doing to facilitate inside transition planning.

The CPA firms are another large category where the various members share some similar disciplines and a host of ancillary consulting and support services. The "franchise" for the public accounting profession is the authority to issue attest financial statements with applicable assurance of the work represented by the CPA's opinion letter. There are degrees of assurance ranging from first the highest level in an audit, next the reviewed financial statements, and finally compiled statements. The profession has exacting standards regarding the reports and level of assurance that accompanies the CPA's opinion. CPA firms often support many complementary services such as:

- Preparing tax returns for clients
- Information systems support and consulting
- Wealth advisory services
- Business valuations
- Litigation support
- Succession planning
- In some cases investment banking capabilities

These are just some of the more common applications. One major concern for the profession is the maturity of the "franchise" and the requirement for audited and reviewed financial statements. The preparation and opinions on financial statements is not growing in revenue nearly as fast as the complementary capabilities. The requirement to be a CPA as a principal in a public accounting firm is no longer the absolute rule as in the past. Many non-CPAs are principals. This fact alone increases the options for succession planning in public accounting companies.

The final category is consulting firms. To a degree, many public accounting firms in part define themselves as management consultants and have substantial teams of professional employees to support client requirements. Consulting firms in this context, however, encompass a wide range of activities such as:

- Employee placement firms
- Organizational change professionals
- Consulting psychologists to industry
- Advertising agencies
- Computer support and installations
- Other niche capabilities

Unlike the A&E firms and CPAs that often have a unifying and identical professional licensing requirement, a similar orientation is often not part of the consulting firm's culture.

General Observations for Professional Service Firms

For professional service firms, having a plan for the inside transfer of ownership over time to other associates is often an outstanding recruiting tool for recent college graduates or any new hire. The key message is that individuals have a career track with the firm. Not everyone is going to be a principal or partner, but the opportunity exists for those individuals wishing to make the commitment and acquire the requisite skills.

Firms committed to an inside transfer will typically champion the training in place for future principals. There should be a process in place to identify and select new owners. An invitation to become a principal typically should not place an unusually large financial burden on candidates. The promising candidates often have families, home mortgages, college educations, and other living standards to address in addition to becoming a principal. The process of becoming an owner is often a long-time horizon. Candidates have to feel confident the firm will be there for the long period, and that they have the requisite skills to lead the firm into the future. An evolving best practice is to have the ownership in the firm broad based. Rather than a few principals with very high percentages of firm ownership, a better risk management strategy is to have many more principals with smaller ownership percentages. This balances the exposure of the firm to the loss in a short period of a number of key individuals.

There is a concern in many professional firms regarding the looming retirement of so many principals in a relatively short period of time, which is related to the disproportionate number of "baby boomers" in ownership positions. Professional firms have to face this reality and develop a succession strategy if they wish to remain independent. Looking 10 or 15 years into the future is not unusual for a successful plan.

ARCHITECTURAL AND ENGINEERING FIRMS

One tremendous advantage of A&E firms is that there are fewer restrictions on firm equity. Ownership restrictions have to be carefully considered and researched depending on applicable state and Federal regulations. There are many options to ownership structures while acknowledging that certain types of professional services may only be provided by fully credentialed professionals.

Viewpoint of the Seller

This chapter assumes that the sellers are in many cases the entrepreneurial founders that have invested most of their career in the development of the firm. Such individuals remember the early years when the firm was small and success was by no means assured. The firm may carry the name of the individual in its masthead, creating a real sense of legacy. If the principals have made it to the point of considering retirement without selling or merging with another firm, the desire to remain independent may be very strong. This statement is dependent on the principals having the confidence in the next generation of managers to assume the mantle of ownership responsibilities.

Transition Options   Not all sellers may have this sense of legacy and a desire for the firm to survive as an independent entity, and those partners may favor a sale or merger with another firm. The sale or merger will often result in a higher payout to the principals in the short term because of the likely high amount of cash that accompanies the transaction. Often the acquiring firm is much larger and is leveraging its position to expand geographically, by services capabilities, or by industry expertise. Selling or merging with a larger firm often has its own substantial benefits, such as offering economies of scale, access to technology, broader client base, and other worthwhile goals.

The seller is looking for a retirement package that optimizes the retirement assets. The orderly transition from one generation of owners to the next generation is the hallmark of many of the most successful A&E firms. This internal transition helps define the culture of the firm. In the A&E industry long-term relationships with clients are routine and represent years of working successfully together on a wide array of assignments. This long-term view builds goodwill within the firm and is a solid basis from which to structure a longer-term buyout of the retiring principals. Once the firm has a history of successfully passing some percentage of ownership to rising associates the process will reinforce itself with a commitment by both the seller and the buyer to continue the process.

Most principals I have met that are committed to internal transition planning are very proud of their new partner training and development programs. It is a source of pride and a feeling of security in addition to being a strong recruiting tool. It is a wonderful marketing vehicle as well suggesting to clients the firm will be there for the long horizon and will continue to grow with the relationship. The training will take on many forms including such items as training courses at universities, programs offered by professional organizations, attendance at trade association conferences, mentoring with principals, outside mentors, and access to expert consultants.

Chapters 12 and 13 considered Employee Stock Ownership Plans and Trust (ESOPs), and that capital structure is particularly applicable to A&E firms. Traditional ESOP benefits apply including tax incentives, employee retention and recruiting, flexibility in structuring a transition plan, remaining independent, and cultural fit. In a recent study by the National Center for Employee Ownership (NCEO), almost 20 of the largest 100 majority owned ESOPs are in the A&E industry. Many of the most recognizable names in the industry have majority ESOPs including CH2M Hill, DLR Group, Weston Solutions, Inc., and HNTB, Inc.

Viewpoint of the Buyer

The buyer is the next generation of employees destined to become the new principals and owners. Many professionals begin their careers following attendance in college and enter at the ground level in the firm. While it is more common to switch firms during a career, it is likely to find the retiring generation of principals to have spent all or most of their career with a single firm. The progression from entry level staff to increasing levels of responsibility to eventually becoming a principal is often the hope and expectation of associates. Many college students study and enter a profession for the perceived stability and progressive increase in responsibility that is typical of the industry.

The buyer has a long view for ownership potential, an expensive education and commitment to time and values is part of the process of entering the profession. After a number of years on the job as employees, it will become readily apparent to the sellers who are members of the next generation of candidate owners. Today, so many of the employees in an A&E firm have advanced technical skills that many if not most have the potential to be owners. Of course, not all of them will have the same ownership potential, but most will have an ability to make a worthwhile contribution to the firm. Having a broad-based participation program can be an exciting development for a firm wishing to develop a proprietary company culture of ownership in fact. For this reason, we often see A&E firms with broad-based participation programs including the application of ESOPs or actual equity ownership.

Companies that actively champion an ownership culture build a proprietary capability that other professional firms without one cannot match. I think an ownership culture is an integral part of long-term success, but not everyone will agree with this position. Today's employees in such companies are well educated and possess portable skills, and this participatory culture is a key to delivering services to clients with a special focus on fostering long-term client relationships. Experience teaches us that professional service firms that take the time to invest in their employees will be in the best position in the long term to succeed.

Valuation Insights

There is no single best way to value an A&E firm. Legally, if the firm has an ESOP the stock must be valued on the basis of fair market value (FMV) as discussed in Chapter 4 on valuations. In other cases there may be long-standing formulas developed to place a value on the equity position of a principal. The formula approach offers the benefit of not having to decide the profitability of the firm. Trying to decide the profitability of the firm invites the question of the "reasonable" compensation of each of the principals. Most principals likely feel they are worth every dollar paid to them, but that is often a jaundiced opinion supported by emotion and not by fact. Compensation surveys are a wonderful way to attempt to place some value on the services of principals. One potential problem with such surveys in my experience is that many firms have a history of paying out most of their earnings to principals for a number of good reasons including not leaving much in the business to be attached in litigation. The surveys may in fact reflect firms "breaking even" at higher and higher levels. Establishing a reasonable salary for the principals before discretionary bonuses is a good first step in determining a value for the firm.

Industry Guidance   The use of a formula has the further advantage of certainty of the computation. Long-term financial planning is often the result of such a formula. In the A&E industry one formula is the "Z" value developed by Zweig White & Associates. The Z value considers such elements as the number of employees, net revenues, gross profit, business backlog, and reported book value to determine a metric to determine a value of the firm. The use of a formula offers the advantages of simplicity, understandability, and cost effectiveness. The formula may not reflect the actual value of the firm as prepared by an independent appraiser in a traditional valuation analysis focused on profitability and the cost of capital. This formal financial model offers the benefit of being more accurate than a formula because it places the emphasis squarely on the profitability of the company. It also considers the economic environment of the moment, which should have an impact on the valuation. There is a cost to a formal valuation that is an item of consideration.

> The application of industry formulas and rules of thumb are good places to begin a consideration of value. Such mechanical methods may be subject to "gaming" the system, or priming the results just before a transaction. Having another source of valuation confirmation is a viable strategy, even if it is only for a sanity check.

Common candidates for funding the purchase include a stock bonus program whereby the value of the stock being acquired is added to the non-cash compensation of the principal, and the principal pays for the income taxes out of personal funds. An annual bonus or increases in compensation may also be a source of funding. If bank debt is part of the equation, the debt should be payable from anticipated bonuses or salary increases. A reasonable period of time to pay for the equity stake is between four and six years. Of course a candidate may wish to purchase or earn a larger share of the firm's equity, in which case the period of time for the acquisition may be correspondingly adjusted.

Risk Environment

Principals are at risk for the catastrophic event that destroys the professional reputation or the financial structure of the firm. A career spent building a firm may vanish in a matter of moments because of one large unforeseen event. I personally witnessed the demise of several excellent A&E firms with the implosion of the housing industry in the recession beginning in 2008. A few areas of the nation were particularly hard hit by the home construction bust such as portions of Florida, California, and Arizona.

A time-honored hedge on the risk is for the individual to continually invest in the personal portfolio of skills and insure that those skills remain robust and relevant throughout an entire career. If the unthinkable happens, the prepared individual will be able to transfer the skills to another firm. Often a premium is placed on being acknowledged as an industry authority or a leading expert. That distinction is often obtained by authoring articles in professional journals and speaking at appropriate industry conferences. The markets move so rapidly that professionals should be planning for a career that typically will last into their late 60s or even early 70s.

Case Study—MSA Professional Services, Inc.   MSA Professional Services, Inc. (MSA) traces its origins back to the 1930s when legacy affiliates started as a land surveying firm. Over time smaller professional service entities were combined and sold, with the Company growing and finally changing its name to MSA in 1996. Today MSA is a full-service consulting firm offering a host of complementary services in the engineering and development arenas. The comprehensive capabilities are summarized into the following operating divisions: construction, planning and development, environmental, engineering, architecture, surveying and Geographic Information Systems (GIS), transportation, water resources, and project administration and funding. Within each of the operating divisions, MSA offers in-depth capabilities and experience. For example the planning and development division will assist with a wide range of capabilities including strategic planning, statutory development requirements, community financing, GIS services, land use planning, transportation requirements, zoning and ordinance compliance, and economic analysis.

Jim Owen, CEO, says, "We work where we live and have a commitment to the communities we serve." MSA has 15 offices throughout the upper Midwest in Wisconsin, Minnesota, Illinois, Iowa, and Upper Michigan. The offices differ in size and local services provided, but every location is able to draw on the extensive resources of the entire Company. This is a strategic advantage because of the local contacts and trust MSA has built over time. The Company has an expansive program of project leader development and recognition of the importance of teamwork in meeting customer requirements. Like all professional service firms, keeping the employees accountable is an ongoing challenge. Jim Owen notes that the branch managers and the various project leaders have incentives to work together and coordinate resources in the interests of MSA and its customers.

MSA fosters the teamwork outlook because the firm is employee owned. There is a combination of employee shareholders and an ESOP. Jim Hendricks, CFO, remarks, "Building and reinforcing the ownership culture is an ongoing commitment because we are in so many different locations across five states." Sharing technical information, customer case studies, and in-field successes is one way MSA fosters the spirit of cooperation. This ongoing commitment is taken very seriously by the senior management team as MSA has approximately 300 associates at the various locations.

As an employee-owned firm there are two levels of ownership participation. First is the ESOP, which permits ownership through the Employee Retirement Income Security Act (ERISA) – centric regulations, so in effect all of the eligible employees have a financial interest in MSA. Other key employees are invited to become shareholders depending on demonstrated capabilities and commitment to MSA. Ownership at this level is broad based and is a source for the future company leaders. MSA carefully champions employee involvement on many levels, including project leadership, team development, branch managers, and senior officers.

Recent challenging economies throughout the MSA market area have reinforced the need for teamwork. The expansive reach of the MSA employees into so many communities was helpful in identifying business opportunities for the various divisions. MSA was able to draw upon its culture of ownership to find additional work. Jim Owen remarks, "Our commitment to communications and team building is a major responsibility of the senior management, but we know the results are worthwhile and at the forefront of helping MSA to grow and provide significant careers for our employees." Living where they work, MSA continues to expand services and provide an enhanced quality of life to the communities served.

Technical Matters

A&E firms enjoy strong flexibility in the ownership of the firm. Many firms are corporations for obvious liability reasons. Other legal entities may be considered with appropriate limits on personal liability within statutory regulations. There is increasingly a trend to have broad-based participation programs within the larger firms. ESOPs are increasingly popular for inside transition planning because of the tax efficiencies already discussed in prior chapters. If the entity is a C corporation there is great flexibility in the capital structure that permits multiple classes of stock. Such equity vehicles as incentive stock options and qualified stock options may be considered for rising professionals. There may be voting and non-voting stock so that equity is shared but the control of the firm resides with the ownership of the voting stock.

Shareholder Agreements   When there are multiple principals, having a shareholder agreement has to be a standard protocol. That agreement must stipulate such things as how the equity positions are valued; how the equity is redeemed from an exiting owner; what happens in the event of a tragedy or unforeseen event; what happens in the event of a divorce; restrictions on the transfer of the equity, and other timely considerations. Most professional trade associations have helpful resources to assist members with succession planning.

Financing   New owners should be able to acquire an equity interest without undue financial hardship. The resources available to the candidate should be disclosed when candidacy becomes a likely event. As mentioned, applying bonuses and salary increases toward the purchase price are customary. The period of sacrifice should be reasonable and limited. Companies may consider inside loans to the candidate amortized from future bonuses. As a pragmatic insight, any program exceeding five years has to be reviewed for desirability. If it takes 5 to 10 years (or longer) to even be considered for an equity position, adding an additional 5 years for the buy-in represents a major portion of a typical working career.

PUBLIC ACCOUNTING FIRMS

Ownership requirements in public accounting firms are typically dictated by the various state boards of accountancy. Pubic accounting as a profession exists as a form of assurance for the readers of financial statements that certain reporting standards are verified. Historically many state boards of accountancy permitted only licensed CPAs to be equity stakeholders in public accounting firms. The advent of complex computer systems for financial reporting and operational requirements meant that certifying financial statements was a function of understanding and auditing information systems. Computer and systems technology skills beyond accounting and auditing became essential for discharging professional responsibilities. In this light most boards of accountancy have amended public accounting ownership rules to permit non-CPAs as principals. Generally, up to 50% of the equity may be held by non-CPAs, but that is a threshold defined by each state. Exemptions from those ownership rules may be granted, but it often requires a special application for an exception to the ownership rules.

Viewpoint of the Seller

Public accounting firms have one common attribute as members of a profession in that the core service, the certification of financial statement reporting, may only be authenticated by a CPA. Traditionally the public accounting firm was dominated by CPAs, often because most of the associates begin their careers in the audit division and with time migrated to other units such as taxes or information systems consulting. This situation has changed dramatically with time and many professionals never become CPAs but nonetheless have critical contributions to the firm. Most commonly the one discipline that is essential but does not require advanced accounting education is information technology applications.

Demographic Changes The principal that is approaching retirement has many of the same concerns as principals in the A&E firms, assuming the firm is committed to an inside transfer program that is typically a core value and is broadly communicated to associates. One interesting aspect of CPA firms today is that over half of the accounting graduates coming from universities are women, and in certain regions the percentage is over 60%. Succession planning now considers the long-term horizon for the female professionals to have a career with the firm consistent with family goals. The historic days of almost unending hours during the "busy season" have to be tempered with the reality that associates in fact have family lives outside the firm.

The profession is currently undergoing a personnel crisis where an unprecedented amount of talent is retiring in the next decade. Many firms are currently top heavy with baby boomer principals that have made a career at the company. As mentioned, the actual professional franchise of certifying financial statements is mature and not rapidly growing. The actual need for CPAs in public accounting firms has not been steadily growing.

Transition to Broader Based Advisory Firms Many CPA firms have addressed this serious shortfall in staff leverage by expanding services well beyond accounting services. Such areas as tax preparation, general business consulting, wealth management, business valuations, and information systems consulting have provided the growth that is needed for the business model based on staff leverage to keep working.

Many principals have a commitment to keeping the firm independent. One fascinating development in the public accounting profession is the development and evolution of public accounting firm networks. Many larger commercial clients have multiple locations in various states and countries. Such clients may prefer the professional service of one firm closest to the corporate headquarters, but equal service must be provided to the various distant operations. Networks of public accounting firms have evolved to provide services to such clients. The networks are typically composed of peer group firms of approximately similar size that have combined to offer national and international service capabilities. This synergistic combining of resources has kept many regional public accounting firms competitive with the industry leaders, often referred to as the "Big Four." Examples of networks include AGN International, CPA Associates International, CPAmerica International, HLB International, International Group of Accounting Firms, Leading Edge Alliance, PFK International, and Praxity Global Alliance. Other networks are aligned under the name of a single firm such as the BDO Seidman Alliance and Crowe Horwath International. There are many other networks that have evolved in the interests of offering multiple location clients a resource of affiliated firms.

The development of the networks means that many firms are free to transition internally while remaining a member of the network without having the need to be acquired by a larger entity. Acquisitions and mergers still have a major presence in the profession, but it is not necessarily a requirement for survival.

Viewpoint of the Buyer

The profession has a discernable brand, which is "CPA." It is one of the most recognized professional designations. It establishes the holder of the designation as a member of one of the largest professional organizations in the country. The entry level educational requirements today have been increased to the point, where it literally takes five years of college to meet the requirements to sit for the uniform CPA exam. Conceptually, that is almost the equivalent of having to obtain a master's degree. After making the educational commitment to obtain the credential, many holders want to have a career in accounting, if not public accounting. They are typically less willing to tolerate the historical business template of suffering through years of business seasons for 10–15 years for perhaps a shot at making partner in the firm.

Often the brightest associates stayed in public accounting for a period of time to amass outstanding technical and professional credentials and left for the more family-friendly embrace of a career in industry or government as a controller, chief financial officer, treasurer, or other comparable position of responsibility. This frequent turnover of the most qualified partner candidates was a crushing burden to the public accounting firms because of the loss of executive-level experience walking out the door. If this loss of talent was to be in part blunted, the lifestyle requirements of younger associates must be addressed. Additionally, career tracks have to be offered for a wide spectrum of associates that will not have equity participation in the firm, but will nonetheless play an integral role in the future.

> There are a number of public accounting firms challenging the traditional template of allowing only a select few to participate in the equity. Chapter 1 considered SSG Financial Services as one "outside-the-box" example of progressive thinking with stellar results.

Progressive public accounting firms today offer far more family-friendly environments than in the past. Many firms are routinely recognized as outstanding places to work because professional and family lifestyle considerations have been successfully addressed. The transition from staff to principal while being more family friendly is available for a greater number of entrants into the profession. Making the ascent to the top management responsibilities within the firm takes time and years of commitment.

Valuation Insights

Public accounting firms are well known to be valued in relation to some industry centric formula. One of the strongest attributes of the profession is the likelihood of recurring work year over year. Once companies and clients have established a requirement for financial statement services, the need is almost always ongoing. Complementary services such as tax preparation and information technology support are often annuitized into ongoing annual services. While the profession is mature the need to continually find new clients to meet the next payroll is sharply reduced due to recurring revenue.

One of the most common metrics of valuation is a relationship between annual revenue and a purchase price. An often quoted relationship is 1 times annual revenue, but that percentage will range between .8 times to 2 times revenue depending on the quality of the clients and likelihood of client retention and repeat revenue. Other operational metrics may weigh into the valuation formula, but most typically the firm is valued on an easily understood computation.

Risk Environment

The most valuable asset of a professional services firm is its reputation. Any risk to the reputation will obviously have a negative impact on the value of the principal's equity. Individual CPAs enjoy one outstanding attribute that may not exist for many other professionals. They may segue effortlessly into industry from public accounting, often being highly desirable by former clients. With time the CPA has grown to know the client almost better than many members of the senior team at the client because of the nature of auditing and certifying financial statements. The most confidential client information typically must be shared with the CPA. Hallmarks of the profession include independence, objectivity, and confidentiality – enviable attributes if you have to go shopping for a new job.

Many college graduates today enter public accounting for the cerebral challenges, adherence to strict values, and a long career. The profession has changed to become far more family friendly, with the result that many CPAs and other non-CPA employees now enjoy a career track without the "up-or-out" mentality of yesteryear.

Case Study—Burr Pilger Mayer Certified Public Accounting   Three professional friends and colleagues, Curtis Burr, Henry Pilger, and Steve Mayer, working for the same Big 4 accounting firm in San Francisco for almost 10 years, decided that the traditional career reward system in public accounting was out of step with reality as they knew it. The time is 1986 and the trio lived in the San Francisco area, home to the exciting Silicon Valley network of technology companies. Something about the traditional highly structured Big 4 public accounting career template was out of step with the California business environment. The founders saw far more exciting ownership developments in their clients compared to the home port of the public accounting domain.

The three formed Burr Pilger Mayer Public Accounting and Consulting (BPM) with the entrepreneurial spirit to try and improve on what seemed to them as a dated business model for the profession. Starting with energy, big dreams, and solid expertise, BPM quickly grew and within 20 years was recognized as one of the largest non-big four public accounting firms in the Bay Area (San Francisco and Oakland). With the growth in staff, the principals also invested in service capabilities. BPM is a full-service public accounting and consulting firm with extensive capabilities in the broad areas of assurance services (traditional CPA focus): tax advisory and preparation internationally and domestic, commercial consulting (valuations, mergers and acquisitions, litigation support, forensic accounting to mention a few), IT consulting, and wealth management.

BPM has been recognized numerous times for its excellence in employee relations and building a distinctive culture. Often recognized as one of the best places to work in the region, BPM is focused on building a dedicated team by focusing on training, development, lifestyle issues, long-term commitment to the staff, and building an environment where people actually smile (the website lists having fun as a goal). The commitment to the staff is exceptional. BPM offers a wide array of benefits including such items as a broad-based insurance program for health and life, a pre-tax cafeteria plan, generous educational benefits, and a 401(k) plan. In addition to these strong benefits, President Steve Mayer and his executive team wanted to make a statement about the BPM difference. In 2010 they became one of the first major public accounting firms to install a traditional ESOP. While ESOPs are common in many industries, they are rare in public accounting. Steve Mayer said, "We are virtually unique in offering some ownership in the firm to all qualifying employees. Many of our clients have similar programs and our team members constantly see it in the field." BPM has joined those far-looking clients by bringing their own employees into a culture of ownership.

One may ask: How is BPM doing in the competitive California professional services market? From a single office in 1986, BPM has grown to 10 offices with over 400 professionals. Recent growth in revenue has been averaging +20% per year. They are now the largest California-based public accounting firm. BPM has addressed the succession issue by migrating away from a rigid formula endemic of many CPA firms, to a more balanced approach that recognizes the equity that the principals have built. The ESOP was installed when a number of principals retired in 2010. Exiting principals will sell a portion of their stock to the ESOP at the annual valuation amount, which recognizes the fair market value of their equity. The balance is redeemed by the firm. The ESOP is currently a minority shareholder, and will always be in a minority position. The stock of retiring principals sold to the ESOP is redeemed with tax-deductible dollars.

BPM seeks to recruit the best and brightest associates. The firm has high expectations, and those that find the challenges and rewards of a career at BPM are pleased with their decision. BPM attracts new college graduates, but a substantial number of the professional team has Big 4 experience. This exposure to experienced staff has evolved into a substantial SEC practice area, which is often unusual with regional public accounting firms.

There are three driving principles for BPM: Provide a full range of services to clients, commitment to community, and have fun. Clearly BPM backs the principles with action on a daily basis by giving back to the communities it serves and placing people first. BPM is a member of the Leading Edge Alliance, an affiliation of likeminded public accounting and consulting firms worldwide.

Technical Matters

This overview of CPA firms cannot begin to address the issue of succession planning to the extent studied by the American Institute of Certified Public Accountants (AICPA). The AICPA offers excellent resources for public accounting firms. The Private Companies Practice Section (PCPS) of the AICPA offers two outstanding books. William Reeb has authored *Securing the Future: Succession Planning Basics* (American Institute of Certified Public Accountants, 2010), and the PCPS has sponsored *Securing the Future: Taking Succession Planning to the Next Level* (American Institute of Certified Public Accountants, 2010). Those books provide an excellent overview of the succession-planning process with insights into such matters as accountability for all professionals in the firm, training future leaders, setting expectations, and formalizing the transition process.

When a CPA firm explores ownership options one of the first requirements is to verify the state Board of Accountancy regulations pertaining to equity participation. Those state regulations are not necessarily the final word as exceptions may be authorized. Anticipate an additional application to seek a waiver of the regulations, and wait. It will likely take months for the review process and eventual decision to be made.

MANAGEMENT CONSULTING FIRMS

There is a wide spectrum of professional service firms under this general banner. The intended common element is that such firms are populated with well-educated practitioners that provide specific and often customized services for clients and customers. There are few disciplines in this general category that require participants to have mandatory professional certifications. Many professions offer designations as an indication of minimum attainment of skills. Such designations may be subject to passing a rigorous examination and meeting experience requirements.

Viewpoint of the Seller

Management consulting often does not enjoy a requirement for services. A market for services obviously exists, but it is typically up to the professional to identify the market and sell the services. There is typically a high requirement for the ability to be a consistent new business producer. Not only does new business have to be consistently developed, few of the professions offer the security of the ongoing business that public accounting firms enjoy. One of the few subsets of firms that come close regulatory compliance whereby there is an ongoing requirement for services. Some environmental or safety testing firms are examples.

Internal transition planning will typically have a high emphasis placed on the ability to generate new business. Many principals have to be guarded about transition planning. The failure to keep communications open with the promising new business development achievers (rainmakers) may result in one day having your former superstars as new competitors. The best associates often possess strong attributes in self-confidence and risk tolerance. They may not be particularly entrepreneurial, but why take the risk? If those associates are that good it makes sense to invite them to become equity stakeholders in the company.

Typically, once a consulting firm has reached critical mass beyond a few professionals, the organization has been the majority of the adult career of the principals. There is a commitment to the organization as most of the senior associates are often good friends as well as business partners. The need to provide services and produce billings is a bond that ties associates together. This is particularly the case when the firm has weathered the turbulence of recessions and other challenges. The firm is the people, and often developing a long-term succession strategy involving them as partners often produces acceptable value for a retiring principal.

Viewpoint of the Buyer

Many of the most promising candidates for equity participation have outstanding capabilities essential for the firm. To retain their services, it is a best practice to communicate a transition strategy before frustration levels reach a point where they leave. These associates often have strong portable skills in demand by other employers and they will consider options if they feel overlooked or neglected.

As discussed in earlier sections of this chapter, the inside key employees often do not have the financial resources to acquire the firm with after-tax dollars. The transition process may take years, but if it is gradual and does not pose unduly harsh sacrifices on the part of the candidate buyers the end result will be a successful transfer of ownership.

Valuation Insights

Similar to the other professional service forms discussed, there is no best way to place a value on the businesses. Most typical professional trade associations will conduct surveys as a membership benefit on succession-planning and valuation. Often there is some acceptable methodology for developing a benchmark valuation or even a rule of thumb.

With professional service forms, the total valuation is often a function of the terms, and the leading term is retention of clients. In many cases there is a substantial portion of the consideration linked to the retention of clients, and this is a de facto earn-out. If the brand of the firm is particularly strong, client retention is typically much easier. Additionally, client retention is more likely if the transition period from one principal to the next generation begins at least two years before the retirement, or some other designated period of time for the clients to accept change.

Rivalries between senior principals and younger understudies are bound to create friction, but that is part of the transition process. The wise professionals plan for the transition process and work to minimize conflicts in the interest of passing ownership as seamlessly as possible.

Risk Environment

The same admonition applies in this case as with the other professional service firms. One additional comment is that many management consulting firms have a concentration of credit in a few large customers. The relationship has grown with time and the largest clients receive the disproportionate amount of the principal's effort. It is common to see the top few customers comprising half the revenue or more. I have seen situations where a single large account is over 80% of the revenue but it is divided between six autonomous operating divisions. The theory is that the multiple operating divisions are really stand-alone customers that do not communicate with one another. Beware of corporate consolidation or reorganization when suddenly corporate purchasing flexes its authority and consolidates vendors. The loss of one of those large clients is a major financial consideration. This clearly is a major issue for the seller as well as the buyer. While a concentration of credit may not be avoidable, the seller should be aware that such a concentration is a decided negative to value.

The risk is amplified when the consulting firm is regional and the opportunity to replace large accounts is severely limited. Transitioning with inside associates is a delicate subject that must be addressed with candor and pragmatic expectations.

Technical Matters

The management consulting services industry is dominated at the ownership level by successful rainmakers and individuals often having a high professional profile. If there is an internal transition process in place it is essential to secure a non-solicitation and non-competition agreement from the seller. The seller is unlikely to turn against the former employer, particularly if it is a firm that the seller founded. In rare instances, bitterness may linger at having to retire or being forced out by younger associates, but it is unlikely to result in a challenge to the company. Obtaining the non-competition agreement is typically much easier to enforce if the violator is given significant consideration in return for the promise.

SUMMARY

The increasing demands of a competitive society and the higher educational and experience barriers to entry for most professions means that the newest members of the firms have exceedingly portable skills. Traditional templates for advancement and eventual equity participation are being challenged by many firms with positive results. The retention and recruitment of qualified associates is forcing a rethinking of dated methods in many sectors. Progressive professional firms recognizing this new reality sooner will likely be the marketplace leaders tomorrow.

CHAPTER 15

Buyouts Using Parallel Companies

Put all your eggs in one basket, and watch the basket.

—Mark Twain

Prior chapters have focused on shareholders transitioning the company to a new group of owners, but still maintaining the identity of the original business. As we have seen, there are often compelling reasons for maintaining the existence and the identity of the company regarding such things as industry goodwill, reputation, the ability to sell stock, among other reasons previously described. There may be instances when creating or employing another separate entity is appropriate to facilitate the succession of the business.

The most common structure I have seen for this scenario is referred to as the "parallel company" strategy. The idea is to transition the operating activities from a well established company (Firstco) to another recently formed company (Newco). The reason for adopting this two-company strategy is that Firstco may have some of the following attributes: Firstco may be exposed to potentially catastrophic liability; the assets of Firstco are too valuable for an asset sale; liability may make a stock sale impractical; bonding issues may apply. Most of the reasons for adopting the two-company strategy relate to issues regarding the construction industry. A construction firm working on bridges and overpasses may face potentially ruinous liability in the event of a catastrophe. Another construction-related firm may have a significant commitment to capital equipment that is too much of a burden for a new owner, perhaps in the case of road construction. Bonding may be a major issues and the newly formed business may not qualify for the insurance.

Following this general industry application, the owner of the construction firm wants to sell the company to its managers, but the managers are unwilling to acquire the stock of the candidate company because of potential liability issues, or they simply cannot generate the financing to acquire Firstco. Perhaps the current owner is incapable or unwilling to relinquish control until Firstco has been paid in full. Another entity, Newco, is formed to facilitate the transition. Over time the value of Firstco will be transferred to Newco, the successor entity.

Another reason to consider this structure is to provide the seller with the security of retaining the assets of the business in the event of some disastrous event. If the assets are sold to the managers in Newco employing a significant seller note, then the assets and the Newco business could be wiped out, along with the collateral on the seller note,

ADVANTAGES

Establishing another entity addresses the circumstances previously mentioned where there are either tremendous potential contingent liabilities, or the owner wishes to retain control of the key assets of the company until such time as they are relinquished or paid. The owner is not selling the assets or the stock of the primary company; rather the owner is entering into an agreement with the new entity to participate in the revenues and profitability of Newco. The level and amount of the participation in Newco will be a negotiated resolution satisfactory to both the seller and the next generation of owners and managers.

Using parallel companies in this manner permits an orderly transition during a period of time the seller is most comfortable. Using this structure typically will take several years to accomplish the transition. During this time, the seller is typically helping Newco's management build a clientele and a successful reputation. The relationship between the original company and Newco is typically memorialized with an operating agreement between the companies that establishes the interests of both parties and how long the agreement is in effect. There is great flexibility in structuring the relationship to address the goals of all the parties to the transaction.

After a period of time when Newco is established and has a credit capability, the original company may eventually sell its assets to Newco at a negotiated price. Generally, we have not seen a situation where the original company sells its stock to Newco for liability reasons.

Firstco will likely be entering into agreements with Newco for such items as leasing a facility for operations, leasing or renting equipment as needed for jobs, leasing employees depending on job requirements, entering into consulting arrangements for technical support and paying for other services and assistance as appropriate.

Typically the agreements between Firstco and Newco are structured to be operating agreements and tax deductible when paid or accrued by Newco. This is enormously beneficial for Newco because it suggests a pay-as-you-go environment, thereby potentially relieving the Newco management of the burden of trying to raise financing on the front end of the transaction. If the expenses are deductible to Newco that likely means the revenue to Firstco is ordinary income. The ordinary income will be subject to income tax rates and not capital gain tax rates.

CAUTIONS

Using multiple entities requires considerable advanced planning. The owners of Firstco are not selling the original company at first, and therefore they are relinquishing some potential tax advantages. If Firstco could qualify as an asset sale, and it has a strong assets base consisting of substantial capital equipment, much of the purchase price may be ordinary income to the seller because of depreciation recapture. The sale of other assets such as accounts receivable and inventory also typically result in ordinary income to the seller. Only a portion of the sold assets may be subject to capital gain taxes.

When Firstco receives revenue from the lease or rental of its assets to Newco, this ordinary operating income is an acknowledgement by the seller that this is the most pragmatic way to approach the ownership succession issues. Firstco is receiving cash flow and it is up to the seller to be as tax efficient as practicable while converting this cash flow to liquidity.

This structure will typically take a number of years to complete. Depending on the ability of Newco to be profitable or to generate significant cash flow, the transition period may be from a few years to a very lengthy period of time. The seller may be at risk for several years waiting for the agreements with Newco to provide the anticipated liquidity. The construction industry is known for its volatility and this strategy may be subject to considerable delays in the event of an unforeseen recession or other negative event.

> Using parallel companies to implement a transition plan promises significant flexibility in meeting the objectives of the buyer and the seller. The plan is most typically linked to business volume and is a natural fit for companies in volatile or cyclical industries. The planning cycle may take years to complete, but it avoids potentially ruinous debt levels.

The parallel company strategy may be acceptable to the seller and the management of Newco from an operating standpoint. If Newco requires bonding, it may be unlikely that it has the financial resources to secure bonding by itself. Newco may need the guarantee of Firstco to secure work. Newco may be charged a fee for relying on the bonding capacity of Firstco.

Firstco should be a pass-through entity for tax purposes if it is not already when the operating agreements are executed. Revenue from Newco will go to Firstco as operating income. It is important that the income from the revenue not be taxable to Firstco at the entity level, as with a C corporation. If Firstco is an S corporation or some other form of a pass-through tax entity, income will flow to the seller and be eligible for a distribution. The distribution may be taken in lieu of a salary thereby bypassing Federal Insurance Contribution Act (FICA) taxes. Tax advice should be secured to verify the potential tax liability of whatever structure is adopted.

VALUATION INSIGHTS

Using parallel companies means that there is typically an overall understanding of how to value Firstco from a cash flow standpoint. The intent is to have the revenue from Newco to Firstco taxed as ordinary income. The ultimate value of Firstco to the seller will be taxed at ordinary income rates. This relative tax disadvantage may be compensated by having operating agreements between the parallel companies extended for a longer period to provide a reasonable return to the seller.

At some point once Newco is sufficiently well established with credit availability, Firstco may eventually sell assets to Newco. In this event, there may be some capital asset considerations resulting in capital gain treatment to the seller. While this is a possibility, capital gain treatment resulting from the sale of assets is often not a driving attribute of the deal.

The valuation of the original company is typically a function of a number of revenue-sharing agreements that define costs to Newco and income to Firstco. It will likely be a number of years for the owners of the original company to realize the overall value for the business, and during that time they are in essence providing financing to Newco by agreeing to lease or rent various assets.

One hedge on the future on the part of the owners of Firstco is to enter into a royalty program with Newco that is an "evergreen" agreement having no defined ending date. Perhaps the royalty program includes the use of a brand or trade name that is widely recognized in the business community. There are many opportunities to structure long-term agreements that will provide the value required by Firstco while allowing Newco time to become established.

VIEWPOINT OF THE SELLER

The structure of the transition plan is open to creative thought, but there are some time-honored general principals regarding structure. The seller wants to convert the ownership interest in Firstco to liquidity. It is important to structure Firstco as a pass-through entity for taxes as mentioned. The strategy is to establish a relationship with Newco so that it is paying rental rates or leases to the original company. The idea is to insure that the sellers are paying a single tax rate at the personal level.

One strategy mentioned is to have Firstco lease or rent assets and equipment to Newco. This will result in a deductible expense to Newco, and it is ordinary income to the original company. Classifying as much cash flow as possible as rental income or lease income to Firstco will have the benefit of income to the original company that is not subject to payroll withholding taxes. Often the goal is to have Newco paying deductible expenses to Firstco that largely consume the profitability of Firstco. For example, if Newco is renting equipment, the rent may be computed by the hour, the day, or some other negotiated period. Leasing equipment may be attractive to the seller because it provides a more certain cash flow, but Newco may not have the business to support a lease. Renting allows the relationship to fluctuate with business activity.

If Firstco occupies facilities owned by the shareholder and leased back to Firstco, those same facilities may be a candidate to be leased instead to Newco. The lease revenue is likely to be passive income to the owner, which may have desirable tax-planning attributes. The existence of a lease for facilities from the owner of Firstco (often a separate limited liability company), and renting equipment, and perhaps employees from Firstco represents tax planning for multiple entities. Clearly, the relationship between Firstco (and perhaps a related real estate company) and Newco could become legally complex involving several tax entities. This suggests there are multiple agreements to be coordinated. Again, having professional advisors experienced in such transactions is highly recommended.

VIEWPOINT OF THE BUYER

The successor team in Newco will typically appreciate the opportunity to run a parallel company and be able to acquire Firstco in spirit (if not in name), using tax-deductible dollars in the form of a combination that may include rents, lease payments, royalties, commissions, consulting agreements, or any other form of fee arrangement. From a tax standpoint, this is very efficient for the stakeholders in Newco. Buying an existing business using this strategy is much easier than attempting to begin a totally new company without support. A startup company has an exceedingly difficult time securing the resources it needs to operate at almost any level. The cost of major pieces of construction equipment or the lease on a suitable facility is almost prohibitive.

The Newco management will often need the cooperation and assistance of Firstco to work with customers throughout the transition period. It is common for planning to be communicated to key customers to let them know this is a strategy for business continuity that is tax efficient. The operating essence of Firstco is not changing, as the management is the ownership of Newco.

PROFESSIONAL ADVISORS

This structure is one that in effect has a buyer and a seller and at least two separate entities. If another entity owning facilities or real estate used in the business is involved, the number of relationships increases along with a corresponding requirement to maintain accounting records. Clearly there is assistance required in a number of disciplines in this case. Those disciplines are legal counsel, accounting and tax expertise, and insurance.

First, having legal counsel familiar with these types of transaction structure is important. The relationship between Newco and Firstco may involve a number of agreements that are transferring cash and revenue from one company to another. Those agreements have to be drafted, reviewed, and executed to the acceptance of all parties. Newco has to be formed, and the legal entity must be thoroughly considered.

Understanding the tax environment for each of the entities and the shareholders in them requires a strategic tax planner. That tax advisor may be the attorney or it may be another financial advisor, most often a certified public accountant (CPA) or a public accounting firm. While most of the agreements are likely to result in ordinary income (and a tax deduction to the payer); there may be planning opportunities to convert some ordinary income to taxable capital gain income at a much lower tax rate.

These agreements often take a number of years to accomplish. The longer the term that Firstco is providing support, the stronger the case for some insurance on the owner of the Firstco. Contacting suitable insurance representation will uncover potential financial exposure that may be covered with an insurance product.

RISK ENVIRONMENT

This parallel company structure is often used when Firstco is difficult to sell for any number of reasons. Since one of the most commonly encountered applications is with construction companies, clearly there is a risk consideration with that industry. Construction firms are often notoriously exposed to highly volatile fluctuations in revenue and income. The benefit of using parallel companies is that conceptually it is a pay-as-you-go environment. It is very difficult and often not wise to heavily leverage a construction firm with long-term debt. Debt obligations, particularly from a third party such as a bank, come with loan covenants that may be subject to violation during periods of economic uncertainty. If loan covenants are violated or if there is a payment default on the loan, significant trouble accrues to the debtor.

Taking the longer view that considers industry volatility is appropriate. Without putting the underlying business activity at undue risk, having reasonable agreements in place is a tremendous positive that helps insure an orderly transition. The recession beginning in 2008 is a lesson in not leveraging a construction-related company with fixed obligations. Using parallel companies offers a great deal of flexibility with adjustments that may be enacted as circumstances demand.

If the underlying business entity is construction oriented and subject to bonding capabilities, the acceptance of the plan by a bonding company is paramount. Communicating with the bonding company and retaining an approval from them is essential for a successful transition. The use of parallel companies with the original company guaranteeing the bonds, or providing acceptable assurance during the transition period is a critical detail to confirm.

FIRSTCO CONSTRUCTION

Firstco Construction, Inc. (Firstco or the Company) is a road-building and resurfacing construction company in the Midwest with approximately 80 employees. Firstco uses the trade name of "Allweather Construction" as its brand, which is a well-recognized name in the marketing area and lettered on all the equipment. Only 30 of the employees are full time for the entire year; the balance are seasonal and receive layoff notices each winter. Most of the work is subject to bidding on State Department of Transportation projects, which requires

posting performance bonds. Located in a metropolitan area and region
with over 2 million people, Firstco has enjoyed a strong market share
of available business based on an analysis of bidding results the past
10 years. Firstco is one of three major regional competitors. The current recession has decreased operating revenues over 30%, but activity
is beginning to rebound.

Mr. Smith, age 64, is the sole shareholder of Firstco, an S corporation for income tax purposes. He is the sole principal of Buildings, LLC (a limited liability company) that leases facilities to Firstco
that include an 8,000 square foot facility with a complete maintenance garage for heavy construction equipment overhauls, administrative offices, and parts warehouse. Buildings, LLC owns 10 acres
of land that is used for outside storage. The storage is essential during the winter when substantially all of the equipment is back on
the lot.

Firstco was founded in 1980 and has amassed a reservoir of new
and used construction equipment that includes such pieces as bull-
dozers, graders, profiling equipment, front end loaders, flat bed de-
livery trucks, pick-up trucks, and various other support units. The
maintenance garage refurbishes the equipment during the winter keeping several mechanics busy. While many of the major pieces are
older, they are well maintained and functional. The useful life for
much of the major equipment is 10–15 years. The equipment is 70%
depreciated.

Mr. Smith wants to pass Firstco to a trio of capable managers that have on average 15 years of experience with the Company. Mr. Smith has no children in the business. The managers are
all under 50 years of age and have demonstrated a capability to
work together. Mr. Jones is currently the Chief Operating Officer
and is the leader of the management team. The three managers will
form Newco, an S corporation, to enter into a number of operating agreements with Firstco and Buildings, LLC. The management
team has invested between them $250,000 to capitalize Newco and
fund working capital needs and meet payroll for the first several
months. All of the management team members have taken second
mortgages on their homes and contributed some savings to the capital
contribution.

The management team feels confident there is enough business to
enter into a sublease with Firstco and Buildings, LLC for the use of
the facilities including the building and outside storage. Newco enters
into a sublease for five years with renewals for two additional five-
year periods. After just 10 years, Mr. Smith will consider extending

an option to the management team to acquire the facilities at its fair market value. Mr. Smith suggested he would consider a seller note on the facilities when the time comes. Mr. Smith remarks: "What am I going to do with a maintenance garage that can refurbish CAT equipment? I want the management team to have the building once they can afford it."

Firstco and Newco have agreed on rental rates for all of the construction equipment. Some of the equipment is rented on an hourly basis as needed, and other pieces are rented for an entire work season. The hourly rates are more expensive to Newco, but the additional cost provides flexibility to meet peak demand without incurring fixed costs. Newco is responsible for the maintenance of the equipment and insurance. The rental and lease agreements are beneficial for Firstco because most of the equipment is paid with little outstanding debt. Newco may acquire the equipment as they have the ability to pay for it. Pricing will be negotiated at the time of sale.

During the first three years while Newco is establishing credit and building net worth, Firstco agrees to lease certain full-time employees to Newco. After three years Newco will decide how many employees it will be able to support. Finally, Mr. Smith has entered into a 20 year royalty program whereby Newco pays 1% of revenue for the exclusive use of the name "Allweather Construction."

Mr. Smith wanted to sell Firstco and Buildings, LLC for a combined $10 million as part of an asset sale, but that structure was not workable. He is in essence providing seller financing through leases, rentals, and a royalty program to Newco. Based on projections and considering the current recession, it will take Newco between 8 and 11 years to pay Mr. Smith the $10 million fair value of the business.

This illustration will eventually prove to be valuable to Mr. Smith and the management team with time. Mr. Smith will realize the fair value of Firstco and Buildings, LLC. The transition of Firstco is largely at ordinary income tax rates. The eventual sale of Buildings, LLC may result in some ordinary income and capital gain liability. Firstco is a substantial company and under this illustration it will take almost a decade to pass ownership. Planning of the long horizon is appropriate. Mr. Smith is delighted because Allweather Construction will be in business for decades to come.

TECHNICAL MATTERS

The Firstco illustration suggests that the parallel company strategy for substantial entities will likely take years to complete, during which time any number of unforeseen events may complicate the intended outcome. Having experienced professional advisors assisting with a plan that is flexible yet binding, is an art form that results in a successful transition.

Careful financial and tax planning is indispensable. The parallel company plan should be modeled over many years to illustrate the cash flows that can be anticipated and the likely tax on them. The successor team should be invested in the transition and should be required to make a significant personal financial commitment. The significant personal commitment is in relation to the individual's net worth and not necessarily in relation to the size of the transaction. The successor team must demonstrate a willingness to stay focused to insure the program works.

SUMMARY

The parallel company strategy in this chapter is targeted primarily for construction-related organizations. In the right circumstance, the strategy will work well transitioning a company that may prove very difficult to sell to a third party. The planning is predicated on a long-term time horizon and a great deal of trust between the parties. With so much uncertainty in the economy, placing so much faith in trust and a long-term payout may not be acceptable to the seller. An option for the seller is to reduce the price or hold out hoping for an improved economy that allows for more leverage in buyouts. For owners with an interest in pursuing a succession strategy where they have worked hard to build a management team capable of succession responsibilities, reducing the price and working with the management leaders over a longer period of time may be one of the best decisions ever made if it provides an exit vehicle.

CHAPTER 16

Buyouts with Family and Management

If you put off estate planning long enough, you won't need it.
—Arthur Bloch

You never know how soon it will be too late.
—Anonymous

This chapter assumes the intent is to have the business stay within the family, or within its control. Several key assumptions are part of the strategy to keep the business within the family. First, we assume there are capable members of the family to run the company and provide leadership into the next generation. Second, the company has to be financially viable. One of the benefits of a family company is that even financially weak firms may be transitioned to the next generation, whereas poor financial performance is often not an option for most of the other buyout strategies. A company that is profitable will typically result in the next generation having an interest in owning and managing the business. Finally, we assume that the founding generation or the generation passing ownership actually wants to pass control to the next generation.

2010 TAX LAW UPDATE

The biggest news for privately held family companies in the immediate short term is the passage of the Tax Relief, Unemployment Insurance Reauthorization and Job Creation Act of 2010 (2010 Tax Relief Act), which greatly expanded the limits for gifting. By way of sharp contrast before the passage of the 2010 Tax Relief Act, the practical limits for gifting any material amount of wealth to a next generation was $1,000,000 for individuals ($2,000,000 for a couple), a substantial but often largely insignificant amount compared to the value of most middle market financially successful companies. This prior gifting limit was a function of the Federal unified exclusion amount, and while the limits on the unified exclusion amount were increasing recently, a sunset provision in the tax code was going to revert to limits in 2001. The 2010 Tax Relief Act increased the unified exclusion amount to $5,000,000 or $10,000,000 for a husband and wife. This legislation will be discussed in more detail shortly, but the key thing to emphasize is that the generous gift tax limits have been increased only until December 31, 2012. Gifting to the next generation is by far the most tax efficient method of passing wealth, and the time to take advantage of the legislation on the books currently is very limited.

Many smaller family-owned businesses will stay within the ownership of the family; there are also a number of circumstances when the business has grown and is sufficiently complex that outside managers may be called upon to provide leadership for the company until the family regains the skills to run the business. For example, the next generation may still be in school or simply has not been given enough time to gain the skills necessary to run the company. In such instances, an interim strategy of employing experienced management to run the company until such time in the future that a family member is qualified to assume the most senior responsibilities is adopted.

This chapter will explore some of the more traditional methods of succession planning entirely within the scope of family members, and also a number of practices to consider when outside management is employed to lead the company. When outside management is employed, one critical issue is the compensation of such managers. One mistake often made is that the managers are not provided any significant incentives to increase the value of the business; rather it seems their role is custodial and to not lose value. This unfortunate development may lead to a company that has limited leadership and no apparent future. This can be a decided negative development for the key employees with portable skills.

ADVANTAGES

Going back to our chapter assumptions, the founding generation decided to keep the business within the family and pass the ownership to a new generation. This is a major assumption, because this is by no means the norm. Most family businesses have significant concerns regarding such issues as the willingness of the founding members to relinquish control, the competence of the designated successor family members, the participation of inactive family members (particularly if the company is a substantial percentage of the family wealth), and the financial retirement requirements of the departing generation. Many of these issues are behavioral and are beyond the scope of the book. If there is a level of family stress brought on by family member conflicts, there is help from the professional ranks. There are trained behaviorists that specialize in the dynamics of family businesses, and they will provide guidance and insights on managing the conflicts. Dysfunctional families have effectively destroyed many companies to the point they are no longer competitive or they simply cease to exist.

If the family business is smaller, passing the financial interest to a next generation is relatively straightforward using gifting strategies, or gifting in concert with other financial programs. When the family business has grown to encompass many millions of dollars, far more elaborate tax planning is required to avoid potentially ruinous gift and estate taxes. With enough advanced planning guided by the expertise of professionals literate in family succession planning, most family businesses can be structured to survive until the next generation takes control of ownership and management. Occasionally, a family business simply outgrows the ability of the family to finance its operations and growth. In those circumstances, the company is a candidate to be sold to a third party.

Long-Term Horizon

Absent immediate health issues placing key family members at risk of becoming incapacitated or dying, another tremendous advantage is having a long-term time horizon. Passing the symbolic reins of control to a next generation of owners is a process that may take many years. The family may be thinking strategically over a time horizon that allows for long-term investment in the company and not a short-term focus on optimizing profitability. Often many of the wonderful commercial brands have been carefully built over time under the watchful eyes of family members that have elected to adopt a long view to wealth generation. Wealth and control of the business will pass to a next generation of family members with enough time. With many individuals living into their 80s and 90s, the time that control rests with such patriarchs may place generational interests at conflict. Think of founding family members that hold on until their senior years and the children are well into their 50s or 60s without the control or ownership passing to them. Motivation on the part of the succeeding family members may wane as they are also looking at retirement and may not share the passionate interest in retaining control until a last gasping breath.

When family members may not be ready to assume the mantle of leadership, most typically because of age and lack of opportunity to gain meaningful experience, an option for consideration is to employ senior level managers to fill in for a period of time. The interesting news is that there is often a significant amount of experienced talent available. Many of the largest companies rotate out senior managers because of artificially imposed age limits. There are many senior-level baby boomers that may be available in disproportionate numbers due to the size of that generation. Such members may want to work for a limited period of time; often they are "empty nesters" with no children living at home, and they are flexible on where they live. Such a resource may be invaluable while a next generation of family members matures to the point of assuming control.

CAUTIONS

Hopefully, the most senior family members with control of the business are not blinded to the potentially ruinous shortfalls of some successor family members. Keeping the business within the family at all costs is almost certainly a prescription for ultimate disappointment and financial malaise and decline. Unfortunately, the statistics against family company succession planning are alarming. Statistics suggest that only 30% of family companies will make it to a second generation, and less than 10% will survive into a third generation. These statistics cite instances of the family passing to a next generation; they offer no help on whether the companies successfully passed to the next generation and prospered with the next generation of decision makers. My guess is that a smaller percentage of family businesses enjoy increasing financial success under the leadership of the following generation.

One common concern is that the founding generation has an interest in passing the business to a next generation, but has not been able to extract sufficient wealth to maintain a standard of living to which they have become accustomed. Too often the standard of living is closely related to the ownership of the business and the flow of resources that the ownership provides. Just think of the tremendous benefits that typically accompany such a status such as company provided insurance, transportation, travel, entertaining, and generally having an "inside bank" standing ready to finance unforeseen emergencies. One of the greatest benefits to company ownership is the security of knowing that the business is a ready resource of funding subject to bank participation. Many privately owned companies are very conservatively managed over time, and such companies have significant debt capacity that may be called upon at a moment's notice and at the election of the owner. Separating the real economic value added by the founder from the legacy aspects of ownership is something that many family members are unwilling to broach because such an exercise is personally uncomfortable.

Remaining Competitive

Keeping the business competitive will typically mean that risks must be embraced and some risks are simply not successful. The candidate company may suffer financially as a result of decisions that are made. The family is at a decision point of either retaining the control of the business for future appreciation, the payment of current dividends, or sell the business and invest the liquidity elsewhere.

Unfortunately, one of the worst things the family can do is fail to make the decisions necessary for the company to prosper. This is too often the case where family members are not close enough to the business to understand the challenges facing the company. Indecision is itself a decision to avoid the challenging task of allocating resources.

VALUATION INSIGHTS

This section views the value of the company from the viewpoint of the controlling family. As discussed already in Chapter 4 regarding valuations, when an ownership interest is being passed between family members, the standard of value is fair market value (FMV). This standard has been developed by the Federal government to insure that substantial wealth as represented by family companies passes to a next generation subject to some understanding of how that wealth will be accounted. The Federal government understands that there are natural incentives for families to pass wealth to successor generations in an attempt to minimize the impact of gift and estate taxes. Historically, estate and gift taxes have impacted families at such low dollar amounts that most successful middle-market privately held companies would have significant tax liability. When stock is transferred to family members by way of gifting or an outright purchase, such transactions are subject to Federal review in most cases by the IRS. Such transfers are subject to Federal challenge if the valuation is deemed to be unreasonably defensible.

The FMV standard is a hypothetical definition that is subject to the interpretation of the taxpayer and the Federal government. Clearly, the taxpaying family wants the most conservative assessment of value that may be obtained by a credible appraiser since one key goal is to minimize taxes. Family businesses are one of the few areas of privately held companies where marginally successful firms are candidates for serious financial planning.

Valuations Involving Non-Family Investors

When the valuation is primarily linked to the transfer of ownership between family members, the standard is FMV as previously discussed. There may be instances, typically in larger companies, where there are senior managers with an equity stake in the business. If the relationship between the family and the managers is arm's length, there is great latitude in defining the value of the company for planning purposes. One caution: If the definition of value is unrealistically low, the Federal government has the opportunity to reclassify a portion of a transfer as a gift from the family as owners to the managers as the beneficiaries of the transaction. Often, the standard of value is FMV for ease of understanding and developing a well understood method of determining the value of the business.

If independent managers are retained in the family company and they are provided with equity based programs, the wise family will provide significant incentives for mutually identified performance thresholds. It is assumed that if financial incentives have been carefully considered and memorialized in an appropriate agreement, then meeting such targets is a win-win situation for both the family and the managers. The agreement may also be subject to vesting to keep the manager focused on the future and growing value for all the stakeholders.

VIEWPOINT OF THE SELLER (FOUNDING GENERATION)

In this chapter we do not have a traditional seller and buyer relationship. Rather, the business is being passed to the next generation of family members. For ease of discussion, the seller is referenced as the founding generation. There are many behavioral issues that impact the founding generation. Once such issues as legacy, reputation, addressing family needs, and other requirements have been discharged one of the most important issues is the financial independence of the founders. The founding generation is typically very concerned about maintaining their lifestyle in their senior years. There is typically great pride in being self-sufficient and never having had to ask children for support when the business was built. Correspondingly, once the family business has been established, it is a terrible prospect for the founders to have to be dependent on others for maintaining a standard of living.

The family business is typically closely associated with independence, and the prerequisites that controlling the business affords. The benefits include financial wherewithal, but also may impact social standing, status, and self-confidence. Loss of control to a succeeding generation without first obtaining financial security is a bothersome issue. While some business families have exercised the discipline to retain financial resources outside the company to establish economic independence, such a threshold often represents millions of dollars. Only the smallest minority of family businesses can afford this level of financial independence. Short of this goal, there will be some discussions between generations on the financial division of company generated resources.

Behavioral Issues

One viable strategy to embrace is providing opportunities for the successor family members to prove themselves from a business acumen viewpoint. Such a strategy will almost certainly entail seeing successor family members fail occasionally. It is very difficult to observe such failure when the founding family members have the experience to ameliorate or eliminate the impact. Training successor family managers is at times painful, but it is understandably part of the succession process that builds competence in the long term.

The family hopefully is receiving objective advice regarding the core business. This objective advice consideration is important. Some of the trusted professional advisors may have such a vested ongoing financial interest in the family that they do not want to lose the client by the sale of the business. It may be emotionally painful for the family, but they should be willing to invest the time and some resources to be in an informed place to decide the future of the business.

If the family identifies the need for key outside management, this may entail one or more individuals. A good practice is to retain the services of a strong and experienced compensation consultant. Next it may be appropriate to retain a search firm to locate a candidate if one is not already employed. In our experience this is a bad time to economize with a "we can do it ourselves" mindset. A reminder that hiring the wrong person for the position will likely cost the company years of lost time figuring out the wrong individual was retained, but more importantly the company likely lacked adequate leadership during this period and may be subject to losing market position. Our experience is that good managers respond to well considered compensation programs with suitable incentives. This will be an expense to the company, but it also follows the general belief that good management pays for itself.

VIEWPOINT OF THE BUYER (NEXT GENERATION)

The term "family recipient" or "family beneficiary" is likely more suitable than "buyer" in this chapter. If there are successor family members waiting for the opportunity to assume the mantle of ownership and control, they almost certainly will not buy the company because the tax environment is so hostile to such thinking. Rather, the successor family members will rely on techniques that pass ownership and wealth in the more tax efficient manner embracing a wide selection of gifting, estate planning vehicles, trusts, and perhaps some amount of actual asset purchase.

Founding family members often wish successors to "buy" a portion of the business. Such an action teaches successors the value of hard work, sacrifice, paying for, or earning the opportunity to lead the company, and self esteem among other valuable attributes of self-sufficiency. These are noble developments, but selling the business to family members is just terribly hostile from a tax standpoint. Selling stock means that the buyer must acquire the stock with after-tax dollars and the sale is taxable to the selling parents. The combined tax rate taking into account the taxes paid by both the buyer and the seller may approach 50% of the transaction price. This is nearly confiscatory in businesses that require a certain amount of capital to remain viable.

Practical Experience

A best practice is to embrace some strategy that allows the successor family members to demonstrate business competence. For example, encouraging the family members to gain a practical education that prepares them for the rigors of business today is a good first step. Having an education grounded in information technology, economics, critical thinking skills, and business courses are examples of opportunities.

Another viable strategy is to encourage the successor generation to accept employment in a business away from the family company. Working for a company not dominated by family is an excellent exercise in building self-confidence and business judgment. Earning an advanced degree such as an MBA while employed outside the family company, is another instance of building skills essential to the long-term viability of the family business.

Yes, allowing time for the successor family members to gain employment experience and education outside the province of the family company takes discipline and many years. Assuming there are no immediate health issues driving an earlier entry into the company, this longer-term horizon is still appropriate. Business careers beginning today may span 40, 45, or 50 years with longevity considered. It is much better to build the critical skills outside the family company to help insure the longevity of the business.

The next generation should be reminded that there is a serious responsibility in managing a company, and that responsibility is most appropriately earned. The benefits of ownership are readily apparent, the longer-term responsibility to other business stakeholders may not be. There are many additional things to consider such as treatment of employees, customers, vendors, and community reputation to mention a few.

PROFESSIONAL ADVISORS

The driver for personal advice is typically the controlling shareholder. It is important for the family to employ advisors that demonstrate objectivity and are not retained simply because of tenure and level of comfort with the deciding members of the family. One serious admonition to families is to resist the temptation to grow old together with advisors. Controlling family members will age and grow old, but advisors need to retain current skills and be sensitive to the total needs of the family. Certainly, addressing the requirements of the founding family members is paramount, but it should not be to the exclusion of other important family interests.

As a hedge on succeeding family members being short-changed by advisors with perhaps vested interests relating to the controlling family members, succeeding members are strongly encouraged to seek independent advice. This may run counter to the spirit of absolutely deferring and trusting to the thinking of parents, but it is a recommended step in building self-confidence and asserting a level of independent critical thinking. It is certainly appropriate to understand the succession process through the filter of the parent's perspective. It is also beneficial to view the same process through the filter of the successor generation. Hopefully the advice to the successor generation will strongly champion such things as contribution to the family (values and financial wherewithal), commitment to the business, and community responsibilities.

This is obviously a sensitive subject. Certainly there is substantial merit in retaining long-standing trusted advisors, but the question may eventually become one of very technical considerations regarding such things as complex tax, trust, behavioral, and legal issues. The wise family is always open to new ideas and should evaluate advisors carefully.

In most instances the family will have to retain a literate and strong law firm for these complex family business considerations. When the financial interests are substantial and if a well established law firm is retained with extensive wealth management experience, there is a greater likelihood that the family interests will be legally protected. Protecting family long-term financial interests is often an exceedingly detailed task requiring exceptional training and experience.

RISK ENVIRONMENT

With family companies perhaps the greatest risk is that the business comes between generations and ultimately damages or destroys the sense of trust and love. Having outside trusted advisors, mentors, and friends is a good hedge on this terrible scenario. Unfortunately there are no guarantees. The emotional and human element is not always rational and it is subject to irrational thinking.

Lack of Diversification

Other candidates are having too much of the family wealth committed to the business with little regard to diversification. Diversification may sound great, unless the business is an ongoing call on the resources of the family. It may become difficult to financially diversify the assets of the family if the business is growing. This is a substantial potential paradox. The business is growing (and assumed to be successful), but the resources required to sustain the growth limit the ability to diversify.

The situation is more egregious when the family invests in the facilities (land and building) occupied by the business. Such an investment often makes reasonable sense because the family controls the tenant of the building and thereby controls the rent in such a manner that debt obligations are successfully discharged. Now the family is invested in both an operating company and the real estate. The package looks attractive from the standpoint of generating wealth, but there is often a concentration of that wealth into a single industry. One example of this concentration is with automobile dealers. They have a marketing agreement with at least one major automobile manufacturer, and they typically own the store. The facility looks attractive from the street, but the fact is that the facility is typically a single-use building suitable for only a car dealership. When a major manufacturer such as General Motors or Chrysler decides to streamline operations through bankruptcy, the family that sees its relationship cancelled is in a terrible position having lost the dealership and being stuck with expensive real estate most suitable for a shrinking market.

Closely related to the prior paragraph is a concentration of wealth in the wrong industry. The wrong industry is one that is mature, declining, or one that offers products and services that are becoming obsolete. The industry may represent decades of experience on the part of the founding generation, and they may not know enough about diversification to evolve into other lines of business. Often the founding generation takes the position that substantial risk was assumed when the family business was formed, and there is little appetite to risk the family wealth in newer endeavors.

The sense of uncertainty with unproven strategies is unsettling. Founding family members may stifle initiatives to migrate away from activities that are comfortable and known. Ultimately this thinking may lead to the unraveling of the family business and the corresponding loss of wealth.

Families may counter such risks by activities such as retaining competent advisors, developing critical thinking skills, investing heavily in education, and not losing the perspective that your colleagues are also your loved ones.

Case Study—Charles Machine Company, Inc.   Many readers may not recognize the name The Charles Machine Works, Inc. (CMW). Almost everyone in industry will know the Company by its marquee product line of orange construction equipment, "Ditch Witch®." Started in 1949, Mr. Ed Malzahn, the founder and current President and Chairman of the Board, invented a compact trenching machine to eliminate much of the hand pick and shovel work common with installing utility service. The invention of this machine paved the way for the creation of the compact trencher industry, which today produces all types of equipment for efficiently installing any type of underground utilities. The Ditch Witch organization today has grown into an international leader of underground construction equipment. The equipment is distinguished for its trademark orange paint. Ditch Witch equipment is closely associated with the name and the color. The name for years indicated what the Company did: Build equipment related in some manner to "ditches."

The products today include many state-of-art technology applications in the construction industry. Representative products include heavy duty and compact tractors, vibratory plows, vacuum excavation systems, electronic locating and tracking equipment, compact equipment, attachments, equipment trailers, and parts for all of the above. Perhaps the most technologically advanced product line is referred to as horizontal directional drilling (HDD) equipment. This equipment is engineered to dig horizontally underground for the placement of utility service lines. This is an exceptional advance over traditional trenching that disturbs the surface soil. Utilizing HDD technology, Ditch Witch equipment may dig under such barriers as parking lots, driveways and even bodies of water to reach a desired destination without disturbing the surface (or tearing up existing concrete and asphalt improvements). Through its worldwide dealer organization, Ditch Witch is the market leader in its core businesses.

Located in Perry, Oklahoma, the CMW manufacturing plant is an impressive and virtually self-contained facility capable of producing most of the product line in-house with limited outsourcing. The facility features state-of-art machining, design, and engineering capabilities. Over time the plant has been expanded to provide the turnkey capabilities, which customers and dealers have come to rely on. Perhaps one of the most impressive aspects of CMW is its turnkey capability to design, research, engineer, manufacture, and distribute the product through a worldwide network of authorized dealers.

Since its founding, the Company has enjoyed the leadership of members of the Malzahn family. The family provides a long-term focus for the company and makes decisions based on this strategic international vision CMW has developed. "The Malzahn family is unwavering in our commitment to the pioneering spirit that has positioned Ditch Witch as the innovator in the underground construction market. We are fortunate that we live in a community with bright, enthusiastic people who bleed orange," states Tiffany Sewell-Howard, Chief Executive Officer and granddaughter of the Company's founder, Ed Malzahn.

The long-term commitment by the Malzahn family is a central reason the Company has evolved into the market leadership it enjoys today. A number of the product developments taken for granted were not immediately successful and it took a steady hand to see the potential fully developed. Staying the course and taking a long view has been an integral component to Ditch Witch's success.

The employees also have a stake in the Company. Chief Operating Officer Rick Johnson says, "Our employees have a tremendous sense of commitment and loyalty to the Company. Their contributions and enthusiasm for our vision are reasons for our success." CMW serves as one of the leaders in the small community of Perry encouraging employees to become active in civic affairs in addition to responsibilities to the Company.

TECHNICAL MATTERS

This section will address a number of strategies to transition the family company between generations in addition to a number of elements to consider if the family depends on the services of key managers.

Psychological Considerations

Previously considered, but bearing emphasis again, it is important for the family members to be psychologically ready for the succession process. This state of acceptance is typically a result of considerable discussion with advisors, mentors, and friends; and after a great deal of heartfelt soul searching. Done correctly, this process is the capstone to a business career that results in a financially secure retirement for the founding family members, and strengthened family ties with children and grandchildren. This is the happiest scenario and the dream of many entrepreneurs that suffer the risks and uncertainties of establishing a business with the hope one day of seeing family members take the business to the next level.

Family and market-based dynamics are so complex today that it is a requirement from this perspective to retain the help of professionals thoroughly literate and versed in the survival issues facing family companies. Such advisors exist and they bring to the relationship the expertise to sort through emotional and irrational issues to arrive at a succession strategy that serves the interests of all the family stakeholders.

Tax Efficiency—Gift Taxes and Purchases of Stock

Unquestionably the most tax-efficient strategy for passing wealth to successor family members is by gifting stock. This is accomplished by gifting shares of stock in a closely held company to the next generation of family members. The gift within Federal limits is tax free to the recipient, the recipient of the gift retains the basis of the grantor, and the gift represents assets that must be surrendered by the person making the gift. The limits on gifting have been dramatically impacted by the 2010 Tax Reform Act (Act). The limits have been so substantially increased with this act it is now possible to pass the value of most privately held companies to a successor generation free of all gift taxes—this is the good news. The issue for many families is that the value of the business is potentially passing by way of a gift, and the family members making the gift are losing control of the asset, in this case the stock in the company. Most founding families cannot afford to simply gift the value of the business to successor generations in this amount.

Historical Perspective on Taxes

To appreciate the power of the Act, a brief history of prior tax law is appropriate. This history lesson in prior tax law is still appropriate because the tax changes in the Act relating to Federal gift and estate tax limitations are only temporary. During the Bush Administration two notable tax legislative initiatives were passed that impacted family companies in particular. First the Economic Growth and Tax Relief Reconciliation Act of 2001 (EGTRRA) and second, the Jobs and Growth Tax Relief Reconciliation Act of 2003 (JGTRRA) were passed. These two acts are generally referred to as the Bush Tax Cuts. The major tax cut provisions included decreasing the top Federal personal income tax rate to 35% (from 39.5%) and decreasing the top Federal capital gain tax rate to 15% (from 20%). The gift tax exclusion amount remained constant during the period of the Bush Tax Cuts at $1 million and the gift tax rate was reduced to 35% (from a maximum of 55%). Additionally, the estate tax exclusion amount was slowly increased from $1,000,000 for individuals ($2,000,000 for a couple) eventually to $3,500,000 for individuals ($7,000,000 for a couple) in 2009, and there was no estate tax in 2010. The tax cuts were not made permanent in 2001 and 2003, rather they had a tax "sunset" provision that stated the reductions would reset to the tax rates prior to the Bush Tax Cuts on January 1, 2011.

Shortly before the sunset date during December 2010, Congress passed a two-year extension of the Bush Tax Cuts, and also increased the gift and estate tax exclusion amounts through December 31, 2012. Without further action by the Congress, many of the favorable recent tax rate decreases will reset automatically on January 1, 2013. The highest Federal income tax rate will reset to approximately 39.5% before a consideration of the additional surtax as part of the Patient Protection and Affordable Care Act (PPACA) passed in March 2010 (referred to as the Nationalized Healthcare Legislation), and the highest Federal capital gain rate will reset to 20% before a similar consideration of an additional surtax as part of the same Nationalized Healthcare Legislation. The Act exclusion amount for gift and estate taxes will decrease from $5,000,000 for an individual and a maximum 35% tax rate to an exclusion amount of $1,000,000 for an individual and a maximum tax rate of 55%.

Tax Reform Act—A Financial Benefit to Families

This legislation has many key elements, but for the purposes of this book only a few of the most important sections will be summarized as they relate to succession-planning strategies for family businesses.

Effective with the Act, January 1, 2011, the gift tax exemption amount and the estate tax exemption amount are the same at $5,000,000 million for individuals and $10,000,000 for a married couple. These limits are a material increase over the prior gift and estate tax exemption amounts, but these increase exemption amounts are only legislated until December 31, 2012.

This means that an individual may gift up to $5,000,000 for an individual using the lifetime unified exemption amount to anyone. In our case, the $5,000,000 individual limit may consist of stock in a family business. If there is a husband and wife, together they may gift up to $10,000,000. The application here is to gift up to $10,000,000 in stock to family members with no gift tax exposure. Gifting up to $10,000,000 of FMV stock in a family company essentially means that most privately held family businesses could pass to a successor generation with no Federal gift taxes, as the overwhelming percentage of most businesses are valued at less than $10,000,000. This is a windfall to family companies, but only for an abbreviated time. Assuming the founding generation is comfortable gifting such a material amount to family members, most companies could be transferred with no Federal gift taxes by utilizing this unified exclusion amount.

> The expansion of the lifetime unified exemption amount to $5,000,000 for an individual is an extraordinary concession on the part of Washington to family businesses. Taking full advantage of this amount literally means that most family-owned businesses could pass to the next generation with no tax liability. Surrendering control of a family business in the sole interests of tax efficiency may be a hard sell to the founding family members, but the alternative of paying steep taxes is worth serious consideration.

It is a remarkable family that could make such a dramatic decision and utilize the full extent of the unified transfer credit, keeping in mind that once the gift is made the control of the asset (company stock) is surrendered. There are a number of strategies that a family may embrace to take advantage of this tremendous tax benefit. The family business may have voting and non-voting stock. This distinction may be true even for S corporations assuming that the voting attribute is the only difference between stock classes. Non-voting stock may be gifted to family members and the voting stock retained by the founding family. In this case the founding family may gift a substantial amount of the value of the business while still retaining ultimate control over corporate governance.

In larger family companies, the stock gifted to the next generation may represent a minority block of stock with limited ownership attributes and no ready market. Such a block of stock is likely to be subject to a minority discount and a lack of marketability discount. This is an excellent strategy to remove a significant amount of value from an estate while providing a substantial benefit to succeeding family members.

There are considerable estate-planning opportunities with the Act, but the estate tax window is so narrow (only 24 months beginning January 1, 2011, that during that time a propertied family member must die), that it is likely only a few families will be able to benefit. Only if the estate tax limits are made more enduring or permanent will there be any serious incentive to work with estate planners to build comprehensive tax strategy plans.

One aspect of the Act that is valuable is that the unified exclusion amounts are "portable" between spouses. This means that if one spouse is using the gift tax strategy and happens to die during the enactment period, the surviving spouse may still use the balance of the deceased unified exclusion amount to complete gifts before January 1, 2013.

Gift and Estate Taxes Following December 31, 2012

Failure of families to take advantage of the Act during the narrow window of opportunity will possibly expose them to much higher tax rates. This depends on the automatic legislative sunset provision that resets the applicable tax rates to predetermined amounts assuming Congress is unable to agree on a "permanent" solution. Permanent tax code legislation is an oxymoron as Congress reserves the right to change the law, and there is a long history of Congress making frequent changes. Assuming the Act is not extended or made permanent, the unified exclusion amount for gifts will reset to only $1,000,000 for an individual ($2,000,000 for a couple). This lower amount compares to the combined transfer amount of $10,000,000 for a couple until the sunset date. After the sunset date there is an effective gift-tax rate on amounts in excess of the unified exclusion amount that has a maximum tax rate of 55%. Letting this planning window close may be a very expensive proposition for family businesses.

Tax-Efficient Succession Strategies

Even if the substantial provisions of the Act are not embraced, families still have the option of gifting smaller amounts of stock using an annual exclusion, currently $13,000. This annual exclusion applies to individuals, so a husband and wife could gift up to $26,000 per year ($13,000 × 2). For example from December 28, 2011 until January 3, 2012 is less than a week but that time straddles two tax years. In this instance a total of $52,000 may be gifted by a husband and a wife to a child ($13,000 × 4). If there are three children in the business using this logic a total of $156,000 may be gifted in that period ($13,000 × 12). The math compounds if the children are married so that each child and spouse receives $52,000 per year ($13,000 × 4) or $104,000 in the period that straddles two years ($52,000 × 2). Depending on family dynamics, substantial wealth may be passed over a period of years; particularly if company stock subject to defensible discounts such as minority blocks with a lack of marketability, are used.

Strategies to Provide Income to the Founding Family Members

The current uncertainty with many of the Federal taxes materially impacting family businesses still merits an overview of a few other tax strategies. Many traditional tax strategies were developed to assist with the removal of assets from the founding generation's estate while providing some level of cash flow during lifetime. Removal of assets from the taxable estate of the founding generation is a decided plus because estate taxes were as high as 55% before the Bush Tax Cuts, and with a greatly reduced exemption amount. If the Act is not extended or modified from the current estate and gift tax exemption amounts, it is still appropriate for families to consider strategies to remove assets from the exposure to estate taxes. If the Act exemption amounts are extended, most families will be able to plan with little concern over estate taxes because most businesses are valued below $10 million. With so much political posturing in Washington currently, can you trust our elected leaders to behave rationally or predictably with regard to taxes after December 31, 2012? The most conservative strategy is to assume that the sunset provisions of the Act will apply and tax rates will increase.

Private Annuities   One strategy for a family to consider is the implementation of a private annuity. The transferring shareholder will sell stock in the family business to a family member and will receive annuity payments for the balance of his or her lifetime. The private annuity has several distinguishable features. First, there is no specific transaction amount because the annuity payments continue until the death of the transferring family member. Second, the number of payments is likewise uncertain and related to the longevity of the transferring family member. The annuity rules of IRC Section 72 apply. The stock in the family business is valued for the purposes of the private annuity at FMV. Once the block of stock to be transferred is determined, each year thereafter the transferring family member will receive annuity payments that consist of three elements: return of stock basis, capital gain on the difference between the basis and the FMV per share of the stock and finally some ordinary income.

Several key goals are realized by using a private annuity. The private annuity provides cash to the transferor for life with no stated maximum amount. The private annuity may be structured for a husband and wife together. If the transferor dies before the IRS established life expectancy, the unrecognized deferred is never taxed as ordinary income. The transferred asset, assumed to be stock in the family company, is excluded from the estate of the transferor. Future appreciation of the stock, if any, belongs with the purchaser.

The annuity benefits are only possible if the FMV of the company stock is determined. The private annuity transaction should be unsecured to ensure that capital gain taxes are deferred over the life of the transferor. The transferor must not retain control over the stock being transferred, including voting rights. The private annuity may be combined with a gifting program to achieve an even more tax-efficient means of transferring ownership.

Self-Cancelling Installment Note   Another time-tested strategy to remove assets from an estate and provide income to the founding generation is to implement a self cancelling installment note (SCIN). The use of a SCIN is similar to the private annuity in theory. In this case, the amount of the SCIN is known along with the anticipated interest because there is an established FMV purchase price. The term of the SCIN is subject to Federal rules that state it must be less than the expected life expectancy of the seller.

Several goals may be accomplished using a SCIN. There may be significant deferral of taxes if the transferor dies before the full repayment of the SCIN. The SCIN provides predictable cash flow to the seller, and the SCIN will qualify for installment sale treatment subject to applicable rules. Of course, with the likelihood of increasing tax rates installment sale tax deferral may not be that attractive at the moment. The stock transferred by the SCIN is excluded from the estate of the transferor if there is a death before the full payment of the SCIN. The unpaid balance of the note will be included as income to the estate in the first year. Future appreciation of the stock belongs to the purchaser. The tax benefits of the SCIN are possible only if the cancellation provision is part of the note itself.

The transaction has to include some form of "risk premium" as an incentive for the seller to enter into the SCIN. The risk premium may include a higher than market interest rate or a principal amount in excess of FMV. The amortization of the SCIN cannot be in excess of the IRS-determined life expectancy of the seller. The SCIN is more flexible than a private annuity in such matters as the selection of the interest rate, length of note, and sales price. The SCIN may be secured and the basis of the asset (company stock) to the buyer will be the principal amount of the note, even if all the payments are not made. The SCIN may be combined with a gifting program as an even more tax-efficient means of transferring ownership.

Deferred Compensation and Supplemental Executive Retirement Plan
The founding family member active in the business may enter into a deferred compensation agreement with the company prior to retirement. The agreement has to be reasonable in relation to the size of the company. There should be some justification for the deferred compensation in the company records to protect the company from any IRS audit penalties. It is best to have a stated period covered by the deferred compensation and not just have an undocumented annuity paid until death. The deferred compensation adequately documented will be a tax deduction to the company when paid and ordinary income to the recipient.

If the deferred compensation agreement is reasonable and entered into before the FMV of the company is determined, the agreement may impact the value of the stock. The value of the stock may be reduced because of a significant accrued liability for transition-planning strategies.

In the same tax spirit as deferred compensation, the company may adopt a non-qualified supplemental executive retirement plan (SERP). The retirement benefit must be reasonable, but payments to the former employee are tax deductible to the company and ordinary income to the recipient. In the case of both deferred compensation and payments under a SERP, the payment to the individual is ordinary income, but deductible to the company. Assuming that the deferred compensation and the SERP created unfunded liabilities to the company, such obligations may negatively impact the FMV of the stock. If these programs are part of an overall succession plan, payments with tax-deductible dollars to the company is a much preferred tax strategy rather than incurring after tax payments for the purchase of stock from a buyer.

Strategies such as consulting agreements and deferred compensation are tax deductible to the company when paid, and ordinary income to the recipient when received. If a consulting fee is being paid, some work has to be completed or the agreement may be subject to challenge by the IRS. Similarly, a deferred compensation agreement needs to be defensible and it is appropriate to obtain professional assistance in structuring such an accord.

Consulting Agreement   A consulting agreement may be an open-ended term whereby a family member is paid for services into the future at an agreed fee. The family member is an employee of the company under such an agreement and will be subject to payroll taxes. One major concern with such an agreement is that consulting duties may be stipulated but they are never or rarely provided. It just looks indefensible if the family member is living in a sunny southern location half a continent away from the family business with no apparent real duties. The tax deduction to the company for illusory services may be denied by the IRS.

Trusts and Trust Agreements   There are so many possibilities for the use of trusts in family estate planning that a detailed discussion of trusts is beyond the scope of this book. Generally, trusts are embraced to transfer assets out of the estate of propertied family members that have potential exposure to estate taxes. The prior discussion regarding the Act and the predecessor tax legislation certainly makes the case for significant planning because estate taxes are linked to high marginal tax rates.

This book is primarily focused on buyout strategies that are employed by the sellers of the company with buyers. Preserving individual and family wealth is often linked to the succession planning for the family business, but estate tax planning is not part of that discussion.

Strategies to Compensate Key Employees

Providing a succession strategy for family members has been the near singular focus in this chapter. There are many instances when the family business has one or several key employees whose services are integral to the financial success of the company. The primary consideration is often how much compensation to provide to the key managers. The form of compensation may actually be equity in the business, or opportunities to participate in the future financial success of the business. The opportunities will be driven by a complex consideration of family goals, tax efficiency, and legal requirements. A quick summary of options is reviewed.

Actual Equity versus Phantom Equity   One of the strongest incentives is actual equity in the business. This sends a message to the individual, family members, and professional advisors that the recipient is an important part of the organization with a vested interest in the longer-term success. In my experience it does make a difference if you are a principal as opposed to just a key employee. Significant restrictions may be placed on the equity interest granted to the key employee so that the risk of having an adverse shareholder on the street is greatly minimized. There may be an automatic call provision on the stock if the employee is no longer associated with the company for any reason. The terms on payments for the redemption of the stock may be predicated on the behavior of the employee upon separation from the company. Restrictions should be appropriately part of a shareholder agreement between the employee and the company.

There is more flexibility with C corporations because they can have multiple classes of stock. A special category of stock may be designed for the non-family members with carefully considered restrictions and subject to a strict shareholder agreement. With a C corporation provisions may be made for incentive stock options and non-qualified stock options. Stock options are often found in technology companies that are on the cusp of dramatic growth and a possible initial public offering (IPO). Since technology companies are not really representative of most family businesses, stock options are not a serious consideration. Besides, stock options may be used only in C corporations, and the overwhelming majority of family companies are S corporations.

If the entity is an S corporation, actual equity and the adjoining shareholder agreement must be drawn to not place the S election at risk through some inadvertent action or even a deliberate act of defiance. The point is that there may be some beneficial and powerfully motivating attributes in having the key employee as an actual shareholder in the business.

If actual equity is not a possibility, then other significant financial incentives are appropriately considered. Incentive programs with equity-sounding names are a consideration such as stock appreciation rights (SAR) and phantom stock. These vehicles are really only deferred compensation programs deductible to the company when paid, and ordinary income to the recipient. There is a significant amount of flexibility in designing such programs depending on the goals and objectives of the company. Most goals involve incentives related to the contributions by the employee to make the company more successful. These programs are longer term in their orientation and typically accrue to the key employee with time. They are frequently subject to vesting over a period of specified time. The vesting may be phased in or it may represent zero until some activating event occurs.

> If the company really has a number of key employees, structuring a long-term material benefit program may be in the family's best interest. Suitable restrictions may be placed on the program and a funding mechanism developed. If the intent is to have a business growing in value and that growth is significantly dependent on non-family members, sharing the upside financial potential is a logical win-win situation.

A bonus program that is structured on only a year-to-year basis may have limited motivating appeal for a key employee. Efforts on the part of the key employee to improve the long-term viability of the business are typically not appropriately recognized in a one-time annual bonus. A longer-term incentive program such as SARs or phantom stock with a multi-year horizon provides an incentive that is consistent with building long term value.

SUMMARY

Succession planning in privately held family companies is often a very stressful process because of the myriad of behavioral issues that evolve when the major parties to the process are both work colleagues and loved ones. Due to the closeness of the parties, there are many wealth-transitioning and preservation techniques to consider that are often not part of a process involving independent parties. Planning for financially successful companies will certainly entail strategies aimed at reducing transaction costs including taxes. Unlike the transaction environment involving independent parties, family companies may dictate substantial planning even if the business is not profitable by industry standards. Family businesses may involve both an operating company and another entity with title to the facilities leased by the operating company. The combination of both interests may be significant, especially when real estate is part of the equation.

Succession planning is all the more challenging in many cases because the next ownership generation will have to plan and consider the business involvement of a founding generation. Many founding family members are almost incapable of retirement because the business had to be a sole consuming obsession in order for it to be successful. Having attained the stature of a survivor, and even building a financially successful company, it is often exceedingly difficult for a founder to simply walk away. While this restlessness is often a challenge, it may also be beneficial because it permits a long-term time horizon for succession and the transfer of authority and ownership without overburdening the business with transition related debt. Slow and steady has its benefits as well as its risks.

CHAPTER 17

Buyouts with Employee Cooperatives

Tell me and I'll forget. Show me and I may not remember.
Involve me and I'll understand.
— Native American Proverb

I like the dreams of the future better than the history of the past.
— Thomas Jefferson

The idea of employee cooperatives is not as well known as some closely related cooperatives that have been in existence much longer. The International Cooperative Alliance defines a cooperative as: "An autonomous association of persons united voluntarily to meet their common economic, social, and cultural needs and aspirations through a jointly owned and democratically controlled enterprise." Cooperatives across the country have been a staple in such areas as rural electrification and farming-centric producer cooperatives. One of the aspects surrounding employee cooperatives is that they are dependent on state regulations, and as a result they do not typically gain national prominence. Employee cooperatives have a history of notable financial success within certain regions where states have enacted legislation that makes them possible.

The philosophy of a cooperative is easy to understand and it is an easy communication. Stakeholders with common interests come together and pool financial and human capital interests to form an organization that is beyond the control of corporate entities. Corporate entities reward investors with a return on invested capital. Cooperatives are voluntary affiliations where the stakeholders gain financial reward according to other factors, not necessarily invested capital. Common cooperative models include agricultural cooperatives whereby the producers or the farmers found a cooperative and own the means of production without having to deal with third parties such as corporations. The producers typically participate in the economics of the producer cooperative based on the volume of business that they conduct with the cooperative. To the extent the producer cooperative generates positive cash flow and a financial surplus, the governing body of the cooperative will decide how much of the surplus will be distributed to members in the form of a patronage dividend, and how much of the surplus will be retained as necessary investment to remain viable.

With time, the concept of an employee or worker cooperative has come into fashion. In certain circumstances, the employees are the stakeholders with a high vested interest in the organization. The employees identify common issues and voluntarily join resources and form their own cooperative. Tax advantages for cooperatives are not universal, and will depend on state statutes. Several employee cooperatives have been in existence for many years with impressive financial results, and a number of them are featured as case studies later in this chapter.

ADVANTAGES

The International Cooperative Alliance (ICA) has articulated a number of principals that embody the spirit of cooperative alliances. The ICA has celebrated over 150 years of cooperative involvement, an enviable achievement and a testimony to the enduring strength of their principals. The seven major principals are discussed as part of the advantages of being a cooperative entity.

> *Cooperatives are voluntary organizations. They are open to all persons able to use their services and willing to accept the responsibilities of membership without regard to gender, social, racial, political, or religious discrimination.*
>
> *Cooperatives are democratic organizations controlled by their members. The members actively participate in setting applicable policies and making decisions. Individuals serving as elected representatives are accountable to the membership. In primary cooperatives, members have equal voting rights with one member having one vote. Cooperatives at other levels are also organized in a democratic manner.*
>
> *Members contribute equitably to, and control democratically, the capital of their cooperative. Often, part of that capital is the common*

      property of the cooperative. Members allocate surpluses to any worthwhile purposes including such candidates as: developing the cooperative, establishing capital reserves which may in part be indivisible, benefiting members in proportion to their transactions and involvement with the cooperative, and supporting other activities approved by the membership.

Cooperatives *are autonomous self-help organizations controlled by their members. If the cooperative enters into agreements with other organizations, including governments, they do so on terms that ensure democratic control by their members and maintain their cooperative autonomy.*

Cooperatives *provide education and training for their members, elected representatives, managers, and employees so they can contribute effectively to the development of the cooperative. They inform the general public about the nature and benefits of cooperation.*

Cooperatives *provide the most effective service to their members and strengthen the cooperative movement by working together through local, national, and international structures.*

Cooperatives *work for the sustainable development of their communities through policies approved by their members. There is a longer-term overriding concern for the communities where the cooperatives are active.*

The members of the cooperative (in this case our focus is on the employees) are also the owners. While making money is a primary concern in most cooperatives, meeting the needs of the members is typically more important. There are other issues confronting the cooperative, not just making money and providing employment. The range of issues may encompass such other worthwhile goals such as providing "fair" wages or contributing to a healthier more sustainable environment.

Cooperatives are formed and operated for the benefit of their members. Failure to meet expenses will quickly result in the demise of the organization. Employee cooperatives must meet the customary costs of employment, along with appropriate overhead. Assuming the cooperative is financially well run and it generates positive cash flow (profitability by another name), the income will typically be redistributed back to the employees according to some agreed-upon equitable metric. This redistribution is often referred to as patronage rebates or patronage dividends. In employee cooperatives it is common to measure participation on some equitable formula that considers labor input. The labor input may be a function of such considerations as level of pay, hours worked, employee seniority, or some combination of these items. There is flexibility in designing the patronage participation depending on the leadership of the cooperative.

Most employee cooperatives are organized and operated for the benefit of the employees, subject to the investment requirements of the employer. Excess income beyond the requirements for retaining capital for the employer, is redistributed to the employees. This basically results in a single layer of taxes. The cooperative retains an amount to remain competitive and does not typically amass a tremendous non-operating net worth. This suggests that the redistributions to the employees are taxable once to the employee members at the individual level.

CAUTIONS

There is certainly an attractive philosophy of participation within the cooperative community. The cooperatives are voluntary organizations subject to democratic rule and governance. Perhaps one of the single greatest issues regarding the long-term viability of a cooperative is the governance of the organization. Cooperatives are typically managed by a member-elected board of directors. The senior managers typically report to the board. Since the board will have ultimate authority for the direction of the organization, the election of these board members takes on a heightened importance. Employee cooperatives are voluntary participation organizations. If the employees fail to see or understand the benefits of the cooperative structure, they do not have to participate. This possible lack of commitment may become a factor with employees that are very short-term-oriented in their thinking.

> Governance of employee cooperatives is very democratic with the participants typically electing the board of directors. It is essential for the board to be objective in the discharge of its duties to the organization and not be an extension of an unstable and shifting popularity contest. A best practice is to have a board with several outside members, some with cooperative experience.

One of the challenges of the employee cooperative is to foster and reinforce a culture of ownership. Candidate members of the employee cooperative may have no history of ownership except only a few items of personal wealth, or perhaps a home. If there is a long history of employment with a company where the individual is paid simply for hours worked with no vested interest in the employer, generating an ownership outlook in an employee cooperative is a major challenge.

VALUATIONS

From an ongoing operational viewpoint, the employee cooperative does not require a valuation. The extent to which the employee cooperative generates income, the patronage dividend will be a function of agreed-upon metrics. The determination of the patronage dividend is a more rote computation not necessarily tied to any understanding of the value of the organization.

If a company is being acquired by an employee cooperative, typically the stock of the selling shareholders is being redeemed by the cooperative. Some understanding of transaction price is appropriate as part of smart and responsible due diligence, but a formal valuation is not required.

If the selling shareholders are part of a C corporation with their stock being redeemed by an employee cooperative, the selling shareholders may make an election to have the transaction taxed under Internal Revenue Code (IRC) Section 1042, with a tax-free rollover provision. The attributes of a stock sale under IRC Section 1042 are considered shortly, but such an election will require a valuation of company stock being sold.

Employee cooperatives generally will redistribute the earnings of the company to its members annually. There may be a requirement for the employee cooperative to retain capital for ongoing operating requirements. At some point longstanding members will elect to leave the association with the cooperative and they may have in part some claim on the ongoing capital of the organization. When a distribution is made, it is generally done in consideration of a member agreement that dictates how the payment is computed. Generally the payment is computed according to a formula and not a valuation of the equity.

VIEWPOINT OF THE SELLER

Employee cooperatives are distinctive in that they are formed when significant common interests are recognized among the employees. The employee cooperative is a voluntary member organization, so there is often no one selling the business. There may be a seller orientation when an employee has been a member for many years, and there is a stake in the invested capital of the cooperative.

There are instances when an employee cooperative does acquire a company on behalf of a cooperative structure. Such instances are relatively uncommon, and they are subject to compliance with state laws. Acquisition mechanics of a company by an employee cooperative are considered later in the chapter along with a case study. Again, the relative infrequency of such transactions does not warrant significant consideration at this point.

VIEWPOINT OF THE BUYER

The buyer in our case is the individual thinking of a voluntary affiliation with the employee cooperative. There are certainly a number of attractive selling points for a candidate cooperative member. The individual will become an owner in the organization with at least some voice in its governance. For individuals that have been mere unappreciated employees in a large corporation, this is a very attractive option. Of course, the large corporation may not be particularly sensitive in showing its appreciation for its individual employees, but such firms often enjoy considerable economies due to market share and cost advantages so that the jobs offered may be accompanied with a host of benefits including competitive wages and retirement benefits.

Generally, if the employee cooperative is to be successful longer term, it will embrace significant ongoing communications and educational programs with the members. Employee ownership is a great sounding theme, but the mission needs to be constantly resold and reminded to the members. Successful employee cooperatives typically will have internal newsletters and publications featuring the team members in community activities, helping clients, family announcements, and related endeavors. Being part of an employee community that is enjoying success is a great reward by itself and a significant reason for membership in a cooperative.

Financially, employee cooperatives are organized for the member's benefit. The members enjoy ongoing employment, fair wages, having a say in the governance of the organization, and a quality of life that emphasizes participation. In the cutthroat world of market-based economies, the attributes of the employee cooperative look attractive.

PROFESSIONAL ADVISORS

One significant advantage of cooperatives is that the requirement for professional advisors is reduced. There is no seller in the traditional sense, so there is no requirement for advisors to the seller. There is the requirement for establishing the legal entity, and defining such necessary items as governance, participation, patronage dividends and payouts, and other operating requirements. Accounting for member participation balances is a requirement that is defined by the operating agreements. Someone has to keep "score" of individual accounts, but that should not be an overly challenging discipline.

In the case of the employee cooperative, the emphasis on a democratic form of governance whereby all of the members, however defined, have a voice in the process leads to the observation that a best practice for the board of directors is to have outside members. The risk of having the board of directors dominated only by employees is that the organization will be too inwardly focused and perhaps blinded by forces and events in a broader context. Due to the fact that cooperatives are organized for the benefit of members, having a longer-term focus imbued by a number of outside directors will help insure the cooperative is not penalized by having too singular a focus on short-term events. When the cooperative is employee owned, a longer-term orientation is appropriate because the employees have career aspirations and long-term obligations tied to a stable and reliable job. Ongoing training, upgrading skills to meet competitive market pressure, saving for retirement, and quality of life are all examples of longer-term thinking that may not be part of other stakeholder cooperatives with a focus on producers' interests or interests of consumers.

RISK ENVIRONMENT

Generally, employee cooperatives are clustered in stable and well established endeavors. My examination of the industry finds a number of employee cooperatives in such well established fields as healthcare services, food services and restaurants, smaller endeavors not capital intensive, and other service organizations. The fact that this type of organization is most suited to established industries helps reduce much of the risk.

Perhaps the greatest risk is the management by members and the unique organizational structure of cooperatives. This is a risk because so much of the success of the organization is related to the experience of the board of directors. The board will have the ultimate responsibility for the long-term viability of the cooperative. Yes, the interest of the members is paramount, but is that interest longer term in orientation or shorter term? There is a balancing of strategic interests and immediate standard of living interests. Outside board members may be very helpful in weighing the competing interests of the members.

Cooperatives traditionally have been seen as single member organizations such as producer farmers. As businesses have evolved, there is a strong case to be made for cooperatives with multiple member issues. With time, state laws have been revised to permit multi-stakeholder cooperatives. One clear application of permitting multi-stakeholder cooperatives is that allowing investors to be members enables the organizations to attract the capital required to be competitive without the limitations of only having a single class of members and owners.

Case Study—Select Machine, Inc.

Select Machine, Inc. (SMI or the Company) is a niche manufacturing company near Akron in rural Ohio. SMI manufactures, sells, and distributes machined products and equipment for the construction and demolition industries. The two owners, Bill Sagaser and Doug Beavers, founded the Company in 1994, and they were looking to retire. SMI grew to 11 employees by 2005 and it produced profitable results and positive cash flow. The Company is small, and the only interested outside buyers indicated operations would be closed and the equipment moved to another location. This reality was a concern to the owners because it would mean the employees were to be out of work soon, and this would be a significant impact on the community due to the loss of those jobs.

The Ohio Employee Ownership Center (OEOC) in Kent Ohio got involved and helped coordinate a buyout of SMI with the use of an employee cooperative. The Company would have been a good candidate for an employee stock ownership plan and trust (ESOP) because the owners were concerned about the welfare of the employees, the employees all knew one another and worked together for years. Unfortunately, an ESOP was not a viable solution because of SMI's size; it was simply too small.

William McIntyre, certified public accountant (CPA) and OEOC Program Director stated: "Using the concept of an employee cooperative at Select Machine was an attractive option because of its size. While an ESOP was considered, in most instances you need at least 20–30 employees to justify the costs, compliance and regulatory issues."

This company became an employee cooperative due to changes in the Ohio Cooperative Law in 1998 and 2005 that expanded the concept of cooperatives beyond agriculture. Additionally, the legislation allowed for labor to be a considered as a contributed resource; provisions were permitted to allow a balancing of interests; and retained patronage is in reality sweat equity.

The owners were willing to work with the employees on a succession plan utilizing the services of OEOC and taking a long view regarding transition planning. OEOC assisted the sellers with a feasibility study, organizing a valuation, and coordinating a business plan. SMI was organized as an employee cooperative, the article of incorporation was revised, bylaws adjusted, and company governance implemented that was compatible with an employee cooperative. SMI as a cooperative redeems the stock of the sellers and subject to applicable agreements the stock is sold to the employee members.

The owners were concerned about over-leveraging the Company. They were willing to stay affiliated with the Company for a period of time, and agreed to provide seller funding. The first redemption of stock was for 40% of the outstanding shares. SMI was a C corporation and the sellers elected the IRC Section 1042 tax deferral since the transaction was over the minimum 30% of the stock to qualify for the tax benefit. By staying with the Company during the transition process, both Bill Sagaser and Doug Beavers are participants in the employee cooperative.

The recession beginning in 2008 has had a negative impact on sales. The second redemption of stock by the Company has been delayed until the economy improves. While the transition plan is delayed momentarily by the recession, the SMI owners are pleased with the outcome. According to Doug Beavers, "The OEOC staff provided us with much insight into this transaction. We would not have been able to accomplish our objectives without their assistance." Score one for retaining jobs and converting 11 employees into entrepreneurial owners.

Case Study—Cooperative Home Care Associates

Cooperative Home Care Associates (CHCA or the Company) was founded in 1985 to provide quality home care to individuals who are elderly, chronically ill, or living with disabilities. CHCA is headquartered in the Bronx, New York, and contracts with New York agencies to provide healthcare services. CHCA also provides "private pay" home health care from a minimum of 12 hours per week to 24 hours per day, seven days a week. The Company will work with private pay patients by assigning registered nurses to work with the individual and his doctor to develop a care plan best suited to their needs. The range of services provided by CHCA is expansive and includes such essentials as:

- Bathing
- Dressing
- Assisted walking
- Planning, preparing, and if necessary feeding
- Toileting
- Taking temperature, pulse, and respiration
- Re-ordering and reminding to take medications

- Accompanying the patient on specific errands to the doctor, appointments, and shopping
- Providing companionship and establishing a trusting dependable relationship

Many of the patient functions are completed by paraprofessionals. The paraprofessionals are not typically medically licensed care providers, but they are on the front line of providing in-home support and services. These are often considered entry-level jobs with a lower pay scale and higher employee turnover. The work is challenging because it often does not provide stable and predictable employment, hours are often not full time, work is provided only if there are patients that need assistance, and there are routinely few if any benefits with the job. CHCA has championed offering a quality job to their employees including benefits for both entry level and more skilled associates. Unfortunately CHCA is largely tied to government reimbursement programs, and the ability to offer competitive wages is a function of the reimbursement rates. The fees for the paraprofessional associates are depressed. In spite of this lack of funding, CHCA has been effective in drastically reducing turnover, and CHCA turnover rates are half the industry average. The demands on the employees are often challenging, with lower compensation and a requirement to have transportation.

Since its founding, CHCA has grown into a significant employee cooperative helping to support a national cooperative network. CHCA generates in excess of $60 million in revenue and has created quality jobs for over 2,000 individuals. CHCA provides wages, benefits, and ongoing training for team members wishing to improve their skills. The Company has ongoing training and educational programs. Building a distinctive culture is challenging because most of the employees work out of their homes, travel directly to patients, and rarely come to the main office.

CHCA has developed a number of strategic relationships with other healthcare providers. One such relationship is with Independence Case Systems (ICS), a Medicaid-managed long-term care program generating revenue through its commitment to helping adults with physical disabilities live in their homes independently. Another affiliation is with the Paraprofessional Healthcare Institute (PHI), a national non-profit organization working to insure a stable direct care workforce. CHCA also works with a number of regional employee cooperatives providing substantially similar services, with the leading provider based in Philadelphia. None of the other similar regional employee cooperatives have reached the level of revenue and business critical mass of CHCA. One leading factor is that the success of CHCA is largely a function of being in a major metropolitan area like New York City. This region provides a sufficient number of clients for an organization such as CHCA to exist. The employees have an opportunity to work close to regular 40-hour weeks as much as practicable because of the size and proximity of the metropolitan population.

Mr. Michael Elsas, President, notes: "We are proud of our record of providing quality jobs largely to paraprofessional healthcare workers. At CHCA we have carefully built a working model of success and our employment will only continue to grow as more healthcare providers learn of our capabilities and the population ages." CHCA has succeeded where many others have failed to reach a viable business model. The Company has a strong sense of values and mission, which guides its thinking in serving the community where its employees live. The future looks assured.

TECHNICAL MATTERS

Employee Cooperatives

Generally, cooperatives are formed under Subchapter T of the IRC (Sections 1381–1388). Cooperatives are incorporated to conduct activities on a cooperative basis. Cooperatives may exclude from their taxable income certain allocations of profits attributable to activity completed with the cooperative's members. The cooperative members report this income as though it was received, and this reporting is similar to other tax pass-through entities like S corporations. Similar to other pass-through entities, cooperatives typically distribute sufficient cash for the members to pay their personal income taxes attributed to the prorated allocation of income. In this respect, the members pay the income taxes due when the income is recognized by the cooperative. Correspondingly, when the income is distributed to members, income taxes have already been paid so those redistributions are typically tax free to the members.

Employee cooperatives are not established under Federal laws. State laws must be consulted by informed professionals. Regrettably, state laws are not uniform in this area, and great care must be exercised before proceeding to make sure the plan of succession is legal.

Tax Deferral with IRC Section 1042

As previously mentioned, the shareholders of a privately held C corporation selling at least 30% of the stock to the ESOP may elect to have the taxable gain on the sale deferred under the conditions of IRC Section 1042. While this is a significant advantage for ESOPs, the fact is that there are fewer C corporations in existence to take advantage of the rule. Additionally, there are considerable restrictions deferring the gain because the proceeds must be reinvested in qualified replacement property (QRP) within a designated time period. The tax deferral lasts only as long as the seller holds the QRP.

Corporations subject to Subchapter T of the IRC will permit shareholders selling stock to the cooperative to qualify for the IRC Section 1042 tax-free rollover if they are a C corporation. All other requirements remain in place such as selling 30% of the stock at a minimum. There have been relatively few sales of stock to employee cooperatives and there is not a significant amount of history with such transactions. If the candidate company is an S corporation, the IRC Section 1042 may still be available if the election is made to return to a C corporation prior to the sale of stock. There may be adverse tax consequences to such an election and knowledgeable tax representation should be consulted before such a decision is made.

Employee Cooperative Transaction Considerations

An employee cooperative may acquire a company by one of two common methods. The first method has the selling shareholders encouraging the employees to form their own employee cooperative and that cooperative acquires the stock or the original company over time. For a time there are two organizations while the stock purchases are being completed. The second method is for the subject company to convert into an employee cooperative immediately and the stock of the shareholders is redeemed over time. While an employee cooperative may borrow funds similar to a traditional leveraged buyout, this is likely to be an option with sharp limitations on the amount of acquisition debt. The spirit of an employee cooperative is to be managed for the benefit of the patrons, the employees. The benefit of the employees may be at a high degree of risk if the company is burdened with too much debt. Time is an ally of a company considering becoming an employee cooperative, because departing shareholders may sell their stock back to the cooperative over time and avoid placing an undue amount of debt on the company. It is also noteworthy that the acquisition debt incurred by the employee cooperative must be repaid with after-tax dollars.

There is generally no requirement for a formal business valuation in the case of the employees forming an employee cooperative to acquire their employer from selling shareholders. The purchase price may be negotiated between the various parties. Of course, the buyer should exercise appropriate due diligence to insure the purchase price and the terms of the transaction are reasonable. The terms may involve seller financing on the part of the departing shareholders. A stock valuation will be required if the sellers elect the IRC Section 1042 tax-free rollover because the fair market value of the replacement property must be determined in relationship to the sale price of the stock in the privately held corporation.

One key consideration is that once a corporation is organized under Subchapter T, corporate governance changes from rule by shareholders with invested capital to governance by the members as stipulated in the articles of incorporation. If the selling shareholders are providing financing or they are only selling a percentage of their stock, they may have trouble accepting the loss of control prior to selling all their stock or having their notes paid.

Multi-Stakeholder Cooperatives

While the discussion is largely focused on employee cooperatives, there is an increasing interest in multi-stakeholder cooperatives. In this regard, such multi-stakeholder cooperatives have more than one class of members. For example, a multi-stakeholder cooperative may have as members both employees and outside investors. The outside investors may place capital into the cooperative for such things as facilities and equipment in the case of a medical cooperative. The outside investors may have allocated to them preferred stock that returns a stipulated but limited dividend amount before the interests of the other members are quantified.

Comparison with Employee Stock Ownership Plans and Trust

At first examination, one may well ask what are the significant differences between an employee cooperative and a corporation with an ESOP. ESOPs were considered in Chapters 12 and 13. This question may be more sharply focused because of the discussion regarding the strong attributes of 100% ESOP S corporations where the trust owns all the stock of the corporation for the beneficial interest of the plan participants. There are a number of key distinctions to be made, but by no means is the following a comprehensive list.

- An ESOP is a qualified retirement plan under the Employee Retirement Income Security Act (ERISA) that is governed by a trustee with fiduciary responsibilities. The trustee has a key purpose of maximizing the plan assets, the value of the corporation's stock, for the benefit of the employees. This often encompasses a longer view to creating value in the company because that will increase the value of the plan assets. Even in a 100% ESOP company the trustee is oriented to increasing the value of the plan assets and is not primarily motivated by the individual interests of the employees. For example, an ESOP trustee may not place undue emphasis on protecting the jobs of ESOP participants if it means the company would incur operating losses to retain those employees. The ESOP is not exclusively about guaranteeing full employment; rather it is about remaining financially successful and optimizing the assets in the plan. An employee cooperative has as a guiding principal the interests of the members taking into consideration such things as fair wages, guaranteeing employment as much as practicable, and the impact of actions on the community as defined by member input.

- ESOPs enjoy oversight and tax benefits at the Federal level. ESOP-related regulations and tax code incentives are universally applied throughout the country with little deference to state and local regulations. This is a significant advantage because the Federal regulations are well understood by a substantial pool of professional advisors. There is significant competition among ESOP professional advisors offering a thoroughly vetted option to selling shareholders and the acquiring ESOP. Employee cooperatives are not well known and there are relatively few professional advisors as thoroughly versed on the legal aspects due to a high emphasis on state regulations. There is often insufficient critical mass of client potential for professional advisors to specialize in the cooperative development.

- ESOPs enjoy many tax advantages that place them in a competitive advantage when deciding to purchase an existing employer. Assuming the candidate company is profitable on an adjusted basis as previously discussed, the ESOP is able to engage in a heavily leveraged transaction with the likelihood of having the acquisition debt principal repaid rapidly with tax-deductible dollars. Many major employers have become ESOP companies because of this favorable treatment of acquisition related debt. Employee cooperatives do not participate in heavily leveraged buyouts in most cases. They grow and evolve with time as the employee members authorize such focus.

- Many ESOP companies have become exceedingly successful, and the value of the stock has been a substantial benefit to the participants. ESOP companies have a history of being very profitable, and it is common for those firms to retain significant capital to grow the company in the interests of creating substantial long-term value for a growing body of participants. ESOP companies have a material consideration in the stock repurchase obligation. This orientation may in fact be in conflict with the charter of an employee cooperative that has not established the long-term growth of the entity as a key part of the operational mission. Employee cooperatives may distribute most of its current year earnings to its members so that there really is not much left to invest aggressively in future growth. Employee cooperatives redistribute most of their earnings annually to the members.

- An ESOP may be only one of many investors in the corporation. Correspondingly, the ability of the trustee to exert much influence on the board of directors may be very limited. ESOPs participate in a corporate environment with investors, and the investors are rewarded according to their capital in the corporation. Investors have a weighted vote at the shareholder meeting according to the number of shares owned.
- ESOPs are likely to be significantly more expensive to establish and to maintain than an employee cooperative. Establishing an ESOP is often associated with the sale of stock by a shareholder in a privately held corporation, whereby the ESOP incurs acquisition debt to purchase the stock. The origination costs typically include the preparation of legal documents such as the trust agreement, the employee stock ownership plan, stock purchase agreement, loan documents, and other transaction related provisions; a valuation of the stock by an independent appraiser; often a fee for the independent transaction trustee; fees for the administration of the plan and other ancillary expenses. Ongoing, the ESOP will incur annual costs for a valuation, plan administration, and depending on the circumstances the fees for an independent trustee. ESOPs must be in ERISA compliance and are subject to audits by both the IRS and the department of labor. Employee cooperatives will have origination documents such as establishing the cooperative, but there is often no requirement for a valuation or for a trustee.

> As evidenced in the case of Select Machine, Inc., an employee cooperative is less costly to install than an ESOP and is an option for companies with less than 20 employees. Unfortunately, restrictive cooperative legislation prevents this option in many states currently.

SUMMARY

Employee cooperatives are establishing some track record of success. Progress is coming slowly, and will be in part limited by the lack of state legislation permitting their existence. With time both employee cooperatives and multi-stakeholder cooperatives will become more common. Many people are discouraged by the excesses of Wall Street and the concentration of wealth into the hands of a few. They seek a more just and balanced capital structure and cooperatives promise such a worthwhile goal.

CHAPTER **18**

Buyouts of the Smallest Companies

The road to success is always under construction.
—Lilly Tomlin

I have not failed. I've just found 10,000 ways that won't work.
—Thomas Edison

This chapter is included to offer insights into the smallest category of businesses. This category is arbitrarily defined as companies with less than 20 employees and sales under $1 million. The intent is to isolate a broad category of companies that comprise a substantial number of candidates, but are typically so small they will not easily absorb significant professional advisor fees. The spectrum of candidate companies is virtually limitless and the intent of this chapter is to offer overall insights into the planning process.

ADVANTAGES

One strong advantage of this category of candidates is the size of the business. Such small firms may often literally be transacted on good faith and a handshake of the parties who know and trust one another. Of course, the handshake should be memorialized with a purchase agreement that details the terms of the transaction. If the company has enjoyed a degree of financial success, there is an enviable lifestyle consideration on the part of the seller. Often there is a significant commingling of business enterprise activities and personal activities. This commingling happens and it is ultimately up to the business owner to justify reasonable costs as necessary for the operations of

283

the business. The employment of family members or friends is one prerequisite among a vast array of other benefits. The businesses under consideration for our purposes are really a lifestyle selection. The business prospects are often financially capped at a comfort level of the owner. Another limitation may be the owner's unwillingness to delegate responsibilities. If the owner insists that a direct hands-on approach to virtually all decision making is required, the financial future will be severely restricted.

Often the owner has personally owned real estate leased to the company, so there may be a consideration of an asset company in addition to the operating company. This offers an opportunity to do the transactions in stages. The first stage is to transact the operating company while a long-term lease is in place and negotiated on the real estate. A second stage may be the acquisition of the real estate at a point in time by the key employee. A solid operating company will always be able to attract the resources to acquire a building if appropriate. Trying to negotiate the acquisition of a building and an operating company, often results in a total package that is too much for the key employee to manage. Breaking the transaction into smaller and more manageable parts is more risk adverse.

CAUTIONS

Our experience is that owners often confuse the lifestyle with value. The ability to lead a comfortable lifestyle often by commingling business and personal expenses makes objective financial analysis of the company very difficult. The next owner may not believe commingling activities are warranted and will not see the value of such behavior. If success is to be realized, the seller must have some objective idea regarding an arm's-length value of the company. Absent this basic tenant, it is very difficult to broach the topic of structuring a transaction. It is almost impossible to begin the conversation. There is some help in the area of valuations discussed shortly.

Limited Transition Options

There is a very high likelihood that the successor key employee(s) have little in the way of financial resources to acquire the company. Often, if they did have some financial wherewithal, and are entrepreneurially oriented, they would already be competitors. It is very common to have some type of an earn-out provision as part of the buyout. The attributes of the earn-out have to be reasonable with regard to the cash flow generated by the company.

If the seller is considering the sale of the company to an outside buyer and looking past key employees that may be a terrible mistake. It is safe to say that only a smaller percentage of the smallest companies will ever be sold to third parties. The statistics from business brokers attempting to sell such businesses suggests that approximately only 25% to 33% of all companies listed with a broker are ever successfully sold. It is almost impossible to verify that range of percentages because no one likes to admit failure, but that range represents a best estimate from talking to many business brokers over the years.

VALUATION

Due to such issues as the size the business, the avoidance of professional fees, and commingling of costs, it is very challenging to place a value on the business using traditional valuation techniques. There is also likely to be a significant issue with accurate financial statements. It is unusual for small companies to produce financial statements reviewed by a public accounting firm with the applicable footnotes and timely accruals. For these reasons perhaps one of the best ways to think about valuation is by industry rules of thumb as a first approach and sanity check.

Industry Rules of Thumb

One excellent place to begin the analysis is with the annual *Business Reference Guide: The Essential Guide to Pricing Businesses and Franchises* written and compiled by Tom West and published by the Business Brokerage Press as mentioned in Chapter 4 on valuations. This is an annual publication that is literally the standard in the business for determining a useful range of value for these smaller companies. The book has grown with time to include many business categories. The table of contents in the 2010 edition is 14 pages in length and includes descriptions of hundreds of businesses and also a significant number of franchises.

The key benefit of the book is that the data on the businesses is compiled from the business broker community reporting literally thousands of transactions over time. One aspect is that the transactions are reported during a spectrum of economic considerations. Another key aspect is that the overall "consideration" is indicated, but there is not much specific guidance on the terms of the transactions. Due to the size of these companies it is an assumption that typically assets are sold in combination with some sort of earn-out provision that provides income to the seller for a period of time. In essence we often have a transaction that is largely seller financed.

The rules of thumb often equate the value of the business in terms of commonly understood terms. Most frequently, the candidate companies are valued as a percentage of revenue with adjustments for such things as inventory and fixed assets if applicable. In such instances, the intent is not to identify the earning power of the business because that may be very difficult to pinpoint. The company is typically a lifestyle selection on the part of the buyer, and the buyer will have to make a determination if the sale price is acceptable in relation to the sacrifice required to enter into a purchase agreement.

Another commonly used term in the *Business Reference Guide* is seller's discretionary cash flow (SDCF). Mr. West provides guidance on an understanding of SDCF from the definition by the International Business Brokers Association (IBBA). The IBBA defines this as the earnings of the business enterprise prior to the following items: income taxes, non-recurring income and expenses, non-operating income and expenses, depreciation and amortization, interest expense or income, owner's total compensation for one owner/operator after adjusting the total compensation of all owners to market value.

Once a rule of thumb is applied, then a decision to possibly proceed with a more formal assessment of value may be considered or to proceed with an offer to purchase. The *Business Reference Guide* is often most valuable with helpful insights on the terms of transactions for selected industries. Unfortunately the historical statistics do not permit Mr. West to offer insights into all of the listed business categories, but when they exist it provides outstanding information such as the suggested range of years for seller financing, gross margins by product line, industry profit margins, and other benchmark data.

> The reliable industry valuation guides are excellent places to begin for business owners to establish a realistic expectation of value. It is unlikely that the suggested formula will result in a cash offer, rather the seller should anticipate an earn-out, seller note, and other terms intended to permit an affordable amount from the buyer.

VIEWPOINT OF THE SELLER

Often the seller waits too long to begin thinking about the succession process. As the case with so many smaller companies, the owner is closely associated with the business. Often the owner works in the business for lack of planning to do something else. The business is frequently an all-consuming enterprise that occupies a substantial amount of time. This is particularly true in retail enterprises with their long hours including weekends.

I have seen countless examples of the owner holding on to the company just to have someplace to go every day. When the company is finally available for transition planning it may be due to a "mortality event." A sudden change in life's circumstances such as the death of a spouse, a change in personal health, or just a change in the industry are common reasons driving the decision to sell. For any number of reasons, the owner decides it is time to move on. Unfortunately, most owners think it is easy to sell the business and they are not prepared for the process of selling something with such emotional attachment. While the owner may be imbued with the attributes of the business, finding another party similarly minded may be difficult, particularly if the hours are long and the industry carries significant risks.

Realistic Outlook

Many smaller companies are vulnerable to changes in technology, and the owner may not be current on the latest applications. Absent the appropriate investment in the latest technology, an already difficult assignment becomes almost impossible to sell.

The seller may be making a terrible mistake by assuming the broader market is stacked with individuals dying to become heavily indebted entrepreneurs. Many qualified buyer candidates have home mortgages, children, college educations to finance, and perhaps aging parents to provide care for. Adding the burdens of acquisition obligations and even longer hours may not be that attractive. This may be particularly the case in two-income households where there is already a comfortable standard of living without excessive hours.

VIEWPOINT OF THE BUYER

Most candidate inside buyers in such smaller companies have little if any readily available liquidity. While there may be a few exceptions to this general statement, I have not found many. Too often the candidate to acquire the business is the same approximate age as the owner and is unwilling or uninterested in assuming the liabilities of the company. The upside potential is not worth the trade-off of assuming significant liabilities and debt for the acquisition.

If an inside employee is interested in earning the ownership of the company, he or she will need to be convinced of the upside financial return. This financial return may include such obvious things as cash compensation, but also participating in ownership benefits. It is important for the owner to communicate the difference between pre-tax benefits and after-tax living costs. If the buyer is in fact purchasing a job, then the advantages of the job ownership has to be understood.

PROFESSIONAL ADVISORS

Due to the size of the transaction and the more limited nature of the dollar amounts involved, there is typically a hesitancy to engage the services of professionals. Of course there will be a need for an attorney to draft the purchase agreement and any loan documents that are applicable. The seller should also be consulting a financial advisor or a certified public accountant to review the tax impact of the transaction. There is a very high likelihood the sale will be an asset transaction and the tax issues are often more hostile to the seller. Some appropriate tax planning will surely pay for itself.

Appropriate tax advice is essential. As mentioned, there is an overwhelming likelihood of an asset sale. Since most small companies are either S corporations or some variation of limited liability companies (pass-through tax entities), there is a strong chance that a significant part of the sale price will be taxed as ordinary income. This is because such items as depreciation recapture, accounts receivable, and inventory are all taxed as ordinary income to the seller. Structuring the sale proceeds to minimize taxes is one of the strongest recommendations I can make.

Perhaps one of the most important advisors is not subject to fees; and that is family members and most significantly a spouse. Planning for retirement security is a concern of family members, and family support is very valuable to have when making such a serious decision.

RISK ENVIRONMENT

These are smaller companies with a limited number of parties to the transaction. Something may happen to the buyer for one reason or another. The seller is typically banking on a single individual for the transition, and any number of things can happen to have the transaction unravel. Just thinking of things like a divorce or adverse turn in health are instances of risk. While the seller is likely to have an earn-out or other contingent payments, there is always the risk of events in the industry or the location. The margin for error in such matters as selecting an inside buyer, hoping that there are no material changes in the industry during the transition period, no adverse health, and a myriad other issues is very thin. Considering that the life expectancy of owners is lengthening, holding on too long is one of the major risks for the owners of small companies.

TECHNICAL MATTERS

There are many ways to approach the ownership transition in a small company. There is the situation described of selling the business to a key employee. Perhaps an alternative is to make the key employee a partner, and then institute a cross buy-sell agreement. This is a common occurrence among professionals. The idea of a "partnership" has attractions as a strategy because it suggests a long-term horizon and adequate planning. The succession plan may proceed over a number of years with adequate time to make key financial decisions.

There are a few technical matters to consider. If there are partners (or co-shareholders), as suggested, one common item is to have a cross buy-sell agreement funded with life insurance. This works best with a limited number of parties. The insurance is there to provide liquidity during the transition period in the event that a catastrophic event occurs. The partner in the company may hold the insurance. Often insurance is obtained to provide liquidity on the life of the major shareholder, and the source of the major liability to the company should that person die unexpectedly. The most typical structure is to have term insurance on the life of the major shareholder. In this instance, it is assumed that the major shareholder is the elder partner and represents a significant ownership stake in the company.

> Owners are advised that marginally successful operations will be exceedingly hard to sell. The long hours, risks of failure, and uncertain future may not be a sufficient inducement for a buyer. In such cases the business is really a job and has little stand-alone value.

Financing the Transaction

Planning for the financing of the succession has to be a priority. In the current market, traditional banking sources are loath to extend funds for risky credits, and buyouts are typically considered risky. These companies are often too small to attract creative and expensive sources of financing. Typically the candidate to provide financial support is the seller. The term "financial support" has been selected carefully to suggest there are many strategies to consider in financing the succession plan. One method is to sell the business to the key employee and evidence the sale with a note. The note must be repaid with after-tax dollars and as prior discussion has suggested, this is a particularly hostile tax environment for the buyer. The tax environment for the sales of smaller companies is often particularly harsh for the buyer and the seller. Typically the sale is an asset-based transaction with a significant amount of ordinary income taxed at unfavorable rates to the seller. The transaction is often financed with an acquisition note and the debt principal is repaid with after-tax dollars. Unfortunately, that is the status of most transactions that are completed. Remember, the object of the IRS is to collect tax receipts, not make life easier for business owners and candidate buyers.

Depending on an analysis by a tax professional, another option is to price the business based substantially on an earn-out that is contingent on results. The metrics of computing the earn-out are subject to negotiations, but the important point of emphasis is to make the payments tax deductible to the company. Tax-deductible payments for the company typically suggest ordinary income to the seller, but the income tax rate for the seller may not be that high based on the relatively low amounts associated with the price for these small companies. There are many ways to accomplish the succession plan to be the most tax efficient for both the buyer and the seller. An earn-out agreement may be combined with a deferred compensation program or a consulting agreement. The benefit of such arrangements is to make the succession plan tax deductible to the fullest extent.

Facilities

Many companies lease their facilities from a limited liability entity owned by the seller. If there is real estate involved, folding a consideration of the facility into a long-term succession plan is appropriate. The fact is that the real estate may be the most valuable part of the company in total. The operating company may be impacted by any number of negative events, but investment theory often holds that real estate is a good long-term financial strategy. This is particularly the case if the real estate is favorably located and maintained.

Offering a more than fair deal on the operating company in return for a long-term lease on the real estate may be an excellent option. The lease will be tax deductible to the operating company, and it is ordinary income to the landlord. The landlord may have several options to in part shelter the income. The building will typically be generating depreciation, which helps shelter income. If the real estate is generating income, such income is typically not subject to payroll taxes and is passive income for tax purposes.

The overall transaction may be structured to produce more passive income for the seller and still have the cash flow deductible to the buyer.

At some point the seller may want to sell the real estate. The buyer is a logical candidate and will typically have a self-serving interest in acquiring the facility. Once the operating company has been sold, selling the real estate may be an attractive long-term program to convert the equity in the business to cash flow for retirement. It is my overwhelming experience that a seller will realize more for the business by selling the operating company and the facilities (if applicable) in two separate transactions. This strategy takes discipline and patience. One of the tremendous benefits of the strategy to the seller is risk management. It is assumed that the operating company will be able to afford the rent on the facility. The wise real estate owner will acquire facilities that can be readily converted to any number of commercial applications. If the operating company falters or at some point is unable to meet lease payments, the facilities may be repackaged and sold to someone who can use it more productively.

If the seller has not planned for a longer-term time horizon, then both the facilities and the operating company may be sold together. This places a substantial burden on the buyer because now the acquisition price balloons to include more assets.

SUMMARY

This chapter introduces a few of the more common elements of transition planning with smaller companies. Such firms are often very difficult to sell to unknown third parties because the financial reporting is suspect, the valuation is unrealistic, or the true entrepreneur will decide it is much easier to begin the business alone and on a thin budget. It is helpful when the seller and the buyer have some knowledge of each other in order to establish a degree of trust and credibility.

CHAPTER 19

Inside Buyouts Compared with Sale to Outsider

Every time a deal is made, somebody is wrong.
—Dennis Roberts

This is a summary chapter that compares the differences between the many types of buyouts developed in this book in comparison to selling a business to a third party. The emphasis in this book has been on describing the mechanics and concerns regarding passing the company to a consortium of potentially inside managers, managers and a private equity firm, employees, and family members. The first major section of this chapter discusses many of the most common elements of sales to third-party buyers. The second major section considers the relative range of third-party candidates and some of the key attributes.

RELATIVE NEGOTIATING STRENGTH

In the world of transactions the actual outcome is a heavily negotiated environment, and the most advantageous and more preferential outcome will typically go to the strongest negotiating position. For a candidate seller, remember that a third-party buyer wants to know why the company is for sale. The buyer also wants to gain every advantage in negotiations by understanding the weaknesses in the seller's position. If a real material weakness is suspected on the part of the buyer, the seller will substantially be hurt in negotiating strength, lessening the chances for the most favorable result.

Other factors impacting the relative negotiating strength of each side will play a major role in the outcome. The list of issues is endless, but a few examples will help drive the point. A change in technology will negatively impact software and systems support firms if they are not versed in the new processes. The candidate firm may not have the resources to keep up with technology and is at high risk of falling behind. The loss of a major account or the addition of a national relationship may be material.

One thing to keep in mind: To the buyer most acquisitions are discretionary actions. They are typically not required, and the willingness to move ahead is often a function of the overall terms. The more favorable the transaction to the buyer, the more likely they have an interest in closing. This may be particularly the case if the buyer is a privately held company that is insulated from the pressures to grow (often at almost any cost) that a publicly held company faces. Many proposed transactions fail to materialize at the last moment when a "deal breaker" event progresses to its conclusion. There may be tremendous pressure to get the transaction completed by the seller lest the buyer gets away. This is artificial pressure that in many instances is initiated by the buyer to try and negotiate the most favorable terms of the deal right up to the closing date.

> The best prepared will typically walk away with the more desirable result. Many smaller companies are controlled by owners with limited exposure to transactions and they are often ill-suited for hard-edged negotiations. Often such owners do not understand the need for an experienced professional to assist with the process. As companies are larger and worth more, my experience is that owners are more savvy regarding value and do not hesitate to enlist professional help.

When the owner is negotiating with the inside-led team, the likelihood that relations remain more cordial are greatly enhanced. It is in no one's interest for the discussions to become rancorous and bitter. This fact is particularly heightened when it is a near certainty that in most instances the inside buyer will need financial assistance from the seller.

WHERE'S THE MONEY?

An outside buyer may be an attractive option if the offer is accompanied with a substantial percentage of the proposed transaction to be paid in cash at closing. This was more likely to occur before 2008 as I have previously mentioned. In today's economic environment, the availability of traditional sources of financing is stressed. Banks and financial institutions have tightened their credit standards and in general they are not actively seeking leveraged buyouts. In some cases private equity firms may have their own funds to invest, but they will still find it challenging to partner with a traditional bank for a significant part of the proposed sale price.

Seller "Skin in the Game"

If an offer from a third party is accompanied with the requirement for a material percentage of the transaction to be financed with seller notes, the terms of the proposed transaction must be carefully weighed. Instead of seller notes, the terms may include a host of other negative covenants to the seller. Such things as excessive holdbacks, inordinately high earn-out amount, significant consulting or deferred compensation are examples of techniques used by buyers to insure as much seller "skin in the game" as possible. The seller is vulnerable in such circumstances because he has crossed over from being in control of the operations to being a major creditor with sharply restricted access to the checkbook.

In addition to seller financing, the offer may insist on a significant escrow account, an aggressive earn-out (contingent payment), and the terms may impose a significant tax liability in the year of sale that requires cash. When an escrow account is required, claims against the balance must be clearly understood. Any contingent payment must be reasonable and easily verified. If the seller is surrendering the control of the company to a third party, it is imperative to do a thorough examination of the other parties to the transaction. Such things as exhaustive credit checks of the principals, prior business experience, previous acquisitions, relationships with banks, and in certain instances the credit of spouses is important.

When control of the company is sold and the seller has left a material percentage of the transaction consideration in the business to be paid over time, there is a considerable risk being assumed. In my experience if there is a dispute regarding terms, the buyer has most of the negotiating strength and control of the company purse strings. Sellers rarely prevail to their satisfaction in such matters. The moral is to know with whom you are dealing.

The seller providing credit in the form of notes will be subordinated to most or all the other major secured lenders in the transaction. The seller obligations will be paid last if some dispute arises or if unforeseen developments impact operations and the ability to honor obligations. It is appropriate to insist on security for the seller obligations beyond any security provided by the assets in the company being sold. It is appropriate to make sure the seller note is secured in some manner. If the note is not secured with additional assets of the buyer, it is not likely the seller will be able to negotiate the much higher interest rates associated with commercial unsecured lenders. A best practice is for the seller's attorney to draft the seller loan agreement that provides for a range of lender options if the loan is in default. The legal documents relating to the seller note should include provisions for personal guarantees from the buyer.

ASSET OR STOCK SALE

Many sales of closely held companies to third parties are asset-based transactions. The buyer wants the asset sale for the benefit of writing up the acquired assets to the transaction price and then depreciating or amortizing them. Another time-honored benefit of properly structured asset acquisitions is that unknown liabilities will remain with the seller. If the buyer is acquiring assets, it is common that the buyer will also insist on the seller agreeing to the asset allocation reporting required for the IRS (IRS Form 8594) and the exposure to transaction-related taxes. The buyer is often most concerned with allocating the price in a manner that permits the rapid recovery of purchase price through depreciation and asset turnover. The buyer's allocation will almost certainly conflict with the allocation preferred by the seller that is biased to capital gain tax treatment. The tax consequences may be enormous depending on precisely how the transaction is structured. Asset sales are more common with smaller companies. Asset-based transactions are almost always more hostile from a tax standpoint to the seller.

Stock sales are more frequent when private equity firms are involved due to the relatively short time horizon for investment. Many acquisition candidates by private equity firms are technology centered and the assets may be largely composed of goodwill. Goodwill is an IRC Section 197 intangible asset, and subject to 15-year amortization. Few if any private equity firms have an investment horizon approaching that amount of time, and the combined depreciation and amortization may not be that critical to the transaction. The private equity firm will have a significant negotiating advantage if they offer to buy stock, which is taxable as a capital gain to the seller.

The seller must be careful that the terms of the transaction are not so onerous as to impose material cash outlays (taxes, escrow withholding amount, seller finance, retire existing debt, etc.) that erode the receipt of proceeds on the date of closing. Many cash requirements to the seller are required at closing or shortly thereafter. In asset sales, typically all depreciation and amortization recovery is taxable in the year of sale as ordinary income, and are not subject to installment sale treatment. The current year taxes may be very high to the seller with cash income deferred due to seller notes, contingent payments, and the repayment of the escrow account. The unwary seller may be surrendering control of the company to a buyer, and at the date of closing have little cash in pocket to evidence the transfer of control. It is true that the buyer may have significant obligations to the seller, but that fact will be of little comfort to the seller.

What Are You Really Getting?

A best practice for the seller is to have a closing statement prepared before the actual closing. This statement will indicate exactly how much cash is being provided by the buyer at closing, and to plan accordingly for living expenses into the future.

If a stock sale is proposed, the good news is that the transaction will likely be taxed at more favorable capital gain rates. If payments are received over time, the proceeds may be subject to an installment sale. In most instances, the installment sale is a positive because it means that some sale proceeds are received in the future with the benefit that tax obligations may be deferred over a number of years. Of course, the historical benefit of an installment sale may not be advantageous if future tax rates are higher than today's rates. The specter of rising tax rates is a near certainty, so an installment sale is not likely to be attractive. A selling owner may opt out of the installment sale election and pay the taxes up front in the year of the closing. This may save some dollars by avoiding future tax increases, but it takes cash to pay those taxes, and identifying the source for that cash is important.

The point to be emphasized in this section is that the seller needs to be wary of the terms extended by a third party with substantial elements of deferred and contingent payments. Control has been surrendered and it is very difficult to prevail in litigation against a buyer once things unravel. If the seller is dealing with an inside buying group it is far more likely there will be more opportunities to retain elements of control in the company until the debt is repaid. There is seller risk in both scenarios, but looking across a table at your management and its backers is more comforting than a law firm representing a buyer that cannot be reached.

CONTINGENCY PAYMENTS

Contingent payments have in part already been considered, but they merit separate mention here. Contingent payments are another tactic by the buyer to insure that the seller is still invested with the future success of the business. A portion of the sale price is contingent in some manner on a future payout to be earned. After the company is sold the seller often has no control over the accounting and the production of management reports. It is often a safe bet that reporting functions will be consolidated at the buyer's main facility. Sellers often think collecting the contingent payment is a done deal, but it must be remembered that the buyer has a strong incentive to help insure that the overall purchase price for the business is as low as possible. The extent that contingent payments do not have to be paid is money in the buyer's account.

There is likely to be less risk to a seller when transacting with the inside buyer. The seller is less likely to agree to a significant earn-out because there is little pressure to make the concession to the management. The seller is typically extending significant credit to get the deal accomplished with the inside buyer and we rarely see significant earn-outs in such transactions.

THE DAY AFTER

One of the most important considerations for a seller is the realization that life continues the day after the sale of the business. Many sellers are consumed with the business, and it may be a hard psychological adjustment to wake up and no longer be in control of the company and directing the resources of the business. After years of often unfettered control, having little or no authority is something that must be carefully considered.

The buyer often indicates that the seller's services are required for a period of time following the transaction. In most instances, the seller's assistance is required for a very short period of time. The buyer may have committed to several years of payouts, but those payouts may not be linked to real duties provided by the seller. Of course there are exceptions to this, particularly when the seller has extraordinary technical skills or has commanding customer rapport.

> I cannot emphasize strongly enough that a seller must think about life the day after control of the business is sold to a third party. Going from the "captain of the ship with unquestioned authority" to insignificance within a short period of time is an adjustment that few easily make.

When selling to the inside team, however identified, there is the greater likelihood that the seller will structure the exit on terms most favorable to his goals. Often, a gradual pull-back from daily responsibilities is negotiated, with the inside team picking up the obligations. An ongoing seat on the board with authority is a real benefit since it permits an exit with dignity and legacy.

TIME UNCERTAIN—GETTING TO THE CLOSE

Dealing with a third party is often a harrowing experience, with the proposed transaction having a life of its own. Every transaction goes through the uncertainties of closing or not closing. A myriad of influences may put the transaction at risk of failing to close, and the seller often can do little about it. There is a long history of transactions failing to close at the last minute (literally the day of the proposed transaction), or failing to close ahead of schedule. In the event that a closing does not happen, it may mean back to the market for the sellers and the months of effort such action leads to. This uncertainty may extend to years, and will wear on the seller.

In the event there are multiple candidates for the company, the failure for the leading suitor to close may suggest to other candidates that something fundamental is wrong. If this is the case, expect rigorous due diligence from the next candidate. A successor candidate will be wondering what the first buyer did not see in the business that was a reason for not closing.

The anxiety of dealing with a third party is very stressful. The level of stress is typically greatly reduced when an inside buyout is contemplated where the major players know one another, and there are far fewer chances for surprises.

INVESTMENT BANKERS AND INTERMEDIARIES

One time-honored method of selling a company is to engage the services of an investment banker. This book is focused on middle market companies and the services of an experienced investment banker will prove to be valuable. While there is a cost to having this resource, that cost is typically a success fee and the fee is often not earned until the transaction is closed. The terms of an engagement with an investment banker are subject to some negotiation. Many investment bankers insist on a commitment down payment as a sign of good faith that the company really is for sale before a great deal of effort goes into marketing the business. The commitment fee is subtracted from the success fee when the company is sold. This arrangement protects the investment banker from sellers that experience seller's remorse and kill transactions at the last moment after considerable work has been completed.

My experience is that knowledgeable investment bankers pay for themselves. They approach assignments with the objectivity, financial incentives, and pragmatism that get transactions closed.

To optimize the services of an investment banker always ask questions such as: Do they have experience in your industry? How many transactions have been closed (especially in this recession market)? How large are the companies sold? Finding someone that speaks the industry language is an integral ingredient to a successful sale.

COMMON THIRD-PARTY BUYERS

As the name suggests, the buyer is not known to the business owner, and the company is being sold to this new investor. Candidate buyers may include a strategic buyer, a competitor, a vendor, a key customer, or a private equity firm. The risks and rewards of the buyer candidates are reviewed.

Strategic Buyer

This possibility is the business owner's dream-come-true, and for most it will remain just a dream. Clearly the benefit is often perceived as offering a substantial premium for the business. This potential outcome within certain industries was far more likely prior to 2008, but in today's economy and with most middle market companies this option is unlikely.

The relatively likelihood of a strategic buyer making an offer is centered most typically on businesses with significant upside growth potential in both revenue and profitability. Such businesses are clustered in technology and communications disciplines. It takes special attributes for a buyer to make an outstanding offer for a business. Other candidates include foreign firms wishing to establish an immediate presence in this country and will buy their way into the market with a key acquisition. This is in preference to trying to win market share over time by establishing an internal affiliate and building the organization from the ground floor. In fact foreign acquisitions were a significant percentage of the mergers and acquisitions market prior to 2008. The recession and international uncertainties have eroded this likelihood for the next few years.

Competitors

One of the best time-honored reasons to justify the acquisition of a company is to eliminate a competitor. The more direct the competitor and the closer the proximity, the more likely the advantages of elimination will be felt financially. You may think the competitor is a strategic buyer just waiting to pay a large premium to have a greater sway over the market. Rather, if the buyer is a competitor they may be waiting for the first signs of weakness to become evident. It makes a tremendous psychological difference regarding who communicates the first overture. If the seller makes the first communication, that is almost surely a sign of weakness as it suggests a degree of desperation.

The competitor may only be interested if the price is right, meaning that there is a bargain element to the proposed deal. The major issue to the seller when considering a sale to a competitor is the risk of having the deal fall apart once confidential information has been passed along. Having confidentiality agreements in place with recourse will provide more "feel good" protection, but armed with confidential information a competitor will be hard to stop. Another fear is that employees will know that the company is for sale and many will feel insecure if a competitor buys them. Commonly, many types of functions are redundant on a combined basis. Employees may feel there is no future and begin to look elsewhere. Key employees may be lured away by the competitor in lieu of having to buy the entire business. Loss of key personnel has to be a major concern to the seller, since such a loss almost certainly will have a material and negative impact on the value of the company.

Once a competitor has acquired a company, I have witnessed a "we" versus "them" psychological impact. The acquired company feels like it has been conquered and defeated. In truth, that may be the case. The fear for the seller is that his employees are treated as second-class citizens in the combined entities.

Suppliers and Key Customers

In certain instances the symbiotic relationship between two companies has grown to the point where the need to continue is almost predicated on a combination of the entities. These types of acquisitions are typically friendly, and have a positive outlook.

I have seen several instances when the candidate company has become such an integral part of the acquiring company's business model that the acquisition company cannot afford to lose the relationship. This often happens when the seller has a distinctive skill set or proprietary capability. So many companies have specialized and proprietary processes that finding this type of relationship is common. The smaller company with a commanding niche capability becomes indispensable. A few examples include having specialized high-quality skills for exacting precision, making proprietary tooling, and establishing near-proprietary customer relationships.

Often the topic of a combination, merger, or a sale is broached in a friendly environment such a conference or a meal. Typically the relationship is so strong there is a mutual interest in protecting it. A longer-term horizon that is acceptable to both parties is agreed upon.

Private Equity Firm

Some of these buyers have in part been described in the book, such as the private equity firm or private equity group (PEG). In this instance the PEG is really a buyer of the company with little thought about the managers, employees, or a longer-term time horizon. This PEG is focused on yield in the short term and is typically oriented to acquiring a company with substantial growth potential that has limited access to capital. The PEG is able to provide the short-term liquidity required to boost sales and get the company to the next level of performance (that is often the theory).

The PEG has the knowledge and expertise on managing a business with substantial acquisition debt. The business will be managed to generate a return for the PEG in the most expedient time period available. The PEG may have a management participation program, but it is often relatively small expressed as a percentage of the transaction.

The PEG as represented in this chapter will already have an exit strategy under consideration before the transaction is closed. In the quest to optimize financial returns for the PEG's investors, there is limited consideration to what happens to the acquired company in the longer term. If the seller is comfortable with that likely scenario, the PEG is often an excellent option that promises a significant amount of cash at closing.

SUMMARY

This is a cautionary chapter. There are many parties in the market suggesting that selling a business is a routine matter. Intermediaries and investment bankers in particular are often consummate sales representatives. Remember that they are commissioned sales representatives and have a vested interest in having the seller sign a listing agreement. Once the agreement is signed, getting the company sold is an exercise in applied statistics and hopefully finding a "hit." Yes, there are a number of outstanding representatives that have an admirable track record of closing transactions; those firms typically concentrate in a few selected industries or market segments and have significant standing with the dominant players in those disciplines. If selling to a third party is the realistic option for a business owner, finding an investment banker with industry expertise and a track record of success will usually pay for itself many times over.

Most business owners have no idea how stressful and difficult it is to sell their company. Emotional attachment to the business will blind most sellers to the real worth of the company. It is easy to become discouraged once the business has been for sale for an extended period of time and there have been no qualified buyers. This is particularly true since 2008 and the onset of the recession.

This book is intended to offer an option to business owners that care to immerse themselves in the exit-planning process and work toward an ending that accomplishes their goals.

About the Web Site

Please visit the companion Web site to this book at www.wiley.com/go/millerbuyouts. It provides readers with materials and information to identify resources that facilitate buyouts and an understanding of business transactions. The two main sections on the Web site include Resources and Business Valuations.

The Resources section lists only organizations and books where I, the author, have personal knowledge and experience. The list is not intended to be all-inclusive; such a compilation would by definition include many candidates that are of poor quality or of questionable value. The organizations and books cited have proven beneficial to my professional knowledge. The Resources are arranged by categories and include Web site information and contact numbers that are current as of this book's publication.

The Valuations section includes much of the materials from Chapter 4 on valuations. The material on the Web site has been expanded with additional details regarding the most generally accepted valuation theory. This listing is complements sections under Resources and should be considered together with them. The Resources section includes a section on business valuations, and lists several respected books on business valuations.

I. Resources
   a. Major Professional Organizations
   b. Specialty Professional Organizations
   c. Employee Ownership Organizations
   d. Business Valuation
   e. Investment Banking, Private Equity, and Capital
   f. Books and Printed Material
II. Valuations
   a. Purpose of the Valuation
   b. Determining the Transaction Consideration
   c. Standard of Value for Transactions
   d. Types of Buyers and Sellers
   e. Attributes of Ownership – Control and Minority Positions
   f. Lack of Marketability
   g. Additional Adjustments to Valuation
   h. Three Valuation Approaches: Income, Market, Asset

Index

management and ESOPs and trust
   buyout (*Continued*)
   ESOP and trust tax issues and
      incentives, 184–85
   ESOP as a shareholder, 162–63
   ESOP funding methods and
      contribution limits, 183–84
   ESOPs, 160–61, 165, 181,
      190
   ESOPs, comparison between C
      and S corporation, 189
   ESOP Trustee, 162–63, 168–70,
      172, 181–82, 188, 190
   financing considerations, 167
   IRC Section 1042, 161, 167,
      185–87, 189
   IRC Section 1042 tax free
      rollover, 185–86
   professional advisers, 169–71
   Qualified Replacement Property
      (QRP), 161, 186, 189
   risk environment, 171–73
   S corporation, 161, 163, 165,
      171, 173, 181, 183–85,
      187–90
   seller viewpoint, 166–67
   stock purchase with pre-tax or
      after-tax dollars, 162
   technical matters, 180–90
   valuation insights, 165–66
management consulting firms
   buyer viewpoint, 231
   professional firm buyouts,
      230–32
   risk environment, 232
   seller viewpoint, 230–31
   technical matters, 232
   valuation, 231–32
manufacturing sector, 66
marginal dollar of funding, 30
marginal income tax rates,
   105

marital property state, 81
market
   approach to valuation, 54–55
   discount rate, 122
   prices of comparable companies,
      44
   rate, 90
marketing manager, 75
Market Value of Invested Capital
   (MVIC), 48
   to book value, 56
   to EBIT, 56
   to sales, 56
Martell Construction, Inc.,
   139–40
The McLean Group (TMG), 73
MDI. *See* Molded Dimensions, Inc.
   (MDI)
mediation, 89
Medicaid, 100
medical coverage, 133
medical practices, 215
Mergers & Acquisition: An
   Insider's Guide to the
   Purchase and Sale of Middle
   Market Business Interests
   (Roberts), 73
mezzanine
   bank, 34
   debt, 34, 157
   financing, 167
   funds, 33–34
   lender, 33–34
   package, 34
middle market
   characteristics of, 2–3
middle market companies
   credit, collateralized, 33
   defined, 3
Middle Market Investment
   Banking Association, 3, 73
middle market transactions, 128